2nd International Workshop on Designing Meaning Representations (DMR 2020)

Held online due to COVID-19

Barcelona, Spain
13 December 2020

ISBN: 978-1-7138-2825-9

DMR 2020

The 2nd International Workshop on Designing Meaning Representations

Proceedings of the Workshop

December 13, 2020
Barcelona, Spain (online)

Preface

While deep learning methods have led to many breakthroughs in practical natural language applications, most notably in Machine Translation, Machine Reading, Question Answering, Recognizing Textual Entailment, and so on, there is still a sense among many NLP researchers that we have a long way to go before we can develop systems that can actually "understand" human language and explain the decisions they make. Indeed, "understanding" natural language entails many different human-like capabilities, and they include but are not limited to the ability to track entities in a text, understand the relations between these entities, track events and their participants, understand how events unfold in time, and distinguish events that have actually happened from events that are planned or intended, are uncertain, or did not happen at all. "Understanding" also entails human-like ability to perform qualitative and quantitative reasoning, possibly with knowledge acquired about the real world. We believe a critical step in achieving natural language understanding is to design meaning representations for text that have the necessary meaning "ingredients" that help us achieve these capabilities.

This workshop intends to bring together researchers who are producers and consumers of meaning representations and through their interaction gain a deeper understanding of the key elements of meaning representations that are the most valuable to the NLP community. The workshop will also provide an opportunity for meaning representation researchers to critically examine existing frameworks with the goal of using their findings to inform the design of next-generation meaning representations. A third goal of the workshop is to explore opportunities and identify challenges in the design and use of meaning representations in multilingual settings. A final goal of the workshop is to understand the relationship between distributed meaning representations trained on large data sets using network models and the symbolic meaning representations that are carefully designed and annotated by CL researchers and gain a deeper understanding of areas where each type of meaning representation is the most effective, and how they can be linked.

We received 15 valid submissions and accepted 10 papers for oral presentations. One paper has since been withdrawn from the workshop after it was accepted. The papers address topics ranging from meaning representation methodologies to issues in meaning representation parsing, to the adaptation of meaning representations to specific applications and domains, to cross-linguistic issues in meaning representation. We thank the authors and reviewers for their contributions. In addition to the regular program, we also have three invited speakers, Daniel Gildea, Lori Levin, and Mark Steedman, to speak on topics ranging from meaning representation and knowledge, to cross-lingual issues in meaning representation design, to meaning representation applications. We look forward to a stimulating and exciting online workshop.

Nianwen Xue, Johan Bos, William Croft, Jan Hajič, Chu-Ren Huang, Stephan Oepen, Martha Palmer, James Pustejovsky

Organizers:

Nianwen Xue, Brandeis University
Johan Bos, University of Groningen
William Croft, University of New Mexico
Jan Hajič, Charles University
Chu-Ren Huang, The Hong Kong Polytechnic University
Stephan Oepen, University of Oslo
Martha Palmer, University of Colorado
James Pustejovsky, Brandeis University

Program Committee:

Omri Abend, The Hebrew University of Jerusalem
Emily Bender, University of Washington
Claire Bonial, US Army Research Lab
Johan Bos, University of Groningen
William Croft, University of New Mexico
Valeria de Paiva, Nuance Communications
Lucia Donatelli, Saarland University
Jan Hajič, Charles University
Dag Haug, University of Oslo
Daniel Hershcovic, University of Copenhagen
Elisabetta Ježek, University of Pavia
Aikaterini-Lida Kalouli, University of Konstanz
Kenneth Lai, Brandeis University
Alex Lascarides, University of Edinburgh
Lori Levin, Carnegie Mellon University
Bin Li, Nanjing Normal University
Fei Liu, University of Central Florida
Sara Moeller, University of Colorado at Boulder
Joakim Nivre, Uppsala University
Timothy O'Gorman, University of Massachusetts at Amherst
Weiguang Qu, Nanjing University
Nathan Schneider, Georgetown University
Zdenka Uresova, Charles University
Ashwini Vaidya, Indian Institute of Technology Delhi
Chuan Wang, Google
Anssi Yli-Jyrä, University of Helsinki

Invited Speakesr:

Daniel Gildea, University of Rochester
Lori Levin, Carnegie Mellon University
Mark Steedman, University of Edinburgh

Table of Contents

This page intentionally left blank.

Workshop Program

Sunday, December 13, 2020

14:00–15:20 **Session A:**

14:00–14:50 **Invited Talk by Mark Steedman: Unsupervised Design of Explainable Meaning Representations**

14:50–15:00 *A Continuation Semantics for Abstract Meaning Representation* **ID: 12**

Kenneth Lai, Lucia Donatelli and James Pustejovsky

15:00–15:10 *Separating Argument Structure from Logical Structure in AMR* **ID: 3**
Johan Bos

15:10–15:20 *Building Korean Abstract Meaning Representation Corpus* **ID: 4**

Hyonsu Choe, Jiyoon Han, Hyejin Park, Tae Hwan Oh and Hansaem Kim

15:50–17:10 **Session B:**

15:50–16:40 **Invited Talk by Lori Levin**

16:40–16:50 *Cross-lingual annotation: a road map for low- and no-resource languages* **ID: 14**

Meagan Vigus, Jens E. L. Van Gysel, Tim O'Gorman, Andrew Cowell, Rosa Vallejos and William Croft

16:50–17:00 *Refining Implicit Argument Annotation for UCCA* **ID: 1**

Ruixiang Cui and Daniel Hershcovich

17:00–17:10 *K-SNACS: Annotating Korean Adposition Semantics* **ID: 9**

Jena D. Hwang, Hanwool Choe, Na-Rae Han and Nathan Schneider

17:40–19:00 **Session C:**

17:40–17:50 *InfoForager: Leveraging Semantic Search with AMR for COVID-19 Research* **ID: 13**
Claire Bonial, Stephanie M. Lukin, David Doughty, Steven Hill and Clare Voss

17:50–18:00 *Semantic parsing with fuzzy meaning representations* **ID: 8**

Pavlo Kapustin and Michael Kapustin

18:00–18:10 *Representing constructional metaphors* **ID: 11**

Pavlina Kalm, Michael Regan, Sook-kyung Lee, Chris Peverada and William Croft

18:10–19:00 **Invited Talk by Daniel Gildea: Translation and Evaluation of AMRs**

A Continuation Semantics for Abstract Meaning Representation

Kenneth Lai[1], Lucia Donatelli[2], James Pustejovsky[1]
[1]Department of Computer Science
Brandeis University, USA
[2]Department of Language Science and Technology
Saarland University, Germany
{klai12, jamesp}@brandeis.edu
donatelli@coli.uni-saarland.de

Abstract

Abstract Meaning Representation (AMR) is a simple, expressive semantic framework whose emphasis on predicate-argument structure is effective for many tasks. Nevertheless, AMR lacks a systematic treatment of projection phenomena, making its translation into logical form problematic. We present a translation function from AMR to first order logic using continuation semantics, which allows us to capture the semantic context of an expression in the form of an argument. This is a natural extension of AMR's original design principles, allowing us to easily model basic projection phenomena such as quantification and negation as well as complex phenomena such as bound variables and donkey anaphora.

1 Introduction

Abstract Meaning Representation (AMR) is a general-purpose meaning representation that has become popular for its simple structure, ease of annotation and available corpora, and overall expressiveness (Banarescu et al., 2013; Knight et al., 2019). Specifically, AMR focuses on representing the predicative core of a sentence as an intuitive representation of the semantics of a sentence, advantageous for parsing and matching algorithms. As an example, the AMR for the English sentence "Everyone in the room listened to a talk." is given in example (1), in three equivalent formats.

(1) a. Everyone in the room listened to a talk.

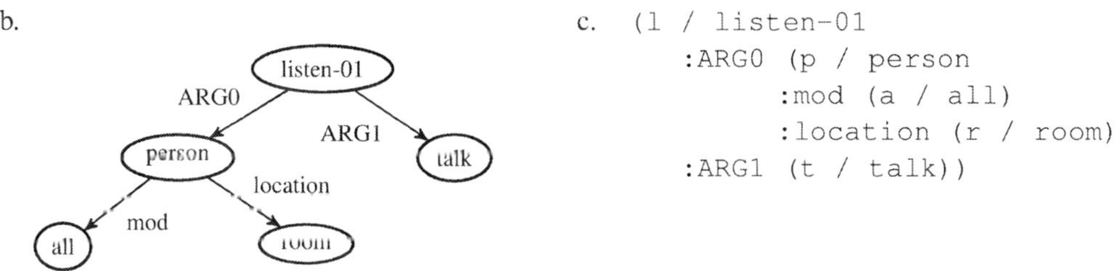

d. instance(l, listen-01) $\wedge$ instance(p, person) $\wedge$ instance(a, all) $\wedge$ instance(r, room) $\wedge$ instance(t, talk) $\wedge$ ARG0(l, p) $\wedge$ mod(p, a) $\wedge$ location(p, r) $\wedge$ ARG1(l, t)

For the sentence in (1a), the predicate and its arguments are represented as nodes in the AMR graph in (1b), while the edges represent the relations between the predicate and each of its arguments. PENMAN notation in (1c) provides a more readable version of the AMR (Matthiessen and Bateman, 1991).

By design, AMR emphasizes argument structure over logical structure, distinguishing it from several other meaning representations based on formal semantic frameworks (Kamp and Reyle, 2013; Copestake et al., 2005). Although AMRs can be represented as conjunctions of logical triples, as seen in (1d),

Proceedings of the 2nd International Workshop on Designing Meaning Representations, pages 1–12
Barcelona, Spain (Online), December 13, 2020

such representations cannot be used directly for drawing valid inferences such as textual entailment or contradiction. Quantifiers, for example, are not given any special semantics, being represented as simple modifiers. Furthermore, AMR does not represent quantifier scope in any way, leaving open the question in (1) of how many talks were listened to in the room.

Several proposals have been put forth to provide AMRs with more meaningful logical forms, driven both by parsing and theoretical concerns. Artzi et al. (2015) present a CCG-based grammar induction technique for AMR parsing; a learned joint model integrates classical lambda calculus and underspecification to improve search for compositional and non-compositional elements of AMR, respectively. Semantically speaking, each AMR variable gets its own lambda term (scoped as low as possible) and each AMR role becomes a binary predicate that is applied to those variables. More strictly theoretical work also provides systematic mappings from AMR into logic. Bos (2016) defines a syntax of AMR and provides a recursive translation function into first-order logic (FOL) that is able to handle scope phenomena. In a similar vein, Stabler (2017) adds tense and number information into AMR leaves and makes explicit quantificational determiners as a basis for a mapping to a higher order, dynamic logic. Finally, Pustejovsky et al. (2019) add scope itself to AMR graph structure, representing it relationally in the form of a scope node that attaches to the predicative core when necessary.

Adding to the discussion about the expressive capacity of AMR, Crouch and Kalouli (2018) argue that any purely graphical representation of meaning is unable to capture basic natural language semantics such as Boolean operators. Instead, the authors propose layering graphs based on the Resource Description Framework (RDF) (Schreiber and Raimond, 2014) and named graphs (Carroll et al., 2005) such that the interaction between different layers can capture Booleans (such as negation and disjunction), modals and irrealis contexts, distributivity and quantifier scope, co-reference, and sense selection (Kalouli and Crouch, 2018). However, in this work, we will show how we can give AMR a semantics expressive enough to handle at least some of these phenomena, namely quantification and negation, without needing to introduce additional graph structure.

Here, we build on previous work and present a translation function from AMR to FOL using continuations. A continuation of an expression encodes surrounding contextual information relevant to its interpretation. More specifically, the *continuation hypothesis* assumes that some natural language expressions denote functions that take their own semantic context as an argument (Barker, 2002; Barker and Shan, 2014). In the present discussion, continuations have interesting consequences for the representations associated with the predicative core in an AMR graph structure. Namely, the continuation effectively allows the graph to be rooted at the predicate level, while treating the continuation as an associated argument to the relation associated with that predicate. Thus, our methods allow us to work with standard AMRs without adding features or modifying the graphs, yet still permit us to draw valid inferences.

We take as our starting point the work presented in Bos (2016), as it is the most similar to ours in translating AMR to FOL without significantly altering the AMR feature inventory. We consider the semantics of basic AMRs and show how Bos (2016)'s translations can be naturally formulated in terms of continuations (Section 2). We then demonstrate how continuations allow us to give a simpler, more transparent semantics that can handle scope phenomena (Section 3). We go on to discuss our treatment of universal quantification (Section 4) and negation (Section 5) before examining how our continuation semantics deals with "donkey sentences" (Section 6). Finally we discuss implications of our work and conclude (Sections 7 and 8).

2   A Basic Continuation Semantics

Continuations capture important contextual information surrounding an expression useful for disambiguating the expression's interpretation. In the same way that the generalized quantifier interpretation of an entity is the set of properties true of that entity, the continuation of an expression is the set of *contexts* that, when combined with that expression, result in a true sentence. Alternatively, in terms of the characteristic function of that set of contexts, the continuation of a word or phrase is the entire future of the computation of that expression, packaged as a function over the expression itself (Barker and Shan,

2014; Reynolds, 1993).

With the goal of integrating continuations into our methodology, we begin in the same way Bos (2016) does, by considering the semantics of basic AMRs. Basic AMRs are comprised of constants c (used in, e.g., proper names) and instance assignments (x/P) where a variable x is declared to be an instance of a predicate P. Instance assignments may also have out-going roles $R_i A_i$, where the instance denoted by the AMR A_i fills the role R_i of its parent. We provide a semantics for these basic AMRs below in Definition 1:

Definition 1 (Semantics of Basic AMRs)

$\llbracket c \rrbracket = \lambda\phi.\phi(c)$

$\llbracket (x/P) \rrbracket = \lambda\phi.\exists x.P(x) \wedge \phi(x)$

$\llbracket (x/P : R_1 A_1 \ldots : R_n A_n) \rrbracket = \lambda\phi.\exists x.P(x) \wedge \llbracket A_1 \rrbracket (\lambda y.R_1(x,y)) \wedge \ldots \wedge \llbracket A_n \rrbracket (\lambda y.R_n(x,y)) \wedge \phi(x)$

The above definition is nearly identical to that given by Bos (2016) for basic AMRs, and also, in turn, very similar to that of Artzi et al. (2015). In fact, our definition can be seen as a notational variant (namely, an eta-conversion) of Bos' definition: where our translations have the general functional form $\llbracket A \rrbracket = \lambda\phi.f(\phi)$, Bos' translations have $\llbracket A, \phi \rrbracket = f(\phi)$. Bos describes ϕ as a "λ-expression for roles"; the purpose of ϕ is to "delay the translation of roles" until we have evaluated the meaning of the instance to which we are assigning the role. But it is also possible to consider ϕ from another perspective: in a formula such as $\phi(c)$, ϕ contains contextual information, namely, about the role c plays in relation to its parent node. In other words, ϕ is a continuation. In Definition 1, we thus define the meanings of AMRs directly, as functions of their continuations. We note that the first two meanings in Definition 1 are those of generalized quantifiers (Montague, 1973; Barwise and Cooper, 1981), or continuized noun phrases (NPs) (Barker, 2002), for "c" and "some P", respectively.

A very simple example is given below. An AMR for the sentence "A dog barked" is given in example (2). The calculation of the FOL formula from the AMR is then shown in (3).

(2)   a.   A dog barked.

     b.
```
(b / bark-01
     :ARG0 (d / dog))
```

(3) $\llbracket \text{a dog barked} \rrbracket = \lambda\phi.\exists b.\text{bark-01}(b) \wedge \llbracket (d/\text{dog}) \rrbracket (\lambda y.\text{ARG0}(b,y)) \wedge \phi(b)$

$\qquad\qquad = \lambda\phi.\exists b.\text{bark-01}(b) \wedge (\lambda\psi.\exists d.\text{dog}(d) \wedge \psi(d))(\lambda y.\text{ARG0}(b,y)) \wedge \phi(b)$

$\qquad\qquad = \lambda\phi.\exists b.\text{bark-01}(b) \wedge \exists d(\text{dog}(d) \wedge (\lambda y.\text{ARG0}(b,y))(d)) \wedge \phi(b)$

$\qquad\qquad = \lambda\phi.\exists b.\text{bark-01}(b) \wedge \exists d(\text{dog}(d) \wedge \text{ARG0}(b,d)) \wedge \phi(b)$

$\qquad\qquad \rightsquigarrow \exists b.\text{bark-01}(b) \wedge \exists d(\text{dog}(d) \wedge \text{ARG0}(b,d))$

3   Unifying Assertive and Projective Semantics

Next, we consider the case of projection phenomena, which take wide scope over their parent predicates. Such constructions are very common in natural language; Bos (2016) notes that proper names, appositive expressions, definite descriptions, and possessive constructions all fall into this category, while Stabler (2017), following Champollion (2015) and Landman (1996), points out that arguments of an event in general should scope over the event predicate by default.

As an example, the sentence in (4a), "A dog scratched itself", contains a reflexive pronoun. In its AMR in (4b), (d \ dog) must project over (s / scratch-01), in order for its quantifier to bind the re-entrant :ARG1 d (following Bos (2016), we use the backslash "\" to mark projection phenomena).

(4)   a.   A dog scratched itself.

     b.
```
(s / scratch-01
     :ARG0 (d \ dog)
     :ARG1 d)
```

Bos (2016) accounts for projection phenomena by computing a "projective semantics" and an "assertive semantics" for each sentence. We will not give the full derivations here, but in the above example, the meaning contributed by the projective semantics is $\lambda p.\exists d.\mathrm{dog}(d) \wedge p$, and that from the assertive semantics is $\exists s.\text{scratch-01}(s) \wedge \mathrm{ARG0}(s,d) \wedge \mathrm{ARG1}(s,d)$. The projective meaning is then applied to the assertive meaning, resulting in $\exists d.\mathrm{dog}(d) \wedge \exists s.\text{scratch-01}(s) \wedge \mathrm{ARG0}(s,d) \wedge \mathrm{ARG1}(s,d)$.

One way to look at the above procedure is to note that the projective semantics translates the projective concepts (here, $(\mathrm{d} \backslash \mathrm{dog})$), while the assertive semantics translates everything else. Then, applying the projective meaning to the assertive meaning ensures that the projective concepts take scope over the rest of the sentence. An alternative viewpoint notes that the projective meaning $\lambda p.\exists d.\mathrm{dog}(d) \wedge p$ is an expression that, when applied to the assertive meaning p, yields the meaning of the sentence. This is extremely similar to how an expression is applied to its continuation to yield a sentence meaning in a continuation semantics. In fact, we can write a single translation function that makes this connection explicit, and dispenses with the need for separate projective and assertive semantics.

To do so, we revisit the meaning $[\![(x/P : R_1 A_1 \ldots : R_n A_n)]\!]$. Instead of giving a direct translation as in Definition 1, we decompose it into two parts: an out-going role $[\![:R_1 A_1]\!]$ and the rest of the AMR $[\![(x/P : R_i A_i)]\!]$, where $:R_i A_i$ is a (possibly empty) list of the rest of the out-going roles. From Definition 1, we find that the part of the meaning corresponding to $:R_1 A_1$ is $[\![A_1]\!](\lambda y.R_1(x,y))$, i.e., the meaning $[\![A_1]\!]$ being applied to the continuation $\lambda y.R_1(x,y)$. Now we can consider the rest of the AMR, in particular, its continuation. If we take the continuation to represent the rest of the sentence, then this also has two parts: the out-going role meaning $[\![A_1]\!](\lambda y.R_1(x,y))$, and $\phi(x)$, the original continuation. We can conjoin them, and bind the x with a λ, to get $\lambda x.[\![A_1]\!](\lambda y.R_1(x,y)) \wedge \phi(x)$. Then we can apply the meaning of the rest of the AMR, namely $[\![(x/P : R_i A_i)]\!]$, to this continuation (with a couple of α-conversions to avoid name collisions), to get a recursive semantics for an AMR with out-going roles:

$$[\![(x/P :R_1 A_1 :R_i A_i)]\!] = \lambda\phi.[\![(x/P :R_i A_i)]\!](\lambda m.[\![A_1]\!](\lambda n.R_1(m,n)) \wedge \phi(m))$$

In a continuation semantics, scope and application order are inextricably linked. As such, to make an argument scope over its predicate, we can reverse the order of the role and the rest of the AMR. Now $[\![(x/P : R_i A_i)]\!]$ only gets the λ-expression for R_1 and the original continuation $\phi(m)$, while the projective concept $[\![(y\backslash Q \ldots)]\!]$ is fed the rest of the sentence as its continuation:

$$[\![(x/P :R_1(y\backslash Q \ldots) :R_i A_i)]\!] = \lambda\phi.[\![(y\backslash Q \ldots)]\!](\lambda n.[\![(x/P :R_i A_i)]\!](\lambda m.R_1(m,n) \wedge \phi(m)))$$

We can apply the two rules above recursively until $:R_i A_i$ becomes empty, i.e., we run out of arguments. Then we can use our previous rule $[\![(x/P)]\!] = \lambda\phi.\exists x.P(x) \wedge \phi(x)$, as the base case of our recursion. We also adopt the rule $[\![x]\!] = \lambda\phi.\phi(x)$ to handle re-entrant nodes, such as d in example (4b). Finally, it is important to note that the application order depends solely on whether the argument A_1 is a projective concept $(y\backslash Q \ldots)$ or not, and not at all on whether the parent node (x/P) is projective or not. We can use a vertical bar "|" to denote that a rule applies regardless of whether a concept is projective or not. We summarize our work thus far in Definition 2:

Definition 2 (Semantics of AMRs with Projection)

$[\![c]\!] = \lambda\phi.\phi(c)$

$[\![x]\!] = \lambda\phi.\phi(x)$

$[\![(x|P :R_1(y\backslash Q \ldots) :R_i A_i)]\!] = \lambda\phi.[\![(y\backslash Q \ldots)]\!](\lambda n.[\![(x|P :R_i A_i)]\!](\lambda m.R_1(m,n) \wedge \phi(m)))$

$[\![(x|P :R_1 A_1 :R_i A_i)]\!] = \lambda\phi.[\![(x|P :R_i A_i)]\!](\lambda m.[\![A_1]\!](\lambda n.R_1(m,n)) \wedge \phi(m))$

$[\![(x|P)]\!] = \lambda\phi.\exists x.P(x) \wedge \phi(x)$

As an example, we calculate the meaning of the sentence in (4a), "A dog scratched itself" below. We already know that the meaning of "a dog" is $\lambda\phi.\exists d.\mathrm{dog}(d) \wedge \phi(d)$, so in (5) we focus on the meaning of "scratched itself":

(5) $[\![$scratched itself$]\!]$

$\quad = \lambda\phi.[\![\text{scratched}]\!](\lambda m.[\![\text{itself}]\!](\lambda n.\text{ARG1}(m,n)) \wedge \phi(m))$

$\quad = \lambda\phi.[\![\text{scratched}]\!](\lambda m.(\lambda\psi.\psi(d))(\lambda n.\text{ARG1}(m,n)) \wedge \phi(m))$

$\quad = \lambda\phi.[\![\text{scratched}]\!](\lambda m.(\lambda n.\text{ARG1}(m,n))(d) \wedge \phi(m))$

$\quad = \lambda\phi.[\![\text{scratched}]\!](\lambda m.\text{ARG1}(m,d) \wedge \phi(m))$

$\quad = \lambda\phi.(\lambda\psi.\exists s.\text{scratch-01}(s) \wedge \psi(s))(\lambda m.\text{ARG1}(m,d) \wedge \phi(m))$

$\quad = \lambda\phi.\exists s.\text{scratch-01}(s) \wedge (\lambda m.\text{ARG1}(m,d) \wedge \phi(m))(s)$

$\quad = \lambda\phi.\exists s.\text{scratch-01}(s) \wedge \text{ARG1}(s,d) \wedge \phi(s)$

Then in (6) we combine the meanings of "a dog" and "scratched itself". Note that as an intermediate step, we apply $\lambda\psi.\exists d.\text{dog}(d) \wedge \psi(d)$ to $\lambda n.\exists s.\text{scratch-01}(s) \wedge \text{ARG1}(s,d) \wedge \text{ARG0}(s,n) \wedge \phi(s)$, in a very similar manner to how Bos (2016) applies the projective meaning of a sentence to the assertive meaning.

(6) $[\![$a dog scratched itself$]\!]$

$\quad = \lambda\phi.[\![\text{a dog}]\!](\lambda n.[\![\text{scratched itself}]\!](\lambda m.\text{ARG0}(m,n) \wedge \phi(m)))$

$\quad = \lambda\phi.[\![\text{a dog}]\!](\lambda n.(\lambda\psi.\exists s.\text{scratch-01}(s) \wedge \text{ARG1}(s,d) \wedge \psi(s))(\lambda m.\text{ARG0}(m,n) \wedge \phi(m)))$

$\quad = \lambda\phi.[\![\text{a dog}]\!](\lambda n.\exists s.\text{scratch-01}(s) \wedge \text{ARG1}(s,d) \wedge (\lambda m.\text{ARG0}(m,n) \wedge \phi(m))(s))$

$\quad = \lambda\phi.[\![\text{a dog}]\!](\lambda n.\exists s.\text{scratch-01}(s) \wedge \text{ARG1}(s,d) \wedge \text{ARG0}(s,n) \wedge \phi(s))$

$\quad = \lambda\phi.(\lambda\psi.\exists d.\text{dog}(d) \wedge \psi(d))(\lambda n.\exists s.\text{scratch-01}(s) \wedge \text{ARG1}(s,d) \wedge \text{ARG0}(s,n) \wedge \phi(s))$

$\quad = \lambda\phi.\exists d.\text{dog}(d) \wedge (\lambda n.\exists s.\text{scratch-01}(s) \wedge \text{ARG1}(s,d) \wedge \text{ARG0}(s,n) \wedge \phi(s))(d)$

$\quad = \lambda\phi.\exists d.\text{dog}(d) \wedge \exists s.\text{scratch-01}(s) \wedge \text{ARG1}(s,d) \wedge \text{ARG0}(s,d) \wedge \phi(s)$

$\quad \rightsquigarrow \exists d.\text{dog}(d) \wedge \exists s.\text{scratch-01}(s) \wedge \text{ARG1}(s,d) \wedge \text{ARG0}(s,d)$

4 Universal Quantification

As previously mentioned, quantifiers in AMR are treated as simple modifiers of their head concepts. In a logical form like (1d), all variables are assumed to be existentially quantified. Nevertheless, it is possible to give AMR a proper semantics of quantification. Stabler (2017), for example, is able to translate a number of different kinds of quantifiers into a higher-order logic. In this paper, to stay within the setting of FOL, we will focus on the universal quantifier.

One way of introducing universal quantification into a semantics for AMR, as noted by Bos (2016), is to include a rule such as $[\![(x/P \text{ :quant } \forall)]\!] = \lambda\phi.\forall x.P(x) \rightarrow \phi(x)$, where ":quant $\forall$" denotes any expression that can be interpreted as a universal quantifier. One can verify that, for a simple sentence like "Every dog scratched itself", combining the meaning of "every dog", i.e., $\lambda\psi.\forall d.\text{dog}(d) \rightarrow \psi(d)$, and "scratched itself", from (5), one arrives at $\forall d.\text{dog}(d) \rightarrow \exists s.\text{scratch-01}(s) \wedge \text{ARG1}(s,d) \wedge \text{ARG0}(s,d)$, the correct meaning of the sentence.

However, for more complex NPs, including those that are modified by relative clauses, or even simply by a pre-nominal adjective, the above rule will not provide the right semantics. Consider the sentence "Every brown dog scratched itself" in (7) below.

(7) a. Every brown dog scratched itself.

```
    b.  (s / scratch-01
           :ARG0 (d \ dog
                     :quant (e / every)
                     :mod (b / brown))
           :ARG1 d)
```

Again, we will not give the full derivation here, but the meaning we get if we use the above rule is $\forall d.\mathrm{dog}(d) \to \exists b(\mathrm{brown}(b) \wedge \mathrm{mod}(d,b)) \wedge \exists s.\mathrm{scratch\text{-}01}(s) \wedge \mathrm{ARG1}(s,d) \wedge \mathrm{ARG0}(s,d)$, i.e., "every dog is brown and scratched itself". The problem arises from the fact that in the formula $\lambda\phi.\forall x.P(x) \to \phi(x)$, only the predicate P is allowed to appear in the restriction; everything else is forced into the continuation ϕ, which is interpreted in the nuclear scope.

Our solution to this problem is inspired by Barker and Shan (2008)'s treatment of the universal quantifier, and is also similar to the dynamic meaning of "every" given by de Groote (2006). We will use the below rule for universal quantification:

$$[\![(x|P \text{ :quant } \forall :R_iA_i)]\!] = \lambda\phi.\neg[\![(x|P :R_iA_i)]\!](\lambda m.\neg\phi(m))$$

To understand how this rule works, note that the meaning $[\![(x|P :R_iA_i)]\!]$ will have a logical form like $\lambda\psi.\exists x.P(x) \wedge \ldots \wedge \psi(x)$. Applying this meaning to the continuation $\lambda m.\neg\phi(m)$ eventually results in $\exists x.P(x) \wedge \ldots \wedge \neg\phi(x)$, which we then negate to get $\neg\exists x.P(x) \wedge \ldots \wedge \neg\phi(x)$. Using the logical identity $\neg\exists x.\phi(x) \wedge \neg\psi(x) \equiv \forall x.\phi(x) \to \psi(x)$, we finally get the meaning $\lambda\phi.\forall x.(P(x) \wedge \ldots) \to \phi(x)$, with the "$\ldots$" representing material introduced by an adjective or in a relative clause, correctly interpreted in the restriction of the quantifier. This can be seen in the derivation of the meaning of "every brown dog" below in (8):

(8) $[\![\text{every brown dog}]\!] = \lambda\phi.\neg[\![\text{brown dog}]\!](\lambda p.\neg\phi(p))$

$\qquad = \lambda\phi.\neg(\lambda\psi.[\![\text{dog}]\!](\lambda m.[\![\text{brown}]\!](\lambda n.\mathrm{mod}(m,n)) \wedge \psi(m)))(\lambda p.\neg\phi(p))$

$\qquad = \lambda\phi.\neg[\![\text{dog}]\!](\lambda m.[\![\text{brown}]\!](\lambda n.\mathrm{mod}(m,n)) \wedge (\lambda p.\neg\phi(p))(m))$

$\qquad = \lambda\phi.\neg[\![\text{dog}]\!](\lambda m.[\![\text{brown}]\!](\lambda n.\mathrm{mod}(m,n)) \wedge \neg\phi(m))$

$\qquad \cdots$

$\qquad = \lambda\phi.\neg[\![\text{dog}]\!](\lambda m.\exists b(\mathrm{brown}(b) \wedge \mathrm{mod}(m,b)) \wedge \neg\phi(m))$

$\qquad \cdots$

$\qquad = \lambda\phi.\neg\exists d.\mathrm{dog}(d) \wedge \exists b(\mathrm{brown}(b) \wedge \mathrm{mod}(d,b)) \wedge \neg\phi(d)$

$\qquad \equiv \lambda\phi.\forall d.(\mathrm{dog}(d) \wedge \exists b(\mathrm{brown}(b) \wedge \mathrm{mod}(d,b))) \to \phi(d)$

We can then combine this meaning of "every brown dog" with the meaning of "scratched itself" from (5) below in (9) to get the correct meaning of the sentence:

(9) $[\![\text{every brown dog scratched itself}]\!]$

$\qquad = \lambda\phi.[\![\text{every brown dog}]\!](\lambda n.[\![\text{scratched itself}]\!](\lambda m.\mathrm{ARG0}(m,n) \wedge \phi(m)))$

$\qquad \cdots$

$\qquad = \lambda\phi.[\![\text{every brown dog}]\!](\lambda n.\exists s.\mathrm{scratch\text{-}01}(s) \wedge \mathrm{ARG1}(s,d) \wedge \mathrm{ARG0}(s,n) \wedge \phi(s))$

$\qquad = \lambda\phi.(\lambda\psi.\forall d.(\mathrm{dog}(d) \wedge \exists b(\mathrm{brown}(b) \wedge \mathrm{mod}(d,b))) \to \psi(d))$

$\qquad\qquad (\lambda n.\exists s.\mathrm{scratch\text{-}01}(s) \wedge \mathrm{ARG1}(s,d) \wedge \mathrm{ARG0}(s,n) \wedge \phi(s))$

$\qquad = \lambda\phi.\forall d.(\mathrm{dog}(d) \wedge \exists b(\mathrm{brown}(b) \wedge \mathrm{mod}(d,b)))$

$\qquad\qquad \to (\lambda n.\exists s.\mathrm{scratch\text{-}01}(s) \wedge \mathrm{ARG1}(s,d) \wedge \mathrm{ARG0}(s,n) \wedge \phi(s))(d)$

$\qquad = \lambda\phi.\forall d.(\mathrm{dog}(d) \wedge \exists b(\mathrm{brown}(b) \wedge \mathrm{mod}(d,b)))$

$\qquad\qquad \to \exists s.\mathrm{scratch\text{-}01}(s) \wedge \mathrm{ARG1}(s,d) \wedge \mathrm{ARG0}(s,d) \wedge \phi(s)$

$\qquad \rightsquigarrow \forall d.(\mathrm{dog}(d) \wedge \exists b(\mathrm{brown}(b) \wedge \mathrm{mod}(d,b))) \to \exists s.\mathrm{scratch\text{-}01}(s) \wedge \mathrm{ARG1}(s,d) \wedge \mathrm{ARG0}(s,d)$

We present our translation function thus far in Definition 3 below.

Definition 3 (Semantics of AMRs with Projection and Universal Quantification)

$$[\![c]\!] = \lambda\phi.\phi(c)$$
$$[\![x]\!] = \lambda\phi.\phi(x)$$
$$[\![(x|P \text{ :quant } \forall :R_iA_i)]\!] = \lambda\phi.\neg[\![(x|P :R_iA_i)]\!](\lambda m.\neg\phi(m))$$
$$[\![(x|P :R_1(y\backslash Q\ldots) :R_iA_i)]\!] = \lambda\phi.[\![(y\backslash Q\ldots)]\!](\lambda n.[\![(x|P :R_iA_i)]\!](\lambda m.R_1(m,n)\wedge\phi(m)))$$
$$[\![(x|P :R_1A_1 :R_iA_i)]\!] = \lambda\phi.[\![(x|P :R_iA_i)]\!](\lambda m.[\![A_1]\!](\lambda n.R_1(m,n))\wedge\phi(m))$$
$$[\![(x|P)]\!] = \lambda\phi.\exists x.P(x)\wedge\phi(x)$$

Note that, like other continuation-passing rules, the order in which the rules apply is critical to deriving the correct interpretation. If we interpret the universal quantifier after "brown", rather than before, then "brown" will become part of the continuation of "every dog", and we get the previous incorrect meaning. We will discuss ways to specify the application order in Section 7, but for now, we will process nodes in linear order, i.e., the order they are written in the AMR.

5 Negation

Negation is central to sentence-level meaning, as it directly impacts the assignment of truth values to propositions. In AMR, negation is represented as a predicate rather than a scope operator: a fixed polarity relation is given between the negated concept and negation constant "-". As a result, AMR makes wrong predictions for inferences based on negated sentences; for example, it will allow the inference "a dog barked" from "a dog did not bark." Both Bos (2016) and Stabler (2017) reformulate AMR semantics to allow polarity to act on propositions instead of concepts; here, we expand on the work of Bos (2016) and show the need for two kinds of negation to allow for distinct readings in ambiguous contexts.

Bos (2016) proposes a translation of AMR to FOL in which negation attaches to the quantifier that binds its concept. For example, the AMRs in (10a) and (11a) receive the respective interpretations in (10b) and (11b):

<table>
<tr><td>

(10)   a.   (m / meow-01
        :ARG0 (d / dog)
        :polarity -)

</td><td>

(11)   a.   (m / meow-01
        :ARG0 (d / dog
           :polarity -))

</td></tr>
<tr><td>

    b. $\neg\exists m.\text{meow-01}(m)\wedge\exists d.\text{dog}(d)\wedge\text{ARG0}(m,d)$
       "No dog meowed."

</td><td>

    b. $\exists m.\text{meow-01}(m)\wedge\neg\exists d.\text{dog}(d)\wedge\text{ARG0}(m,d)$
       "It was not a dog that meowed."/
       "A non-dog meowed."

</td></tr>
</table>

Note that a logical form such as $\exists m.\text{meow-01}(m)\wedge\exists d.\neg\text{dog}(d)\wedge\text{ARG0}(m,d)$, with the negation attached directly to the predicate, rather than the quantifier, can also give rise to the interpretation in (11b). In fact, assuming that the meowing event has exactly one ARG0, the two forms are equivalent. It may then seem that any formula with predicate negation can be given an equivalent formula with quantifier negation, and that therefore quantifier negation is sufficient for the semantics of AMRs.

However, there are meanings that cannot be represented with negation only attaching to quantifiers, particularly involving the interaction of negation and universal quantification. For example, a meaning such as "Every non-dog meowed", i.e., $\forall d.\neg\text{dog}(d)\rightarrow\exists m.\text{meow-01}(m)\wedge\text{ARG0}(m,d)$, cannot be generated from any AMR using the rules in Bos (2016). For this reason, we introduce the following two rules for negation:

$$[\![(x|P \text{ :polarity } (n\backslash-) :R_iA_i)]\!] = \lambda\phi.\neg[\![(x|P :R_iA_i)]\!](\phi)$$
$$[\![(x|P \text{ :polarity } (n/-) :R_iA_i)]\!] = \lambda\phi.[\![(x|\neg P :R_iA_i)]\!](\phi)$$

We adopt the same backslash/forward slash syntax as for projective and non-projective concepts, here simply meaning "wide-scope" (i.e., negation attaching to the quantifier) and "narrow-scope" (i.e, negation attaching to the predicate), respectively. An example AMR for the sentence "Every non-dog meowed", with narrow-scope negation, is shown in (12), and the derivation of its meaning is given in (13).

(12) a. Every non-dog meowed.

    b.   (m / meow-01
           :ARG0 (d \ dog
                 :quant (e / every)
                 :polarity (n / -)))

(13) $\llbracket$every non-dog meowed$\rrbracket$

$= \lambda\phi.\llbracket\text{every non-dog}\rrbracket(\lambda n.\llbracket\text{meowed}\rrbracket(\lambda m.\text{ARG0}(m,n) \wedge \phi(m)))$

$\dots$

$= \lambda\phi.\llbracket\text{every non-dog}\rrbracket(\lambda n.\exists m.\text{meow-01}(m) \wedge \text{ARG0}(m,n) \wedge \phi(m))$

$\dots$

$= \lambda\phi.\neg\llbracket\text{non-dog}\rrbracket(\lambda n.\neg\exists m.\text{meow-01}(m) \wedge \text{ARG0}(m,n) \wedge \phi(m))$

$= \lambda\phi.\neg(\lambda\psi.\llbracket\neg\text{dog}\rrbracket(\psi))(\lambda p.\neg\exists m.\text{meow-01}(m) \wedge \text{ARG0}(m,p) \wedge \phi(m))$

$= \lambda\phi.\neg\llbracket\neg\text{dog}\rrbracket(\lambda p.\neg\exists m.\text{meow-01}(m) \wedge \text{ARG0}(m,p) \wedge \phi(m))$

$\dots$

$= \lambda\phi.\neg\exists d.\neg\text{dog}(d) \wedge \neg\exists m.\text{meow-01}(m) \wedge \text{ARG0}(m,d) \wedge \phi(m)$

$\rightsquigarrow \forall d.\neg\text{dog}(d) \rightarrow \exists m.\text{meow-01}(m) \wedge \text{ARG0}(m,d)$

One can verify that reversing the direction of the slash, i.e., changing the polarity to (n \ -), results in the meaning $\neg\forall d.\text{dog}(d) \rightarrow \exists m.\text{meow-01}(m) \wedge \text{ARG0}(m,d)$, i.e., "Not every dog meowed". Definition 4 shows the final version of our translation function:

Definition 4 (Semantics of AMRs with Projection, Universal Quantification, and Negation)

$\llbracket c\rrbracket = \lambda\phi.\phi(c)$

$\llbracket x\rrbracket = \lambda\phi.\phi(x)$

$\llbracket(x|P \text{ :polarity } (n\backslash-) :R_iA_i)\rrbracket = \lambda\phi.\neg\llbracket(x|P :R_iA_i)\rrbracket(\phi)$

$\llbracket(x|P \text{ :polarity } (n/-) :R_iA_i)\rrbracket = \lambda\phi.\llbracket(x|\neg P :R_iA_i)\rrbracket(\phi)$

$\llbracket(x|P \text{ :quant } \forall :R_iA_i)\rrbracket = \lambda\phi.\neg\llbracket(x|P :R_iA_i)\rrbracket(\lambda m.\neg\phi(m))$

$\llbracket(x|P :R_1(y\backslash Q\dots) :R_iA_i)\rrbracket = \lambda\phi.\llbracket(y\backslash Q\dots)\rrbracket(\lambda n.\llbracket(x|P :R_iA_i)\rrbracket(\lambda m.R_1(m,n) \wedge \phi(m)))$

$\llbracket(x|P :R_1A_1 :R_iA_i)\rrbracket = \lambda\phi.\llbracket(x|P :R_iA_i)\rrbracket(\lambda m.\llbracket A_1\rrbracket(\lambda n.R_1(m,n)) \wedge \phi(m))$

$\llbracket(x|P)\rrbracket = \lambda\phi.\exists x.P(x) \wedge \phi(x)$

6 AMR for Donkey Sentences

"Donkey sentences" (Geach, 1962) are known for raising interesting issues regarding the interaction between quantification and anaphora. In the sentence "Every farmer who owns a donkey loves it" in (14a) below, "a donkey" must be able to take scope over the anaphor "it". Furthermore, "a donkey" must also be interpreted as being universally quantified, i.e., every farmer loves every donkey they own. An AMR for this sentence is shown in (14b). In this section, we will show how our continuation semantics can give this AMR an appropriate meaning.

(14) a. Every farmer who owns a donkey loves it.

    b.   (l / love-01
          :ARG0 (f \ farmer
               :quant (e / every)
               :ARG0-of (o \ own-01
                    :ARG1 (d \ donkey)))
          :ARG1 d)

Before we begin our translation from the AMR to FOL, we note that the concepts `(f \ farmer)`, `(o \ own-01)`, and `(d \ donkey)` are all projective. Certainly we want `(d \ donkey)` to take wide scope. Following Champollion (2015), we have, in general, the arguments of an event scoping over the event, hence the wide scope for `(f \ farmer)`. As for `(o \ own-01)`, there is evidence to suggest that events in the restriction should be able to project over the rest of the sentence; e.g., in "Everyone who dined last night got sick afterward", the dining event should take wide scope, in order to be accessible to "afterward".

We now derive the meaning of the subject NP "every farmer who owns a donkey" below in (15). Using the translation rules we defined earlier, we eventually get the meaning $\lambda\phi.\neg\exists d.\text{donkey}(d) \wedge \ldots$. While it may seem odd for the meaning of "every farmer..." to begin with "there does not exist a donkey...", we can use a few logical identities to transform the meaning into a more intuitive form. First, just as in example (8), we can use the identity $\neg\exists x.\phi(x) \wedge \neg\psi(x) \equiv \forall x.\phi(x) \rightarrow \psi(x)$ to rewrite the meaning in terms of universal quantifiers and material conditionals. Then, we can take advantage of the facts that $\phi \rightarrow \forall x.\psi \equiv \forall x(\phi \rightarrow \psi)$ (if x is not free in ϕ) and $\phi \rightarrow (\psi \rightarrow \chi) \equiv (\phi \wedge \psi) \rightarrow \chi$ to move all the universal quantifiers to the beginning (i.e., write the formula in prenex normal form), and move all the terms except $\phi(f)$ into the antecedent of a single conditional. At that point, we can rearrange the quantifiers and the conjuncts to get the more natural-looking meaning at the end of (15).

(15) ⟦every farmer who owns a donkey⟧

$= \lambda\phi.\neg$⟦farmer who owns a donkey⟧$(\lambda m.\neg\phi(m))$

. . .

$= \lambda\phi.\neg$⟦owns a donkey⟧$(\lambda n.\exists f.\text{farmer}(f) \wedge \text{ARG0-of}(f, n) \wedge \neg\psi(f))$

. . .

$= \lambda\phi.\neg$⟦a donkey⟧$(\lambda n.\exists o.\text{own-01}(o) \wedge \text{ARG1}(o, n) \wedge \exists f.\text{farmer}(f) \wedge \text{ARG0-of}(f, o) \wedge \neg\phi(f))$

. . .

$= \lambda\phi.\neg\exists d.\text{donkey}(d) \wedge \exists o.\text{own-01}(o) \wedge \text{ARG1}(o, d) \wedge \exists f.\text{farmer}(f) \wedge \text{ARG0-of}(f, o) \wedge \neg\phi(f)$

. . .

$\equiv \lambda\phi.\forall d.\text{donkey}(d) \rightarrow \forall o.(\text{own-01}(o) \wedge \text{ARG1}(o, d)) \rightarrow \forall f.(\text{farmer}(f) \wedge \text{ARG0-of}(f, o)) \rightarrow \phi(f)$

. . .

$\equiv \lambda\phi.\forall f.\forall d.\forall o.(\text{farmer}(f) \wedge \text{donkey}(d) \wedge \text{own-01}(o) \wedge \text{ARG0-of}(f, o) \wedge \text{ARG1}(o, d)) \rightarrow \phi(f)$

One can verify that the meaning of "loves it" is $\lambda\phi.\exists l.\text{love-01}(l) \wedge \text{ARG1}(l, d) \wedge \phi(l)$, similar to the meaning of "scratched itself" in (5). Then we can combine the two meanings to get the meaning of the entire sentence in (16):

(16) ⟦every farmer who owns a donkey loves it⟧

$= \lambda\phi.$⟦every farmer who owns a donkey⟧$(\lambda n.$⟦loves it⟧$(\lambda m.\text{ARG0}(m, n) \wedge \phi(m)))$

$\leadsto \forall f.\forall d.\forall o.(\text{farmer}(f) \wedge \text{donkey}(d) \wedge \text{own-01}(o) \wedge \text{ARG0-of}(f, o) \wedge \text{ARG1}(o, d))$
$\qquad \rightarrow \exists l.\text{love-01}(l) \wedge \text{ARG1}(l, d) \wedge \text{ARG0}(l, f)$

7 Discussion

Continuations are a natural solution to the challenge of translating AMR to FOL: by treating the continuation of an expression as an associated argument to the relation associated with that predicate, we maintain AMR's focus on the predicative core while still allowing valid inferences from projection phenomena to fall out. Our method avoids the pitfalls of underspecification, allowing us to prioritize the most plausible interpretation of a scope ambiguity yet also to capture less common interpretations when necessary (Bos and Abzianidze, 2019). Our method also does not modify standard AMR nodes, leaves, or edges, which allows us to utilize existing AMR corpora. Formalizing basic projection phenomena in AMR paves the way for more comprehensive meaning representation, allowing simple translation of complex phenomena such as negative raising that evidence speaker belief and intent.

Another interesting advantage of the continuation-passing style semantics introduced here for sentence or utterance level expressions, is the natural way it can be extended to model how AMRs have recently been used in human-robot interaction dialogues (Bonial et al., 2020). The model presented here can easily adopt the dynamic semantics of "discourse moves as continuations", as introduced by de Groote (2001), and extended by Asher and Pogodalla (2010).

As previously mentioned, in a continuation semantics, the order of application determines the relative scope of a predicate and each of its arguments. In this paper, we take the out-going roles of a predicate to be ordered, and the order of application to be the order the arguments are written in the AMR. In contrast, Pustejovsky et al. (2019) attach an optional scope node to the predicate, that explicitly marks the arguments of a predicate with a relative scope ordering.

Ease of annotation is considered one of the major advantages of AMR compared to other meaning representations (Banarescu et al., 2013; Knight et al., 2019). It is possible that introducing a new backslash notation for projective concepts and wide-scope negation may increase annotators' cognitive load. We believe, though, that this effect can be mitigated by specifying default interpretations of projection and negation where possible. For example, Stabler (2017) notes that arguments of an event should be projective in general, and Champollion (2015) comments that negation should take wide scope over event quantifiers by default. In addition to providing guidance to annotators, such defaults can also be used on existing corpora, another area where AMR excels. We plan to conduct a corpus study to evaluate the feasibility of using these defaults to generate logical forms from AMRs in the future.

Although our semantics is able to handle many different kinds of scope phenomena, much more work is needed to capture the plethora of meanings possible in natural language. Extending the translation we present here to logical connectives, conditionals, modality, non-declarative sentences that depend on notions of common ground, and other types of quantifiers (e.g. "most") are all possible next steps. In recent years, there have been a number of proposals to extend AMR to handle definiteness (Stabler, 2017), tense and aspect (Donatelli et al., 2018), and discourse relations (O'Gorman et al., 2018). We look forward to seeing how these proposals and others can be integrated with our semantics.

8   Conclusion

In this paper, we presented a continuation semantics for AMR, building off previous work in translating AMRs to logical forms. We showed that our semantics is powerful enough to handle a wide variety of scope phenomena, including quantification, negation, bound variables, and donkey anaphora. Code for this paper, combining a PENMAN parser based on Goodman (2020), with a computational implementation of our translation function, is available at `https://github.com/klai12/amr2fol`.

Acknowledgements

We would like to thank the reviewers for their helpful comments. This work is supported by the IIS Division of National Science Foundation via Award No. 1763926 entitled "Building a Uniform Meaning Representation for Natural Language Processing". All views expressed in this paper are those of the authors and do not necessarily represent the view of the National Science Foundation.

References

Yoav Artzi, Kenton Lee, and Luke Zettlemoyer. 2015. Broad-coverage CCG semantic parsing with AMR. In *Proceedings of the 2015 Conference on Empirical Methods in Natural Language Processing*, pages 1699–1710, Lisbon, Portugal, September. Association for Computational Linguistics.

Nicholas Asher and Sylvain Pogodalla. 2010. SDRT and continuation semantics. In *JSAI International Symposium on Artificial Intelligence*, pages 3–15. Springer.

Laura Banarescu, Claire Bonial, Shu Cai, Madalina Georgescu, Kira Griffitt, Ulf Hermjakob, Kevin Knight, Philipp Koehn, Martha Palmer, and Nathan Schneider. 2013. Abstract meaning representation for sembanking. In *Proceedings of the 7th Linguistic Annotation Workshop and Interoperability with Discourse*, pages 178–186.

Chris Barker and Chung-chieh Shan. 2008. Donkey anaphora is in-scope binding. *Semantics and Pragmatics*, 1:1–46.

Chris Barker and Chung-chieh Shan. 2014. *Continuations and Natural Language*, volume 53. Oxford Studies in Theoretical Linguistics.

Chris Barker. 2002. Continuations and the nature of quantification. *Natural Language Semantics*, 10(3):211–242.

Jon Barwise and Robin Cooper. 1981. Generalized quantifiers and natural language. *Linguistics and Philosophy*, 4(2):159–219.

Claire Bonial, Lucia Donatelli, Mitchell Abrams, Stephanie M. Lukin, Stephen Tratz, Matthew Marge, Ron Artstein, David Traum, and Clare Voss. 2020. Dialogue-AMR: Abstract Meaning Representation for dialogue. In *Proceedings of The 12th Language Resources and Evaluation Conference*, pages 684–695, Marseille, France, May. European Language Resources Association.

Johan Bos and Lasha Abzianidze. 2019. Thirty musts for meaning banking. In *Proceedings of the First International Workshop on Designing Meaning Representations*.

Johan Bos. 2016. Expressive power of abstract meaning representations. *Computational Linguistics*, 42(3):527–535.

Jeremy J. Carroll, Christian Bizer, Pat Hayes, and Patrick Stickler. 2005. Named graphs. *Journal of Web Semantics*, 3(4):247–267.

Lucas Champollion. 2015. The interaction of compositional semantics and event semantics. *Linguistics and Philosophy*, 38(1):31–66.

Ann Copestake, Dan Flickinger, Carl Pollard, and Ivan A. Sag. 2005. Minimal recursion semantics: An introduction. *Research on Language and Computation*, 3(2-3):281–332.

Richard Crouch and Aikaterini-Lida Kalouli. 2018. Named graphs for semantic representation. In *Proceedings of the Seventh Joint Conference on Lexical and Computational Semantics*, pages 113–118.

Philippe de Groote. 2001. Type raising, continuations, and classical logic. In *Proceedings of the thirteenth Amsterdam Colloquium*, pages 97–101.

Philippe de Groote. 2006. Towards a montagovian account of dynamics. In *Semantics and Linguistic Theory*, volume 16, pages 1–16.

Lucia Donatelli, Michael Regan, William Croft, and Nathan Schneider. 2018. Annotation of tense and aspect semantics for sentential AMR. In *Proceedings of the Joint Workshop on Linguistic Annotation, Multiword Expressions and Constructions (LAW-MWE-CxG-2018)*, pages 96–108, Santa Fe, New Mexico, USA, August. Association for Computational Linguistics.

Peter Thomas Geach. 1962. *Reference and generality: An examination of some medieval and modern theories*. Cornell University Press.

Michael Wayne Goodman. 2020. Penman: An open-source library and tool for AMR graphs. In *Proceedings of the 58th Annual Meeting of the Association for Computational Linguistics: System Demonstrations*, pages 312–319, Online, July. Association for Computational Linguistics.

Aikaterini-Lida Kalouli and Richard Crouch. 2018. GKR: the graphical knowledge representation for semantic parsing. In *Workshop on Computational Semantics beyond Events and Roles (SemBEaR 2018)*, pages 27–37.

Hans Kamp and Uwe Reyle. 2013. *From discourse to logic: Introduction to modeltheoretic semantics of natural language, formal logic and discourse representation theory*, volume 42. Springer Science & Business Media.

Kevin Knight, Lauren Baranescu, Claire Bonial, Madalina Georgescu, Kira Griffitt, Ulf Hermjakob, Daniel Marcu, Martha Palmer, and Nathan Schneifer. 2019. Abstract meaning representation (AMR) annotation release 1.2.6. *Web download*.

Fred Landman. 1996. Plurality. In Shalom Lappin, editor, *The Handbook of Contemporary Semantic Theory*, pages 425–457. Oxford University Press, Oxford, UK.

Christian Matthiessen and John Bateman. 1991. *Text Generation and Systemic-Functional Linguistics : Experiences from English and Japanese*. Pinter, London.

Richard Montague. 1973. The proper treatment of quantification in ordinary english. In *Approaches to Natural Language*, pages 221–242. Springer.

Tim O'Gorman, Michael Regan, Kira Griffitt, Ulf Hermjakob, Kevin Knight, and Martha Palmer. 2018. AMR beyond the sentence: the multi-sentence AMR corpus. In *Proceedings of the 27th International Conference on Computational Linguistics*, pages 3693–3702, Santa Fe, New Mexico, USA, August. Association for Computational Linguistics.

James Pustejovsky, Nianwen Xue, and Kenneth Lai. 2019. Modeling quantification and scope in abstract meaning representations. In *Proceedings of the First International Workshop on Designing Meaning Representations*, pages 28–33.

John C. Reynolds. 1993. The discoveries of continuations. *Lisp and Symbolic Computation*, 6(3-4):233–247.

Guus Schreiber and Yves Raimond. 2014. RDF 1.1 primer.

Edward Stabler. 2017. Reforming AMR. In *International Conference on Formal Grammar*, pages 72–87. Springer.

Separating Argument Structure from Logical Structure in AMR

Johan Bos
University of Groningen
`johan.bos@rug.nl`

Abstract

The AMR (Abstract Meaning Representation) formalism for representing meaning of natural language sentences puts emphasis on predicate-argument structure and was not designed to deal with scope and quantifiers. By extending AMR with indices for contexts and formulating constraints on these contexts, a formalism is derived that makes correct predictions for inferences involving negation and bound variables. The attractive core predicate-argument structure of AMR is preserved. The resulting framework is similar to the meaning representations of Discourse Representation Theory employed in the Parallel Meaning Bank.

1   Introduction

Abstract Meaning Representation, AMR (Langkilde and Knight, 1998), or the PENMAN notation it is based on (Kasper, 1989), puts emphasis on argument structure. In this paper I put forward a proposal to extend AMRs with a logical dimension, in order to—from a formal semantics point of view—correctly capture negation, quantification, and presuppositional phenomena. It is desirable to investigate such an extension, because (i) it would make a comparison of AMR with other semantics formalisms possible (in particular Discourse Representation Theory); (ii) it would make AMR suitable for performing logical inferences; and (iii) it would be an important step in sharing resources for semantic parsing. The aim is to do this in such a way that existing AMR-annotated corpora (Banarescu et al., 2013) can be relatively easily extended with the desired extensions.

This is not the first proposal of extending the PENMAN notation to handle scope phenomena. The need to do so was recognized by other researchers (Bos, 2016; Stabler, 2017; Lai et al., 2020). Pustejovsky et al. (2019) extend AMR with a possibility of adding explicit scope relations. This extension, however, doesn't solve a fundamental problem that AMR faces, namely viewing AMRs as directed acyclic graphs and basing their interpretation on this. Consider examples such as "every snake bit itself" or "all dogs want to swim". In the original AMR graph notation, where quantifiers are expressed as a predicate rather than taking scope, the resulting diagrams are:

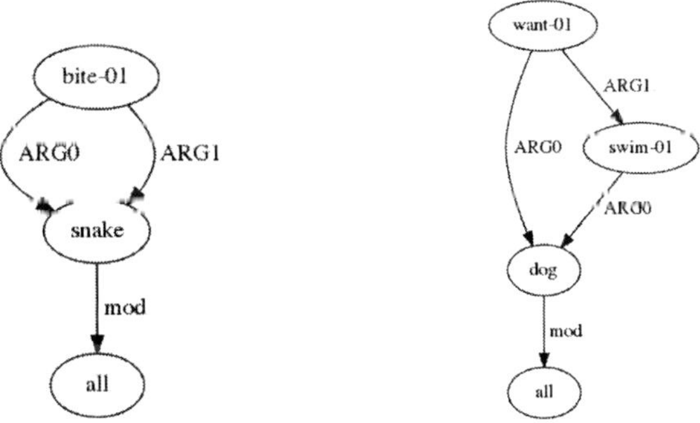

Proceedings of the 2nd International Workshop on Designing Meaning Representations, pages 13–20
Barcelona, Spain (Online), December 13, 2020

The corresponding interpretations for these sentences could be paraphrased as "every snake bit every snake" and "all dogs want all dogs to swim", which are not the meanings that the sentences express. Let's refer to this issue as the *bound variable problem*.

But there is a second, perhaps an even more pressing issue, which could be dubbed the *scope representation problem*. AMRs, in their original PENMAN format (Kasper, 1989), cannot be used directly for drawing valid inferences. Let me demonstrate why this is so. Using the simple conjunction elimination rule (if the conjunction "A and B" is true, then "A" is true, and "B" is true), and assuming that an AMR is interpreted as a conjunction of clauses, AMR will make the right predictions as long as no negation is involved (e.g., it will yield the correct inference "Mary left" from "Mary left yesterday"). But since, in AMR, negation is represented as a predicate rather than an operator that takes scope, it will make wrong predications for negated sentences (e.g., it will allow the inference "Mary left" from "Mary did not leave". This is why AMRs need some kind of reformulation before interpretation, and that is exactly what has been proposed in earlier work (Artzi et al., 2015; Bos, 2016; Stabler, 2017; Lai et al., 2020).

In this paper I seek the solution at the representational level. I think the contribution of this paper is that this extension is simpler of nature than those proposed earlier (Bos, 2016; Stabler, 2017). It bears similarities with *named graphs* for semantic representations (Crouch and Kalouli, 2018). I argue that, if we want to fix the bound variable problem and the scope representation problem, AMR requires explicit scope in their representations (Bos and Abzianidze, 2019). I propose a method to do this by keeping the underlying predicate-argument structure, and adding a second, logical layer (Section 2). In Section 3, a list of examples of extended AMRs demonstrate the approach. Some loose ends are discussed in Section 4.

2 Method

The idea is to extend the AMR with logical structure, obtaining a scoped representation AMR$^+$ with two dimensions: one level comprising predicate-argument structure (the original AMR, minus polarity attributes), and one level consisting of the logical structure (information about logical operators such as negation and the scope they take). This is achieved by viewing an AMR as a recursive structure, rather than interpreting it as a graph, and performing two operations on them:

1. assign an index to each (sub-)AMR;

2. add structural constraints to the AMR via the indices.

AMRs can be seen as a recursive structure by viewing every slash within an AMR as a sub-AMR (Bos, 2016). If a (sub-)AMR contains relations, those relations will introduce nested AMRs. (A constant is also an AMR, following this view.) An AMR (and all its sub-AMRs) will be labeled by decorating the slashes with indices (indices will be indicated by numbers enclosed in square brackets).

Every AMR is augmented by a set of scoping constraints on the labels. This way, a sub-AMR can be viewed as describing a "context". The constraints state how the contexts relate to each other. They can be declared as the same contexts ($=$), a negated context ($\neg$), a conditional context ($\Rightarrow$), or a presuppositional context ($<$). Colons are used to denote inclusion, i.e., $l : C$ states that context l contains condition C.

Note that these labels are similar in spirit to those used in underspecification formalisms as proposed in the early 1990s (Reyle, 1993; Copestake et al., 1995; Bos, 1996). The treatment of presuppositions is inspired by semantic formalism extending Discourse Representation Theory (Van der Sandt, 1992; Geurts, 1999; Venhuizen et al., 2013; Venhuizen et al., 2018).

3 Results

Below I illustrate the idea with several canonical examples involving existential and universal quantification, definite descriptions, proper names, and, of course, negation.

3.1 Existential Quantification

Consider the AMR for "a dog scared a cat" with a transitive verb and two indefinite noun phrases in PENMAN notation:

```
(e / scare-01
   :ARG0 (x / dog)
   :ARG1 (y / cat))
```

Within this AMR we can identify three sub-AMRs. We index and constrain them and arrive at the following AMR$^+$:

```
(e /1/ scare-01
   :ARG0 (x /2/ dog)
   :ARG1 (y /3/ cat)) {1 = 2, 1 = 3}
```

Here, there is just one context shared by all three sub-AMRs, as one would expect with existential quantification: scope does not play a pivotal role here. As equivalent alternative, the following simplified, constraint-free AMR$^+$ can be obtained after eliminating the identity constraints:

```
(e /1/ scare-01
   :ARG0 (x /1/ dog)
   :ARG1 (y /1/ cat)) {}
```

3.2 Definite Descriptions and Proper Names

A sentence like "the bear growled" contains a definite description triggering an existential presupposition. Presuppositions yield new contexts:

```
(e /1/ growl-01
   :ARG0 (x /2/ bear)) {2<1}
```

In other words, the definite article triggers a presupposition that there is a bear (the AMR with index 2) with respect to context provided by the AMR indexed as 1. Proper names can be handled similarly, as the AMR$^+$ for the sentence "Fido barked" shows (the existence of a dog named "Fido" is a presupposition for the barking event):

```
(e /1/ bark-01
   :ARG0 (x /2/ dog
             :Name "Fido")) {2<1}
```

3.3 Negation

Negation introduces a new (negated) context in AMR$^+$. This makes the :polarity- relation in AMR obsolete. As negation is always part of another context in some cases a context needs to be coerced (second and third example below, see also Section 4.1). Consider the representations for "a woman didn't smile", "the woman didn't smile", and "no woman smiled":

```
(e /1/ smile-01
   :ARG0 (x /2/ woman)) {2:¬1}

(e /1/ smile-01
   :ARG0 (x /3/ woman)) {3<1, 2:¬1}

(e /1/ smile.v.01
   :Agent (x /1/ woman)) {2:¬1}
```

3.4 Universal Quantification

Universal quantification introduces a conditional context in AMR^+. Below are examples for quantifiers in subject position, object position, subject and object position, and a quantification with a bound variable. Note that the *mod*-relation used in AMR becomes obsolete.

"Everyone smiled."
```
(e /1/ smile-01
    :ARG0 (x /2/ person.n.01)) {3:2=>1}
```

"A dog scared every cat."
```
(e /1/ scare-01
    :ARG0 (x /3/ dog)
    :ARG1 (y /2/ cat)) {3:2=>1}
```

"Every dog scared every cat."
```
(e /1/ scare-01
    :ARG0 (x /2/ dog.n.01)
    :ARG1 (y /3/ cat)) {5:3=>4,4:2=>1}
```

"Every student revised their paper."
```
(e /1/ revise-01
    :ARG0 (x /2/ student)
    :ARG1 (y /3/ paper
               :poss x)) {2=3,3<1,4:2=>1}
```

3.5 From AMR to DRS

The AMR^+ representations share characteristics with the Discourse Representation Structure (DRS) introduced in Discourse Representation Theory, DRT for short (Kamp and Reyle, 1993). It is important to compare AMR^+ with DRS for various reasons. DRT is a well-studied formalism with a model-theoretic component. If we are able to show that the representations are equivalent then this has positive consequences for AMR, as all inferential properties supplied by DRT could be transferred to AMR.

As a matter of fact, there is a rather straightforward way of converting labelled AMRs to DRS in the style of the Parallel Meaning Bank (Abzianidze et al., 2017). This conversion comprises three main steps (τ is the translation function, $\oplus$ is a DRS-merge operation, and v is a function mapping an AMR to its main variable):

1. Replace each sub-AMR by a DRS. This DRS contains exactly one discourse referent, a one-place predicate, and zero or more two-place relations. The first argument of the two-place relation is the main variable of the sub-AMR; the second argument of the two-place relation is the main variable of the sub-AMR. So given an AMR^+ $(x/i/C :R_1 A_1 ... R_n A_n)$, the corresponding DRS is $\tau(i) = \boxed{x \mid C'(x)\ R'_1(x,v(A_1))\ ...\ R'_n(x,v(A_n))}$.

2. Merge all DRSs that are indexed with the same index. A merge of two DRSs ($\oplus$) consists of taking the unions of their respective domains and conditions. Assign an empty DRS $\boxed{\ \ \mid\ \ }$ to inferred contexts.

3. Construct the final DRS by following the structure expressed by the constraints. For instance, $3:2=>1$ is translated as $\tau(3) \oplus \boxed{\ \mid\ \tau(2) \Rightarrow \tau(1)\ }$, and $1:\neg 2$ is translated as $\tau(1) \oplus \boxed{\ \mid\ \neg\ \tau(2)\ }$.

Here are two examples that illustrate this translation, converting AMR predicates to PMB WordNet synsets, and AMR PropBank relations to PMB VerbNet roles:

"A dog scared every cat."
```
(e /1/ scare-01
    :ARG0 (x /1/ dog)
    :ARG1 (y /2/ cat)) {3:2=>1}
```

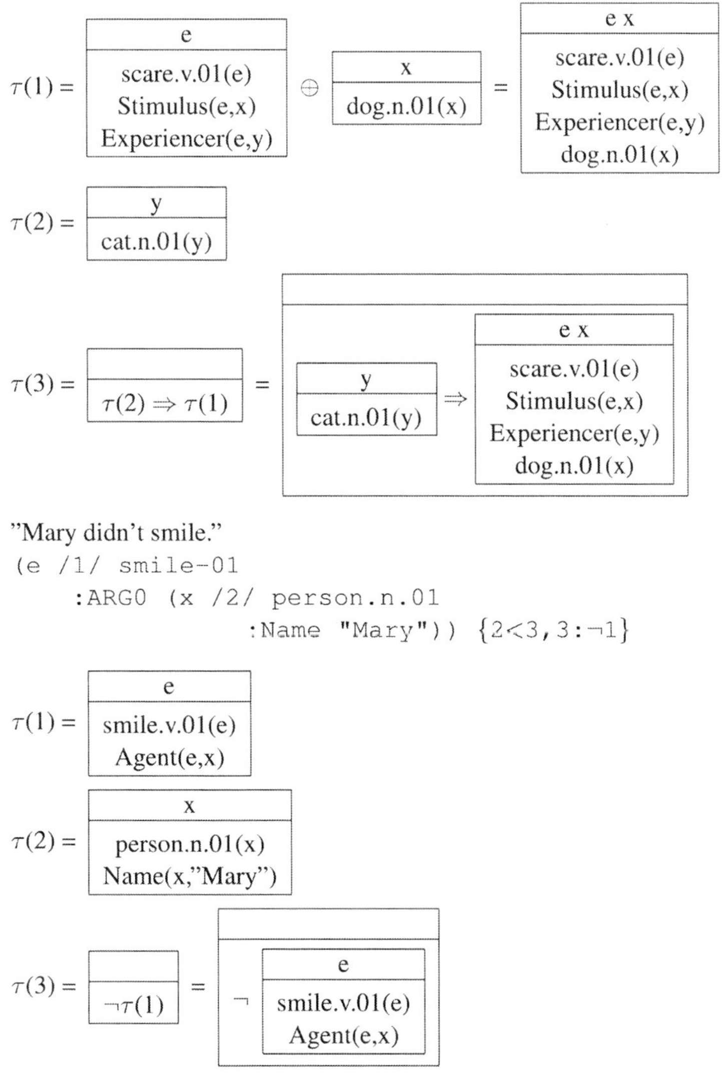

"Mary didn't smile."
```
(e /1/ smile-01
     :ARG0 (x /2/ person.n.01
                 :Name "Mary")) {2<3,3:¬1}
```

In terms of expressive power, AMR$^+$ is equivalent with the dialect of DRS employed in the Parallel Meaning Bank (Abzianidze et al., 2017), where relations cannot have arity larger than two. In general, DRS is a more expressive meaning representation language.

4 Discussion

In this section I discuss some loose ends that emerged when designing AMR$^+$: the issue of inferred labels, annotation work required to implement the approach, and the conversion to triples.

4.1 Inferred Labels

In the current proposal, negation and conditionals introduce new indices, that do not appear in the predicate-argument level of the AMR. These are necessary to ensure a well-formed logical structure. But they are (perhaps) not intuitive, and therefore harder to annotate by coders. It would be useful to investigate whether these labels can be inferred, in such a way that constraints with colons (for negation and conditionals) could be simplified. In what direction could this go? First note that inferred contexts are needed in cases of negation (and conditionals). In DRT, a negation is formed recursively, where the negation material (represented as a DRS) is embedded into the wider context (again, represented as a DRS). But when there is nothing available in the wider context, the corresponding DRS will be empty (and as a result, there won't be a corresponding labelled AMR). As we proposed in Section 3.3, we infer an index to meet the requirements of a well-formed logical structure. Instead, we can adopt a short-hand notation for such cases, i.e., $\{\neg j\}$ meaning $\{i : \neg j\}$, and $\{j \Rightarrow k\}$ meaning $\{i : j \Rightarrow k\}$. But in general, conditionals would require an equivalent notation in terms of negation, so $\{\neg j, j : \neg k\}$ as short for $\{i : \neg j, j : \neg k\}$, which is logically equivalent to $\{i : j \Rightarrow k\}$. This would cover all cases in Section 3.4.

4.2 Annotation Work

Existing AMR annotations can be monotonically extended: all "slashes" that occur in AMRs need to be indexed, and constraints need to be added. Given an annotated AMR corpus (Banarescu et al., 2013), this can be done semi-automatically: first add indices automatically (by replacing "/" by "/1/"). Then manually correct cases of negation (search for ":polarity -"), universal quantification, and definite descriptions, for a sample of the corpus. Finally, use machine learning to annotate the rest (or hire or persuade human annotators to do the job). The polarity and mod relations can be optionally removed from the AMRs. An interesting question concerns the use of existing parsing models developed for AMR (Artzi et al., 2015; Van Noord and Bos, 2017; Damonte et al., 2017). How can these be extended to deal with the extended AMRs as proposed in this paper? As the original AMR is not affected, a sensible approach would be one in a modular fashion, where datasets consisting of AMRs paired with AMR^+s could be used as training material.

4.3 Triple Format of Logical Structure

AMRs are converted to sets of triples for evaluation purposes. Therefore, a sensible question to ask is how the logical constraints in this proposal are converted to triples. There are two new types of triple instances. The indexed sub-AMRs all introduce a membership triple (with the edge named IN) linking an instance with a scope index. Secondly, each scoping constraint introduces one or more "structural" triples. Constraints that involve two indices introduce a single triple. Constraints that involve three indices introduce two triples. Here is an example:

```
"Nobody smiled."
(e /1/ smile-01
     :ARG0 (x /2/ person)) {4:2=>3,3:¬1}
```

This will introduce the membership triples $<$ e , IN , 1 $>$ and $<$ x , IN , 2 $>$, the triple for negation $<$ 3 , NOT , 1 $>$, and the triples for the implication $<$ 4 , IF , 2 $>$, and $<$ 2 , THEN , 3 $>$. As a consequence, standard tools for AMR evaluation (Cai and Knight, 2013) can be used, or extended to more fine-grained scores (Damonte et al., 2017).

5 Conclusion and Future Work

The original AMR notation can be extended by a layer of logical structure that gives correct interpretation of linguistic phenomena that require scope or quantification. The resulting framework bears strong similarities with Discourse Representation Theory as implemented in the Parallel Meaning Bank, and it deals with the *bound variable problem* and the *scope representation problem*. So what's next? Let's get an AMR corpus annotated with logical structure!

Acknowledgements

This work was funded by the NWO-VICI grant *Lost in Translation – Found in Meaning* (288-89-003). I thank the three anonymous reviewers for their feedback. Reviewer 1 rightly reminded me to cite Artzi et al. (2015), and so I did; and I also followed their suggestion to say more about the inferred contexts (they can now be found in Section 4.1), and include more negation examples in Section 3.3 (I added "no woman smiled"). Reviewer 2 was under the incorrect assumption that I was unaware of Crouch and Kalouli (2018), but actually, I already referred to this article in the submitted version of this paper, which indeed shares many points of contact with my work. Reviewer 3 had some excellent suggestions, and also requested a formal definition of the translation, and I thought this was a great idea. I somehow managed to squeeze it in this short paper, forcing me to leave out some of the details. Thanks again!

References

Lasha Abzianidze, Johannes Bjerva, Kilian Evang, Hessel Haagsma, Rik van Noord, Pierre Ludmann, Duc-Duy Nguyen, and Johan Bos. 2017. The Parallel Meaning Bank: Towards a multilingual corpus of translations annotated with compositional meaning representations. In *Proceedings of the 15th Conference of the European Chapter of the Association for Computational Linguistics*, pages 242–247, Valencia, Spain.

Yoav Artzi, Kenton Lee, and Luke Zettlemoyer. 2015. Broad-coverage CCG semantic parsing with AMR. In *Proceedings of the 2015 Conference on Empirical Methods in Natural Language Processing*, pages 1699–1710, Lisbon, Portugal. Association for Computational Linguistics.

Laura Banarescu, Claire Bonial, Shu Cai, Madalina Georgescu, Kira Griffitt, Ulf Hermjakob, Kevin Knight, Philipp Koehn, Martha Palmer, and Nathan Schneider. 2013. Abstract Meaning Representation for Sembanking. In *Proceedings of the 7th Linguistic Annotation Workshop and Interoperability with Discourse*, pages 178–186, Sofia, Bulgaria, August.

Johan Bos and Lasha Abzianidze. 2019. Thirty musts for meaning banking. In *Proceedings of the First International Workshop on Designing Meaning Representations*, pages 15–27, Florence, Italy. Association for Computational Linguistics.

Johan Bos. 1996. Predicate Logic Unplugged. In P. Dekker and M. Stokhof, editors, *Proceedings of the Tenth Amsterdam Colloquium*, pages 133–143, ILLC/Dept. of Philosophy, University of Amsterdam.

Johan Bos. 2016. Expressive power of abstract meaning representations. *Computational Linguistics*, 42(3):527–535.

Shu Cai and Kevin Knight. 2013. Smatch: an evaluation metric for semantic feature structures. In *Proceedings of the 51st Annual Meeting of the Association for Computational Linguistics (Volume 2: Short Papers)*, pages 748–752, Sofia, Bulgaria, August. Association for Computational Linguistics.

Ann Copestake, Dan Flickinger, Rob Malouf, Susanne Riehemann, and Ivan Sag. 1995. Translation using Minimal Recursion Semantics. In *Proceedings of the Sixth International Conference on Theoretical and Methodological Issues in Machine Translation*, pages 15–32, University of Leuven, Belgium.

Dick Crouch and Aikaterini-Lida Kalouli. 2018. Named graphs for semantic representations. In *The Seventh Joint Conference on Lexical and Computational Semantics (*SEM 2018)*, pages 113–118, New Orleans.

Marco Damonte, Shay B. Cohen, and Giorgio Satta. 2017. An incremental parser for Abstract Meaning Representation. In *Proceedings of the 15th Conference of the European Chapter of the Association for Computational Linguistics: Volume 1, Long Papers*, pages 536–546, Valencia, Spain.

Bart Geurts. 1999. *Presuppositions and Pronouns*. Elsevier, London.

Hans Kamp and Uwe Reyle. 1993. *From Discourse to Logic; An Introduction to Modeltheoretic Semantics of Natural Language, Formal Logic and DRT*. Kluwer, Dordrecht.

Robert T. Kasper. 1989. A flexible interface for linking applications to penman's sentence generator. In *Proceedings of the DARPA Speech and Natural Language Workshop*, pages 153–158, Philadelphia.

Kenneth Lai, Lucia Donatelli, and James Pustejovsky. 2020. A continuation semantics for abstract meaning representation. In *The Second International Workshop on Designing Meaning Representations (DMR 2020)*, Barcelona, Spain.

Irene Langkilde and Kevin Knight. 1998. Generation that exploits corpus-based statistical knowledge. In *COLING 1998 Volume 1: The 17th International Conference on Computational Linguistics*, pages 704–710.

James Pustejovsky, Nianwen Xue, and Kenneth Lai. 2019. Modeling quantification and scope in abstract meaning representations. In *Proceedings of the First International Workshop on Designing Meaning Representations*, pages 28–33, Florence, Italy. Association for Computational Linguistics.

Uwe Reyle. 1993. Dealing with Ambiguities by Underspecification: Construction, Representation and Deduction. *Journal of Semantics*, 10:123–179.

Ed Stabler. 2017. Reforming AMR. In *Formal Grammar 2017. Lecture Notes in Computer Science*, volume 10686, pages 72–87. Springer.

Rob A. Van der Sandt. 1992. Presupposition Projection as Anaphora Resolution. *Journal of Semantics*, 9:333–377.

Rik Van Noord and Johan Bos. 2017. Neural semantic parsing by character-based translation: Experiments with abstract meaning representations. *Computational Linguistics in the Netherlands Journal*, 7:93–108.

Noortje J. Venhuizen, Johan Bos, and Harm Brouwer. 2013. Parsimonious semantic representations with projection pointers. In *Proceedings of the 10th International Conference on Computational Semantics (IWCS 2013) – Long Papers*, pages 252–263, Potsdam, Germany, March. Association for Computational Linguistics.

Noortje Venhuizen, Johan Bos, Petra Hendriks, and Harm Brouwer. 2018. Discourse semantics with information structure. *Journal of Semantics*, 35(1):127–169.

Building Korean Abstract Meaning Representation Corpus

Hyonsu Choe,   Jiyoon Han[†],   Hyejin Park[◇],   Teahwan Oh[◇],   Hansaem Kim[†]
Language AI Lab, NCSOFT Corp. / Seongnam, South Korea
[†]Institute of Language and Information Studies, Yonsei University / Seoul, South Korea
[◇]Department of Korean Language and Literature, Yonsei University / Seoul, South Korea
`choehyonsu@ncsoft.com`, {`clinamen35, hjp1010, ghksl0604, khss`}`@yonsei.ac.kr`

Abstract

To explore the potential sembanking in Korean and ways to represent the meaning of Korean sentences, this paper reports on the process of applying Abstract Meaning Representation to Korean, a semantic representation framework that has been studied in a wide range of languages, and its output: the Korean AMR corpus. The corpus which is constructed so far is a size of 1,253 sentences and its raw texts are from ExoBrain Corpus, a state-led R&D project on language AI. This paper also analyzes the result in both qualitative and quantitative manners, proposing discussions for further development.

1   Introduction

This paper aims to prepare the annotation guideline for applying Abstract Meaning Representation (AMR)—the annotation framework to represent the meaning of the sentence in a graph structure—to Korean and construct a corpus based on it as well as to explore the possibility of new Korean semantic annotation methodologies and language resources.

Until now, the field of Korean natural language processing attempts to construct a corpus targeted to specific phenomena such as polysemy disambiguation, Named entities, temporal and spatial information and semantic roles. However, given the complex relationship between the expression and its meaning, integrated meaning representation system and language resources that far exceed the fragmented analysis are necessary.

In response, this study creates annotation guidelines covering sentence structure and grammatical phenomenon in Korean and describes the following result, a Korean AMR corpus with a size of 1,253 sentences. Korean AMR uses predicate frames from Korean PropBank (Palmer et al., 2006) to represent the relation between events and concepts. Parts of the procedures are automated by using feature annotation form preconstructed parallel corpus. As a result, the search cost has been reduced and the annotation process has been simplified. Section 4 will analyze the corpus in qualitative and quantitative perspectives and provide insight for further research.

2   Related Works

Ever since AMR was first proposed in Banarescu et al. (2013), efforts to construct corpus have continued in English-speaking nations. *The Little Prince Corpus*, containing 1,562 sentences, has been continuously providing the foundation for multilingual AMR research; *Bio AMR Corpus*, comprising 6,952 sentences, is known for proving its applicability in the biomedical domain.[1] In particular, the release of *Abstract Meaning Representation (AMR) Annotation Release 3.0* (Knight et al., 2020) demonstrates how the English AMR managed to enter a stable phase.

AMR research in non-English-speaking nations has begun its expansion; recent years have seen concrete developments in corpus construction in various parts of the world. In 2014, 100-sentence-sized Chinese and Czech AMR corpus was first built for basic research on multilingual AMR annotation.

[1]`https://amr.isi.edu/download.html`

Proceedings of the 2nd International Workshop on Designing Meaning Representations, pages 21–29
Barcelona, Spain (Online), December 13, 2020

(Xue et al., 2014) In 2016, Annotation Specification for Chinese AMR (CAMR) and the Chinese version of *The Little Prince Corpus* was released. (Li et al., 2016) According to Wang et al. (2018) and Li et al. (2019), the currently known size of Chinese AMR Bank is 10,149 sentences; such a size can be said to approach the level that allows a significant parsing ability. Follow-up efforts have since continued, including Song et al. (2020), which attempted to expand predicate lexicon in order to improve the Chinese AMR.

Research efforts based on *The Little Prince Corpus* act as a 'calling water' in the multilingual AMR studies. In Spanish, a basic research was performed on how to represent grammatical phenomena that are characteristic of individual languages based on AMR (Migueles-Abraira et al., 2018); In Brazilian Portuguese, *The Little Prince Corpus* (AMR-BR) was constructed (Anchiêta and Pardo, 2018), laying the foundations for the construction of the general-purpose corpus. (Sobrevilla Cabezudo and Pardo, 2019) AMR-based studies that aim to develop semantic representation resources have been done in Vietnamese (Linh and Nguyen, 2019) and Turkish (Azin and Eryiğit, 2019) as well.

In Korean, preliminary studies have been done to illustrate some grammatical phenomena that are unique to Korean, such as Copula construction, its negation, and case-stacking, and address how they can be represented within the grammatical system of AMR. (Choe et al., 2019a) Further studies have developed a Korean Guideline v1.0, thereby laying the foundations for corpus construction. (Choe et al., 2019b) This study expands upon the aforementioned studies by discussing the process and outcomes of the construction of Korean AMR corpus.

3 Towards Korean AMR Corpus

3.1 Guidelines for Korean AMR Annotation

In order to construct Korean AMR corpus, above all, a guideline that is applicable to the Korean language must be set up. Choe et al. (2019a) has already proposed specific but partial annotation guidelines, such as Copula Construction, its negation, and Case Stacking, that must be supplemented and reinforced to better apply AMR in Korean. After that, based on those guidelines, Korean AMR Guideline v1.0 has been developed and released.[2] (Choe et al., 2019b)

Korean AMR guideline was prepared by taking into account a wide array of elements, including morphological and syntactic characteristics of Korean. While its basic structure is derived from that of English AMR, specific representation guidelines regarding some grammatical phenomena such as negation, modality, named-entity representation, and their examples were significantly reinforced. Below demonstrates some of the features of Korean AMR.

Using Korean PropBank – Korean AMR annotation is based on the verb frames of Korean PropBank. (Palmer et al., 2006) This is the result of taking into account that in several languages such as Chinese, Brazilian-Portuguese and Vietnamese AMR is constructed based on PropBank-related language resources and that criteria for determining semantic roles in Exobrain wiseNLU[3], a state-led R&D project, are also based on PropBank style. (Lim et al., 2015) Therefore, such an annotation system may be advantageous in the context of compatibility between different language resources and multilingual research.

Adopting special frames and entities of English AMR as metalanguage – Usage of special frames and entities defined in English AMR will be maximized in Korean AMR corpus. Special frames and entities that can both allow more intuitive annotation (e.g., `rate-entity-91` and `have-org-role-91`) and normalization of meaning will be widely accepted. Reifications such as `cause-01` and `exemplify-01` that correspond to certain relations will also be accepted as the grammar of Korean AMR. These decisions are especially useful in circumstances in which exact correspondence between verb frames cannot be provided due to differences between the two languages. For instance, deontic modality in Korean does not have a lexicalized unit such as the English verb "obligate" but is rather expressed via periphrastic construction such as "-야 하/되-"(*have to (be)*). In cases like this, English verb frame such as `obligate-01` would be used. Such a system would be applied to

---

the counting particles (`:unit`) of `X-quantity` and `X-entity` in the same way, thereby normalizing types of meaning.

Coverage of `:polarity` – Syntactic negation in Korean can be categorized into 1) short-form negation that utilizes adverbial negators '안'(*not*) and '못'(*cannot*) and 2) long-form negation that utilizes auxiliary verb '아니하-'(*do not*), '않-'(*don't*) and '못하-'(*cannot do*). In addition, negation of copula '-이-'(copula *'be'*) uses a lexicalized '아니-'(*be not*). In imperative, '말-'(*desist*), a deontic modal negator, is used to realize the negation. In Korean AMR, `:polarity` is annotated to these basic negators as well as negative prefix such as '비-', '불-', '미-', '무-'(corresponding to *non-, un-, im-, ir-, il-, dis-*) and negative verbs such as '없-'(*not exist*; antonym of adjective '있-', which means *exist*), '모르-'(*not know*; antonym of verb '알-', which means *know*). (e.g. "X를 모른다." → 알-01 `:polarity` - `:ARG1` X)

Expanded usage of `:domain` **for case-stacking** – Korean is a topic-subject prominent language; there are Multiple Nominative Construction, where the nominative marker '-이/-가/-은/-는' is licensed to two or more components, and Multiple Accusative Construction, where the accusative marker '-을/-를' is also licensed to two or more components. Although it is desirable in AMR that relational structure is annotated based on the roleset of an appropriate verb frame and not on the syntactic structure, components that are of topical focus are annotated as `:domain` when it is difficult to determine the semantic role between the constituents. (The detailed discussion on case-stacking in Korean and its representational choice can be found in Choe et al. (2019a).)

Restricted set of NE Types – Current criteria for NE annotation allows for the selection of arbitrary NE Type rather than canonical type based on context. In Korean, the list of basic named-entity types is limited to that presented in English AMR; English vocabulary is adopted when there is a need for expansion. This effectively introduces meta-language in NE annotation and can be helpful for regularized annotation. Furthermore, difficulties in determining canonical form were resolved by annotating wikification for all NE representations within corpus.

3.2 Annotation Overview

3.2.1 Source Texts

The Korean AMR Corpus is composed of texts that are released to the public for research purposes, including a Korean-version text of ⟨*The Little Prince*⟩,[4] example sentences of verb entries in the Basic Korean Dictionary[5], and subset of ExoBrain Corpus v4.0[6]. Most of the texts are from ExoBrain corpus, which is comprised of 19.5M sentences of news texts, Korean Wikipedia documents and web texts. Corpus is highly useful in that it contains various layers of annotation information such as, dependency structure, word senses, NE and semantic roles. Each layer of annotation guideline prepared for the construction of ExoBrain corpus is gradually being accepted as a standard method for automatic analysis of Korean; the analysis engine whose learning is based on a vast amount of data is provided in the form of open API so that Korean NLP researchers and technologists can use it.

3.2.2 Korean PropBank

Korean PropBank (Palmer et al., 2006) comprises 33,295 predicates tokens from Virginia Corpus (54.5K words), Newswire Corpus (131.8K words) and 2,749 Verb Frames. Through the ExoBrain project, Korean PropBank became a customary standard for Korean semantic role labeling, and further research endeavors including an expansion of verb frames followed. (Bae and Lee, 2015) Taking into account that multilingual PropBank resources are already established in diverse languages and that AMR annotation based on this is in trial, Korean AMR corpus was also annotated based on Verb Frames of Korean PropBank. For the Verb Frames of Korean PropBank are limited in size (2,749), additional guidelines are needed when annotating unlisted predicates; therefore, while synonymous predicates are selected when annotating for the unlisted predicates, annotations are made based on the roleset of the verb frame that has similar case-frame information and valency required by the predicates.

---

[4]Text source: *The Little Prince Collection* (`https://phasis68.blogspot.com/2017/03/korean.html`)

[5]Provided by National Institute of Korean Language. (`https://krdict.korean.go.kr/`)

[6]Provided by ETRI. (Electronics and Telecommunications Research Institute) (`http://aiopen.etri.re.kr/service_dataset.php`)

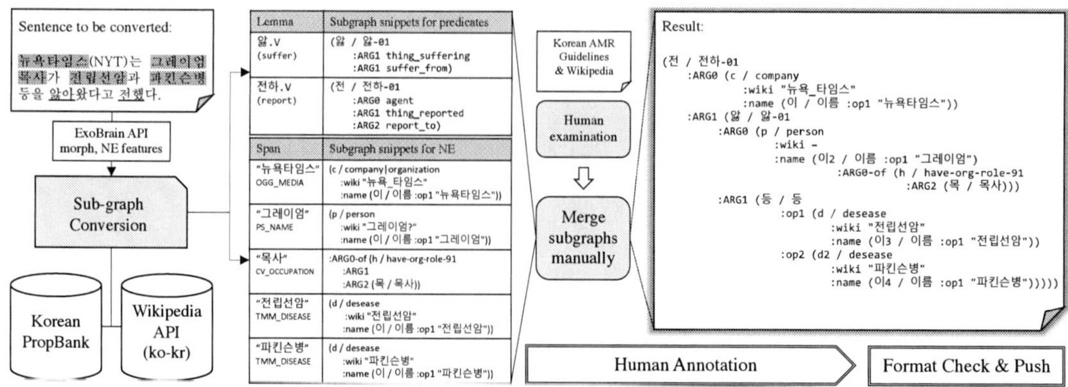

Figure 1: Annotation process: Human annotators take automatically converted subgraph snippets including Korean PropBank frame and roleset, head NE types, name strings and wikification.

3.2.3 Assisted Annotation: Reviewing & Merging Preprocessed Subgraph Snippets

In this study, the corpus was constructed not with AMR Editor (Hermjakob, 2013), a specialized tool for AMR annotation, but rather using text editor with advanced features such as code completion. Such a decision was made to overcome the limitation that AMR Editor was not designed in a way suitable for multilingual annotation as well as reduce the search cost by taking the full advantage of the feature annotation that existing resources have. In the whole annotation process of this study, annotators have completed an AMR graph in a 'assisted bottom-up' process, in which annotator carefully reviewed all the auto-suggested subgraph snippets and merged them manually to the entire AMR graph.

Generating NE subgraphs with API response: When many NEs are included in the raw text, search cost for making AMR increases. To address this problem, substring span of potential NE is used as query of Wikipedia API (ko-kr) to automatically convert NE subgraph, including wikification, thereby reducing the search cost. Without any particular command input, an annotator can examine wikification as well as the type of subgraph that is already created; when required, some can be modified and reflected in the entire graph.

Generating verb frame subgraphs with morphological annotation: Same method of automatic conversion can be applied to verb frame selection as well. Verb Frame of Korean PropBank can be fetched based on verb, adjective, roots of predicative nominals from the morphological analysis result of ExoBrain API response; this verb frame is suggested to the annotator after converted into a PENMAN format subgraph. By doing so, the search becomes simplified and proposing a list of subgraph snippets in advance in such a way can prevent the annotator from omitting certain verbs in long, complicated sentences.

4 Evaluation

4.1 Corpus Specification

The construction process of the Korean AMR corpus can be categorized into trial phase and actual construction phase. In the trial phase, annotators, who were trained based on sentences that are relatively easy to annotate, annotated some parts of the Korean ⟨*The Little Prince*⟩ text and example sentences of verb entries in the Basic Korean Dictionary to verify the feasibility of Korean AMR guidelines. Actual construction was done on a portion of ExoBrain corpus v4.0; The corpus consists of 1,253 sentences was constructed from September 2019 to April 2020. Specific construction sizes of the subgroups are shown below. Constructed corpus was released to the public via online repository.[7]

The constructed Korean AMR Corpus is a size of 1,253 sentences with 20,050 nodes and 18,797 edges. About 6K nodes (30%) represent general concepts, and approximately 3.9K Korean Propbank frames

---

[7]https://github.com/choe-hyonsu-gabrielle/korean-amr-corpus

Source	Subcategory	Snts. (%)
ExoBrain Corpus v4.0	Wikipedia QA Corpus	356 (28.4%)
	Newswire Corpus	256 (20.4%)
	Paraphrase Dataset	253 (20.1%)
	Wikipedia Corpus	234 (18.6%)
Basic Korean Dictionary	Sentence examples of verb entries	120 (9.5%)
The Little Prince (Korean Ed.)	Chapter I (parallel)	34 (2.7%)
		1,253 (100.0%)

Table 1: Organization of the Korean AMR Corpus.

Concepts	Node freq.(%)	Relations	Edge freq.(%)
General Concepts	6,026 (30.1%)	Core roles (`:ARGx/-of`)	6,119 (32.6%)
NE related	3,408 (17.0%)	`:opN` & `:opX`	3,826 (20.4%)
Name span & valid wikification	3,257 (16.2%)	`:name` & `:wiki`	3,032 (16.1%)
Korean PropBank Frames	3,184 (15.8%)	`:mod`	1,469 (7.82%)
Unlisted frames (*-00)	809 (4.1%)	`:time`	595 (3.3%)
Numerics & Scalar	772 (3.8%)	`:location`	395 (2.1%)
Conjunctions	635 (3.2%)	`:manner`	391 (2.1%)
Date-entity & Temporal-quantity	558 (2.8%)	`:quant`	301 (1.6%)
Special frames (*-91/*-01)	455 (2.3%)	`:topic`	251 (1.3%)
Polarity & truth-value	434 (2.2%)	`:poss`	224 (1.2%)

Table 2: 10 most frequent elements in the Korean AMR Corpus.

are used to represent events. Out of the verb frame instances in corpus, 800 instances (554 types) are unlisted entries to Korean Propbank, ending with -00 suffix. About 3.4K (17%) nodes are related to NE representation, including newly added NE Types specific to Korean AMR such as `brand`, `service`, `cultural-asset`, `hospital`, `weapon`.

Out of all relation markers, the core-roles including inverse role accounts for 32.6% in order of `:ARG1/-of`, `:ARG0/-of`, `:ARG2/-of` and the others. As the raw texts contain much information, `:opN` and `:opX`–often used to represent conjunction, enumeration, exemplification, and stretch—are frequently used (20.4%) while `:wiki` and `:name` for NE representation recorded 16.1%. Temporal (`:time`), quantitative (`:quant`, `:unit`) and locative (`:location`) representation are relatively used often. `:ARGA` - `:ARG4`, `:source`, `:location`, `:destination`, `:beneficiary`, `:instrument` for general semantic roles (Saeed, 1997) only accounts for 34.8%.

The Inter-annotator agreement of four annotators who participated in building and editing the corpus, based on 50 sentences, reached Smatch 0.79 comparable to the previously reported 0.79 to 0.83 from English or 0.72 from Brazil-Portuguese.

4.2 Disagreement Analysis

4.2.1 Adverbial Clause and Conjunction

Conjunction is a connection between two or more syntactic units (phrases, clauses, sentences and etc) that can be subdivided depending on whether the relationship is subordinate or not, and if so, what the specific semantic relationship is. However, representing the conjunction is not an easy task because distinguishing between the embedded adverbial clauses and (subordinate) conjunction is difficult, and specifying the semantic relation between two clauses is controversial among annotators, resulting in a lack of consistency among the outputs.

A following sentence (on the left part of Figure 2) demonstrates this issue: *PD 수첩은, "미투 운동이 전개되면서, 피해자들에게 2차 가해를 가하는 것도 많아지고 있다." (The PD Note (said), "As Me-Too movement expands, more and more victim-blamings are inflicted to the victims.")*. The annotators had

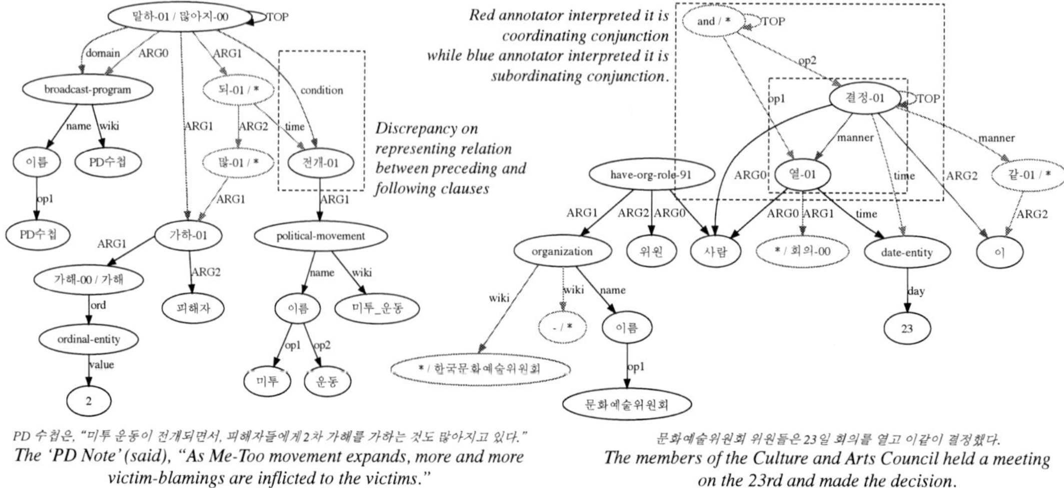

PD 수첩은, "미투 운동이 전개되면서, 피해자들에게 2차 가해를 가하는 것도 많아지고 있다."
The 'PD Note' (said), "As Me-Too movement expands, more and more victim-blamings are inflicted to the victims."

문화예술위원회 위원들은 23일 회의를 열고 이같이 결정했다.
The members of the Culture and Arts Council held a meeting on the 23rd and made the decision.

Figure 2: Annotators showed conflicting views on representing conjunction markers in Korean.

conflicting views when representing this sentence: whether the latter clause (led by '-면서,'; *after*) has temporal relation(`:time`) or logical relation (`:condition` or else). The controversy is due to the fact that a single conjunction marker can represent multiple meanings.

In the following sentence, (on the right part of Figure 2) *"문화예술위원회 위원들은 23일 회의를 열고 이같이 결정했다."* (*The members of the Culture and Arts Council held a meeting on the 23rd and made the decision.*), there was also a difference between annotators as to whether to represent the clause lead by '-고' with coordinate conjunction (`and`) or adverbial clause (`:manner`). In terms of meaning, it is similar to `:manner`; however, '-고' as well as 'and' can represent both coordinate conjunction (enumerate) and temporal relationship (sequential, simultaneous). Therefore, this disagreement among annotators depends on one's perspective: whether to focus on the form ('-고'; *and*) or on the meaning. Further guidelines with detailed examples of specific conjunctive markers are required to solve this issue.

4.2.2 Collocations

The institutionalised collocation in Korean refers to a case in which different morphemes gather to build a semantic unit. The Korean AMR Corpus annotated these cases through 1) using similar Propbank frames 2) using elements from English AMR. For instance, '-ㄹ 수 있-'(*can / be able to*) that represent modality of possibility can be annotated by using 가능-01 similar to the English way of using `possible-01`. In contrast, cases with '-아/어야 하-'(*should be*) that represent deontic modality or '-X을 수록 Y하-' that correspond to 'The X-er, The Y-er' constructions can cite `obligate-01` or `correlate-91` for Korean AMR annotation.

However, the crux of this discussion is that collocations which consist of morphemes with various POS serve diverse semantic functions. For instance, auxiliary verb '하-' from grammatical collocations '-아/어야 하-' function as a part of a unit representing deontic modality, while '하-' in -려(고) 하-'(*in order to / be intended to do*) serve as a part of a unit representing the purpose or intention. Furthermore, '-고는 하-' has a similar meaning to English 'used to', and '-게 하-' functions as English 'make' or 'cause'. Finally, the auxiliary verb '하-' in '-기도 하-' work as a light verb.

Lexical collocations share this complexity. In Korean, a verb '영향받-' (*be influenced*) which is derived by attaching denominal suffix '-받'(*take*) to the noun '영향'(*influence*). However, its relational antonymous expression '영향을 주-' (*give influence*) counts as a collocation. Unlike the antonymous relationship between verb '주-'(*give*) and '받-'(*take*), denominal suffix '-주'(*give*) does not exist in Korean; therefore, annotators did not reach a consensus for representing a sentence such as *"바그너의 음악에 영향을 주었다."* (*It influenced Wagner's music.*) Some annotator used Korean PropBank frame '영향-01' while another used 주-01, considering '주-'(*give*) as a main verb. (See left part of Figure 3.)

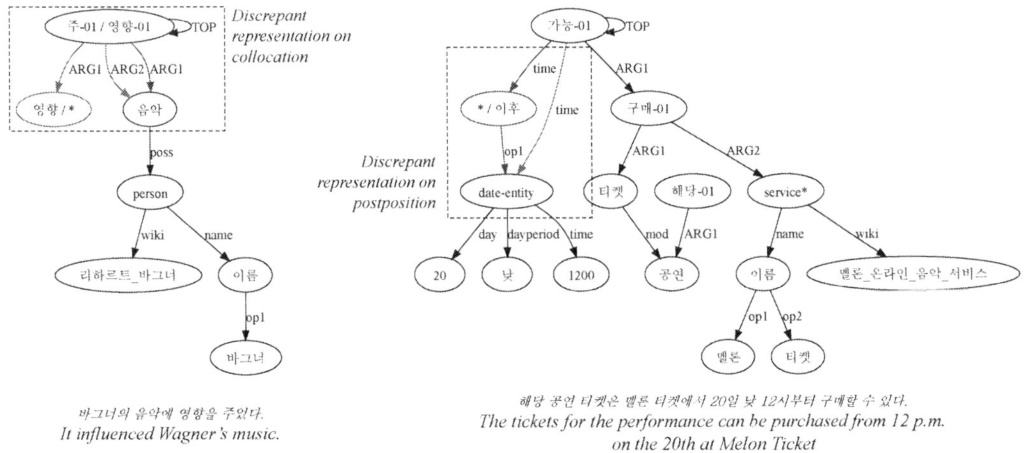

바그너의 음악에 영향을 주었다.
It influenced Wagner's music.

해당 공연 티켓은 멜론 티켓에서 20일 낮 12시부터 구매할 수 있다.
The tickets for the performance can be purchased from 12 p.m. on the 20th at Melon Ticket

Figure 3: Annotators showed conflicting views on representing collocation and postposition.

In Korean, multiple morphemes with various POS often gather to create collocations or periphrastic construction. Without providing detailed guidelines for each of them, it will be troublesome to maintain annotation consistency. The ideal methods would be to obtain a rich collection of examples, such as AMR Dictionary, as well as expanded multi-word predicate frames and rolesets which facilitate intuitive annotations of various constructions in Korean.

4.2.3 Special Postpositions

Postposition of Korean are consists of case postposition, which function as case marker, and special postposition which highlights or adds meaning. Both types of postposition are functional words realized after contents words, establishing postposition cluster. They can be omitted if enough context is provided to interpret the meaning. In such case, case postposition is more frequently omitted than special postposition.

Words that occur independently in other languages including English, (e.g. lexical items such as *'and'* or *'only'*) correspond to special postpositions in Korean. In Korean AMR, these special postpositions are characterized as function words that do not affect the proposition of the sentence. Often, they are omitted in AMR or represented with relations, such as ':postp-는커녕 and :postp-으로-의 because it is not easy to generalize their various uses.

Despite reservations regarding the representation of special postposition, the discrepancy of special postposition interpretation play crucial role in IAA. Special postposition refers to the starting point of the temporal or spatial interval, '-부터' (*from*) illustrates this issue well enough. (See right part of Figure 3.) In "해당 공연 티켓은 멜론 티켓에서 20일 낮 12시부터 구매할 수 있다." (*The tickets for the performance can be purchased from 12 p.m. on the 20th at Melon Ticket*), special postposition '-부터' which combined with temporal expression corresponds to English preposition 'from'. Some annotators considered '12시 부터'(*from 12 p.m.*) as a starting point of the specific time interval and following times; therefore, they added '이후' (*after*) during the annotation. However, some simply omitted '-부터' as '*from 12 p.m.*' meaning 'the start of the sale'.

Special postpositions of Korean vary its meaning and importance, thereby creating different representations depending on the intuition of annotators and types of special postposition. For example, annotators reached to consensus when special postposition '-까지' (*til, until / by*) that marks the end point of the time interval is used alone. (e.g. "9월 25일까지"(*by 25 September*) → date-interval :op2 (date-entity :month 9 :day 25) while "내일까지"(*until tomorrow*) → :time (이전 :op1 내일)). The special postposition words are roughly 30 types in Korean. Even though they are closed set, as multiple special postpositions stacked to add meaning and make syntactic relationships with other grammatical phenomena such as scopal polarity, the generalization of their semantic function is not easy. Therefore, the specific guidelines are needed to capture different usages of special postpositions.

5   Challenges on Korean Sembanking

For Korean AMR to be actually applied to systems that understand and process the natural language, beyond specific tasks such as semantic parsing, there are many challenges to overcome. The Korean AMR corpus presented in this paper is in small size with less specific guidelines. Therefore, it is necessary to set specific goals for both the quality and quantity aspects of data.

The first challenge that Korean AMR is facing is developing several supporting resources for the annotation while simultaneously revising guidelines. To provide more precise meaning representation, ambiguous descriptions in the guideline must be changed to concrete wordings and extensive examples. Moreover, The Korean PropBank should expand its predicates lexicon with enlarged multi-word expression, such as collocation and idioms.

The second challenge is quantitative expansion. To overcome lack of training data, integrated annotation environment that reduces search cost and fosters more intuitive annotation is required, and part of the annotation procedures must be automated to simplify the entire process.

6   Conclusion

This paper introduced the procedure for building a Korean AMR corpus, discussing several issues for further development. The Korean AMR corpus for this study is a size of 1,253 sentences, serving as the first result of foundational studies. Even with small size, the Korean AMR corpus will be the source of empirical clues for developing Korean AMR. It will contribute to laying the foundation for future applications of natural language understanding and generation.

References

Rafael Anchiêta and Thiago Pardo. 2018. Towards AMR-BR: A SemBank for Brazilian Portuguese language. In *Proceedings of the Eleventh International Conference on Language Resources and Evaluation (LREC 2018)*, Miyazaki, Japan, May. European Language Resources Association (ELRA).

Zahra Azin and Gülşen Eryiğit. 2019. Towards Turkish Abstract Meaning Representation. In *Proceedings of the 57th Annual Meeting of the Association for Computational Linguistics: Student Research Workshop*, pages 43–47, Florence, Italy, July. Association for Computational Linguistics.

Jangseong Bae and Changki Lee. 2015. Extending korean propbank for korean semantic role labeling and applying domain adaptation technique. *Korean Journal of Cognitive Science*, 26(4):377–392.

Laura Banarescu, Claire Bonial, Shu Cai, Madalina Georgescu, Kira Griffitt, Ulf Hermjakob, Kevin Knight, Philipp Koehn, Martha Palmer, and Nathan Schneider. 2013. Abstract Meaning Representation for sembanking. In *Proceedings of the 7th Linguistic Annotation Workshop and Interoperability with Discourse*, pages 178–186, Sofia, Bulgaria, August. Association for Computational Linguistics.

Hyonsu Choe, Jiyoon Han, Hyejin Park, and Hansaem Kim. 2019a. Copula and case-stacking annotations for Korean AMR. In *Proceedings of the First International Workshop on Designing Meaning Representations*, pages 128–135, Florence, Italy, August. Association for Computational Linguistics.

Hyonsu Choe, Jiyoon Han, Hyejin Park, Taehwan Oh, Seokwon Park, and Hansaem Kim. 2019b. Korean Abstract Meaning Representation (AMR) Guidelines for Graph-structured Representations of Sentence Meaning. In *Proceedings of the 31th Annual Conference on Human and Cognitive Language Technology*, pages 252–257, Seoul, Republic of Korea, October. SIGHCLT, Korean Institute of Information Scientists and Engineers. *In Korean*.

Ulf Hermjakob. 2013. Amr editor: A tool to build abstract meaning representations. Technical report, USC Information Sciences Institute.

Kevin Knight, Bianca Badarau, Laura Baranescu, Claire Bonial, Madalina Bardocz, Kira Griffitt, Ulf Hermjakob, Daniel Marcu, Martha Palmer, Tim O'Gorman, and Nathan Schneider. 2020. Abstract meaning representation (amr) annotation release 3.0. *LDC Catalog No.: LDC2020T02, ISBN 1-58563-915-X*.

Bin Li, Yuan Wen, Weiguang Qu, Lijun Bu, and Nianwen Xue. 2016. Annotating the little prince with Chinese AMRs. In *Proceedings of the 10th Linguistic Annotation Workshop held in conjunction with ACL 2016 (LAW-X 2016)*, pages 7–15, Berlin, Germany, August. Association for Computational Linguistics.

Bin Li, Yuan Wen, Li Song, Weiguang Qu, and Nianwen Xue. 2019. Building a Chinese AMR bank with concept and relation alignments. In *Linguistic Issues in Language Technology, Volume 18, 2019 - Exploiting Parsed Corpora: Applications in Research, Pedagogy, and Processing*. CSLI Publications, July.

Soojong Lim, Minjung Kwon, Junsu Kim, and Hyunki Kim. 2015. Korean Proposition Bank Guidelines for Exobrain. In *Proceedings of the 27th Annual Conference on Human and Cognitive Language Technology*, pages 250–254, Seoul, Republic of Korea, October. SIGHCLT, Korean Institute of Information Scientists and Engineers. *In Korean.*

Ha Linh and Huyen Nguyen. 2019. A case study on meaning representation for Vietnamese. In *Proceedings of the First International Workshop on Designing Meaning Representations*, pages 148–153, Florence, Italy, August. Association for Computational Linguistics.

Noelia Migueles-Abraira, Rodrigo Agerri, and Arantza Diaz de Ilarraza. 2018. Annotating Abstract Meaning Representations for Spanish. In *Proceedings of the Eleventh International Conference on Language Resources and Evaluation (LREC 2018)*, Miyazaki, Japan, May. European Language Resources Association (ELRA).

Martha Palmer, Shijong Ryu, Jinyoung Choi, Sinwon Yoon, and Yeongmi Jeon. 2006. Korean propbank. *LDC Catalog No.: LDC2006T03, ISBN 1-58563-374-7*, pages 1–58563.

John Saeed. 1997. I. 2003. Semantics. *GB: Blackwell Publishing.*

Marco Antonio Sobrevilla Cabezudo and Thiago Pardo. 2019. Towards a general Abstract Meaning Representation corpus for Brazilian Portuguese. In *Proceedings of the 13th Linguistic Annotation Workshop*, pages 236–244, Florence, Italy, August. Association for Computational Linguistics.

Li Song, Yuling Dai, Yihuan Liu, Bin Li, and Weiguang Qu. 2020. Construct a sense-frame aligned predicate lexicon for Chinese AMR corpus. In *Proceedings of The 12th Language Resources and Evaluation Conference*, pages 2962–2969, Marseille, France, May. European Language Resources Association.

Chuan Wang, Bin Li, and Nianwen Xue. 2018. Transition-based Chinese AMR parsing. In *Proceedings of the 2018 Conference of the North American Chapter of the Association for Computational Linguistics: Human Language Technologies, Volume 2 (Short Papers)*, pages 247–252, New Orleans, Louisiana, June. Association for Computational Linguistics.

Nianwen Xue, Ondřej Bojar, Jan Hajič, Martha Palmer, Zdeňka Urešová, and Xiuhong Zhang. 2014. Not an interlingua, but close: Comparison of English AMRs to Chinese and Czech. In *Proceedings of the Ninth International Conference on Language Resources and Evaluation (LREC'14)*, pages 1765–1772, Reykjavik, Iceland, May. European Language Resources Association (ELRA).

Cross-lingual annotation: a road map for low- and no-resource languages

Meagan Vigus[1], Jens E. L. Van Gysel[1], Tim O'Gorman[2],
Andrew Cowell[3], Rosa Vallejos[1], and William Croft[1]
[1]Department of Linguistics, University of New Mexico
[2]College of Information and Computer Sciences, University of Massachusetts Amherst
[3]Department of Linguistics, University of Colorado, Boulder
{mvigus,jelvangysel,rvallejos,wcroft}@unm.edu,
togorman@cs.umass.edu, james.cowell@colorado.edu

Abstract

This paper presents a "road map" for the annotation of semantic categories in typologically diverse languages, with potentially few linguistic resources, and often no existing computational resources. Past semantic annotation efforts have focused largely on high-resource languages, or relatively low-resource languages with a large number of native speakers. However, there are certain typological traits, namely the synthesis of multiple concepts into a single word, that are more common in languages with a smaller speech community. For example, what is expressed as a sentence in a more analytic language like English, may be expressed as a single word in a more synthetic language like Arapaho. This paper proposes solutions for annotating analytic and synthetic languages in a comparable way based on existing typological research, and introduces a road map for the annotation of languages with a dearth of resources.

1   Introduction: Cross-linguistically informed semantic annotation

In recent years, there has been a surge of interest in annotation schemes that allow natural language texts to be parsed into semantic representations usable for information extraction, machine translation, and other downstream purposes. Good results have been achieved in automatically parsing natural language texts into Abstract Meaning Representations (Banarescu et al., 2013, AMR) and Discourse Representation Structures (Kamp and Reyle, 2013; Bos et al., 2017, DRS), among others, as demonstrated in various shared annotation tasks (Abzianidze et al., 2020; May and Priyadarshi, 2017).

However, most efforts in developing and testing such annotation schemes have focused on a restricted set of (typically Indo-European) languages with large native speaker populations. For example, the shared annotation tasks reported on in Abzianidze et al. (2020) and May and Priyadarshi (2017) were all based on English. Large AMR corpora exist, to our knowledge, only for English and Mandarin - both morphologically isolating languages, with comparatively little inflectional and derivational morphology. PropBank (Palmer et al., 2005) has been extended to large-scale languages with derivational morphology, such as Hindi and Arabic. But the annotation of derivational morphology relies on a thorough documentation of its role in the language, which often isn't available for low-resource languages. For morphosyntactic annotation, this bias is less apparent: the Universal Dependencies project (de Marneffe et al., 2014) has annotated treebanks from 96 languages, representing 20 linguistic families. However, Indo-European languages are disproportionately represented (53/96 languages). In terms of native speaker populations, 62 out of the 96 UD languages have more than 1 million native speakers, belonging to the largest 6% of languages in the world (Eberhard et al., 2020). Only 24 UD languages have relatively small native speaker populations (10 UD languages are ancient languages).

This apparent bias in languages represented in computational linguistic work likely has consequences for the structure of annotation schemes. The World Atlas of Language Structures chapter on the morphological structure of verbs (Bickel and Nichols, 2013) looks at a sample of 145 languages and finds that, on average, languages express 5.52 inflectional categories within the verb. The 19 UD languages

Proceedings of the 2nd International Workshop on Designing Meaning Representations, pages 30–40
Barcelona, Spain (Online), December 13, 2020

with more than 10 million native speakers that are also included in Bickel and Nichols' (2013) sample express only an average of 4 inflectional categories within the verb - exemplifying a known correlation between morphological complexity and demographic factors (Lupyan and Dale, 2010). The annotation schemes developed in the context of high-population, typically Indo-European languages, may therefore not carry over well to smaller-scale, often more morphologically complex languages. Many smaller-scale languages do not have a long history of linguistic analysis, and therefore understanding of their structure may be progressing in tandem with annotation efforts.

Expanding annotation efforts to such morphosyntactically diverse languages may, apart from simply expanding typologically sound coverage of annotation efforts, improve the overall utility of annotation schemes. Cross-linguistic annotation schemes must incorporate a certain amount of flexibility in order to deal with differences in conventionalized semantic distinctions, and the morphosyntactic expression of these distinctions. This flexibility in design can also benefit monolingual annotation, by allowing for flexibility with annotators who have different levels of linguistic training.

For that reason, this paper proposes solutions for extending AMR to as many languages as possible, including a "road map" for languages with few existing resources. This provides a starting point for flexible but consistent annotation of a number of semantic categories. It also describes how the cross-linguistic diversity in morphosyntax, paired with pre-existing linguistic analyses and resources, can inform the design of a flexible annotation process. This road map provides steps towards more detailed semantic annotation, as the linguistic analysis of the language progresses and computational resources are created, in order to eventually arrive at the same level of specificity in annotations as in high-resource languages. The creation of a comparable cross-linguistic semantic annotation scheme is of course a larger topic than can be covered in a single paper; this paper sets forth a general approach for dealing with differences in linguistic properties and resource availability (the road map), and specific annotation solutions for certain semantic categories and morphosyntactic phenomena (e.g., synthesis).

In this paper, examples are drawn from three no- or low-resource languages: Sanapaná, Kukama, and Arapaho. Sanapaná (Enlhet-Enenlhet) has about 1000 native speakers living in Paraguay. Aside from an ongoing documentation project (Van Gysel, 2020), there are only exploratory analyses of the morphology (Gomes, 2013; Van Gysel, 2017). Kukama (Tupian) has about 1000 native speakers living in Peru. Existing linguistic resources include a descriptive grammar (Vallejos, 2016), a Kukama/Spanish bilingual dictionary (Vallejos and Amías, 2015), translated and morphologically analyzed texts (Vallejos, 2014), and some pedagogical materials. Arapaho (Algonquian) is spoken by two communities in the United States, the Northern Arapaho in Wyoming and the Southern Arapaho in Oklahoma. Among the Northern Arapaho, there are around a hundred native speakers, and several hundred with passive knowledge of the language. Linguistic resources include a grammar (Cowell and Moss Sr, 2008), an online lexical database with detailed part-of-speech labelling and argument structure information, and an annotated text database of nearly 100,000 sentences with accompanying audio and/or video.

2 Cross-linguistic annotation: Typological issues

Certain typological issues arise when constructing a semantic annotation scheme that can, in theory, be applied to any language. Three general types of issues are described here.

First, some types of morphosyntactic differences do not hinder the annotation of semantic information, and can therefore largely be ignored in a semantic annotation scheme. For example, languages may indicate grammatical roles via constituent order or case affixation of argument phrases, but argument phrases in both types of languages can be annotated for their semantic roles in the same way.

Next, there are major typological differences in the conventionalized semantic distinctions that languages make in their grammar, i.e. how languages 'carve up' conceptual space. For example, some languages distinguish only SINGULAR from NON-SINGULAR nominal number, other languages distinguish SINGULAR, DUAL, TRIAL, and PLURAL (more than three), still other languages have a FEW (including singular) vs. MANY nominal number system (Corbett, 2000, chapter 2). For these types of semantic differences, the use of lattices of category values has been proposed to allow flexible but consistent annotation (Van Gysel et al., 2019); we adopt this approach and incorporate it into the road map in §3.

Finally, languages differ in terms of how concepts are packaged into words and sentences. As discussed in §1, languages that are more synthetic, packaging many morphemes/concepts into a single 'multiconcept' word, have not been well-represented in past annotation efforts. This also presents a practical issue: for languages at an earlier stage of documentation, it may not be possible for annotators to morphologically decompose multiconcept words. Therefore, the issue of how to maintain consistent annotation across both more analytic and more synthetic languages will be the main focus of this section.

Even 'word' does not have a consistent definition across languages. Most languages have a language-internal concept of 'word', at least as a cognitively salient unit of the language (Bolinger, 1963). But these units do not share consistent linguistic traits across languages, nor is there a widely-accepted definition of what should constitute a word across languages (Dixon et al., 2002), but see Zingler (2020).

2.1   One predicate instead of two

In many languages, a single verb with derivational morphology may express what is expressed by two verbal words (e.g.., main verb, complement, auxiliary) in English and other analytic languages. In general, we treat derivational morphology as a single predicate along with the verb to which it attaches. Derivational morphology may express phasal aspect, as in 1 from Arapaho.[1] The aspectual marking, whether an affix or a separate word, is not annotated as a separate predicate, since it selects a phase of the event.[2] Derivational morphology may also express an external causing event, shown in 2 from Kukama. For causatives, either a single event with causative semantics is identified or two events are identified, one for the causing event and one for the caused event. This is based on whether negation can apply to the causing event and caused event separately. For derivational morphology, as in Kukama, negation would scope over both events, meaning that it is construed as a single event and annotated as such. In English, causative auxiliaries can be negated separately from the caused event (e.g., *Grandmother didn't make the kid drink / Grandmother made the kid not drink*); therefore, two events are identified.

(1)   ceesisnoo'oebiicitiit.
      ceesis-noo'oe-biicitii-t
      IC.begin-around-bead.s.t.-3S
      'She is starting to bead around it.'

(c / biicitii 'bead s.t.'
   :Actor (a / '3S')
   :Undergoer (u / '3S')
   :aspect Activity
   :modstr Aff)

(b / bead s.t.
   :Actor (s / she)
   :Undergoer (i / it)
   :aspect Activity
   :modstr Aff)

(2)   nai   kurata-**ta**   churan=ui uni=pu
      grandmother drink-**CAU** kid=PST   water=INS
      'Grandmother made the kid drink the water.'

(k / kuratata 'make drink'
   :Causer (n / nai 'grandmother')
   :Actor (c / churan 'kid')
   :Undergoer (u / uni 'water')
   :aspect Performance
   :modstr Aff)

(d / drink
   :Cause (m / make
      :Actor (g / grandmother)
      :aspect Performance
      :modstr Aff)
   :Actor (k / kid)
   :Undergoer (w / water)
   :aspect Performance
   :modstr Aff)

For modality, as shown in 3 from Arapaho, we apply semantic criteria to determine whether a single predicate or multiple predicates are identified; see §3.3 for a discussion of the modal annotation. If the

---

[1] We present examples with annotations for predicate-argument structure, modal strength and polarity, and aspectual structure; temporal annotations have been omitted. The annotations make use of the general 'Stage 0' participant roles; §3 explains the relevant annotation categories in more detail. Abbreviations used in glosses are the following: 2 = second person; 3 = third person; ALLAT = allative; APPL = applicative; APPRX = approximative; CER = certainty; CAU = causative; DEF = definite; DISTR = distributive; IC = initial change; IMPERF = imperfective; INF = inferred; INS = instrumental; LOC = locative; M = masculine; NARR = narrative; PAS = passive; PL = plural; PST = past; REDUP = reduplication; S = singular; SBJ = subjunctive.

[2] The aspect indicated by the morphology is reflected in the aspect annotation. Inceptive phasal aspect is annotated as ACTIVITY to reflect that the event may be ongoing.

modal can itself be modalized (i.e., appear under the scope of another modal), then it is annotated as its own predicate. Since English allows this (e.g., *they **might want** to take it...*), *want* is annotated as a predicate. But, in the Arapaho, this is not possible, and therefore the modal is annotated in the same predicate as the main verb. While this criterion generally correlates with the expression of the modal as a complement-taking predicate versus an affix on the verb, it relies on semantic criteria that can be applied across languages. In both cases, the modal informs the modal strength annotation of the verb.

(3) xonouu niibeetwon3eiinein.

xonouu
immediately
nii-**beet**-won-3eiin-ein
IMPERF-**want.to**-ALLAT-put.inside.a.place-3S/2S

'Right away he wants to go and put you in jail.'

(n / beetwon3eiin 'want to go and put s.t. inside a place'
   :Actor (a / '3S')
   :Theme (t / '2S')
   :aspect Habitual
   :modstr Neut)

(w / want
   :Experiencer (h / he)
   :Stimulus (g / go
     :Actor (h)
     :aspect Habitual)
   :Stimulus (p / put
     :Actor (h)
     :Theme (y / you)
     :Goal (j / jail)
     :aspect Habitual)
   :aspect Habitual
   :modstr Aff
   :modal g
   :modal p)

Associated motion is treated similarly. Whether or not motion events are considered a single predicate with the verb or a separate predicate depends on whether locative or directional expressions that occur in the clause correspond to arguments of the motion event (as opposed to arguments or circumstantial locatives modifying the main event). When they are arguments of the motion event, it is identified as a separate predicate; when they are not, it is considered a single predicate with the verb. In the Sanapaná example in 4, no *arrive* predicate is identified in the annotation. The associated motion morphology *-angv-akm* indicates that the seeing event occurs after arriving at a location other than the deictic center. A locative expression can occur with this construction, but there is no evidence that this is an argument of the motion event rather than a circumstantial locative of the *see* predicate. Therefore, only a single predicate is annotated in Sanapaná. In English, this location can be expressed as an unambiguous argument of the motion event (e.g., *we arrived **home** and saw...*), so a separate *arrive* predicate is annotated.

(4) netamen   apk-el-vet-**angv**-ay-**akm**-e'   hlema nenhlet, ang-kelvana.
    afterwards 2/3M-DISTR-see-**LOC**-PST/HAB-**APPRX**-V1.NFUT one   person 2/3F-woman

'Afterwards, they arrived and saw a person, a woman.'

(v / engvetangvayam 'arrive and see'
   :Experiencer (a1 / apk-el- '3PL.M')
   :Stimulus (n / nenhlet 'person'
     :mod (a2 / angkelvana 'woman')
     :quant 1)
   :aspect State
   :modstr Aff)

(a / arrive
   :Actor (t / they)
   :aspect Performance
   :modstr Aff)
(s / see
   :Experiencer (t)
   :Stimulus (p / person
     :mod (w / woman)
     :quant 1)
   :aspect State
   :modstr Aff)

2.2 One word containing predicate and arguments

Languages can also package together concepts that cut across the event-participant distinction that is fundamental to semantic annotation schemes that rely on predicate-argument structure, such as AMR. For these types of multiconcept words, namely pronominal indexation and noun incorporation, both a predicate and an argument are identified at all stages of the road map.

In many languages, participants are indexed on the verb; this is often called agreement or pronominal affixation. In certain constructions, participants are signalled only through indexation and not expressed elsewhere in the clause. We treat the indexed participants as pronouns and identify both a predicate and an argument (or arguments) for a single word. This can be seen in examples 1, 3, and 4 above.

Noun incorporation involves a word that expresses both a predicate and an argument. Mithun (1984) identifies four types based on their structure and function across languages. These types of noun incorporation exist on a grammaticalization cline, with languages that exhibit the more grammaticalized types also exhibiting the less grammaticalized types. Example 5 shows Type I incorporation, the least grammaticalized, and 6 shows Type IV incorporation, the most grammaticalized, both from Arapaho.

(5) he'ih'iixooxookbixoh'oekoohuutoono'

He'ih'ii-xoo-xook-
NARR.PST.IMPERF-REDUP-through-
bixoh'oekoohuutoo-no'
act.so.that.hand.appears.quickly-PL

'they were sticking their hands right through them [the ghosts] to the other side'

(b/ bixoh'oekoohuutoo 'stick hands through'
  :Actor (a1 / '3PL')
  :Theme (t / 'hands')
  :Undergoer (g / '[ghosts]')
  :aspect Endeavor
  :modstr Aff)

(6) hoono' nuhu' tihciinii'eihiinit, he'ih'etoocein
     nuhu' hitiine' nuhu' hoote.

hoono' nuhu' tih-cii-nii'eihiini-t
not.yet this   when.PST-NEG-be.eagle-3.S
he'ih-'etoocein   nuhu'
NARR.PST-pull.**rope-like.thing**.out this
hi-tiin-e'   nuhu' **hoote**
3S-mouth-LOC this   **sinew**

'At the [time] when he wasn't yet an eagle, he took [it] out of his mouth, the sinew.'

(e / 'etoocein 'pull rope-like thing out'
  :Actor (a / '3S')
  :Theme (h1 / hoote 'sinew')
  :Material/Source (h2 / hi-tiin-e' 'his mouth'
      :part-of a)
  :Temporal (h3 / have-role-91
      :ARG0 (a)
      :ARG1 (n / nii'eihiini 'be eagle')
      :aspect State
      :modstr Neg)
  :aspect Performance
  :modstr Aff)

Type I noun incorporation doesn't allow the addition of a syntactic argument that corresponds to the incorporated noun. Type IV noun incorporation, often called classificatory constructions, incorporates a more general noun into the verb, whose referent can be made more specific by the addition of a syntactic argument in the clause. In the less grammaticalized types of noun incorporation (Types I-III), both a predicate and arguments are identified, as in 5. The more grammaticalized types of noun incorporation, as in 6, are treated like derivational morphology and only a predicate is identified.[3]

2.3 Nonverbal clauses: Different packaging of "predicate" and arguments

Nonverbal clauses, such as locative, possessive, object, and property predication, and equational clauses, vary across languages in terms of how concepts are packaged into words (Stassen, 1997; Stassen, 2009). There are three nonverbal clause strategies, two of which are problematic for the predicate-argument structure of AMR.[4] These strategies are shown in 7 and 8 from Kukama. In 7, the theme participant and the noun 'shaman' each correspond to a single word, but the predication does not map to a specific word, though it is inherent in the construction. This poses a problem in annotating the "predicate" of the clause. In 8, the possessum and the predication correspond to the same word, that is, an "argument" is predicativized. Like participant indexation and noun incorporation, these types of constructions pose a problem for the annotation of predicate-argument structure. From a semantic perspective, it's important that the different strategies receive comparable annotations, since they have the same meaning.

---

[3] Due to space limitations, the English translation annotations for these examples are included in the supplementary material.

[4] The third strategy is the use of a verb separate from either participant, such as *have* in the English translation of 8, or the copula in the translation of 7.

These two different problematic strategies require different solutions. In the case of predicativized arguments as in 8, we use the same solution as for pronominal affixes and less-grammaticalized noun incorporation: both a nonverbal clause function and argument are identified and annotated separately. When there is no predicate, as in 7, then we assume that the annotator is able to recognize the type of nonverbal clause function, and use an abstract predicate in the annotation.

(7)   ajan kunumi   tsumi
     this young.man shaman

     'This young man is a shaman.'

```
(h / have-role-91
  :ARG0 (k / kunumi 'young man')
  :ARG1 (t / tsumi 'shaman')
  :aspect State
  :modstr Aff)
```

(8)   Mijiri-tin   iara-yara
     Miguel-CER canoe-owner

     'Miguel does have a canoe.' (Lit. 'Miguel is a canoe-owner')

```
(e / iara-yara 'has canoe'            (h / have-03
  :ARG0 (m / Mijiri 'Miguel')           :ARG0 (m / Miguel)
  :ARG1 (i / iara 'canoe')              :ARG1 (c / canoe)
  :aspect State                         :aspect State
  :modstr Aff)                          :modstr Aff)
```

Some of the nonverbal clause functions have specialized predicates in AMR, but not all; we propose additional predicates for those functions (see Table 1, ARG0 is always an argument, but ARG1 may be predicativized). The first four types in Table 1 describe possession and location. Possession and location may be predicated of the possession and the spatial figure, as in *This bicycle belongs to my brother* and *The bicycle is in the garage*. However, possession and location may be used in a context in which the information is presented as 'thetic' or 'all-new' in the terms of Lambrecht's (1994) theory of information structure (cf. the contrast between 'have' and 'belong' possession in Heine (1997)). One common thetic function is presentational, as in *I have one brother* or *In the garage was a single bicycle*. AMR has predicates for thetic possession (HAVE-03) and predicative location (HAVE-LOCATION-91); we add predicates for thetic location (EXIST-91) and predicative possession (BELONG-01).

The predication of properties (*Susan is smart*) and object categories (*Susan is a professor*) can be distinguished straightforwardly. AMR uses HAVE-MOD-91 for property predication and some types of object predication; we propose to restrict it to property predication. Other types of object predication are expressed in AMR with HAVE-REL-ROLE-91 or HAVE-ORG-ROLE-91; we propose a superordinate predicate HAVE-ROLE-91 that covers all object predication clauses. Finally, equational sentences (*He is the father of the bride*), corresponding to Lambrecht's identificational information structure, are challenging to distinguish from object predication in context (see Stassen (1997, 106-111)). Where this can be done, we propose to use the predicate IDENTITY-91

Clause type	Predicate	ARG0	ARG1
thetic/presentational possession	have-03	*possessor*	*possession*
predicative possession	belong-01	*possession*	*possessor*
thetic/presentational location	exist-91	*location*	*theme*
predicative location	have-location-91	*theme*	*location*
property predication	have-mod-91	*theme*	*property*
object predication	have-role-91	*theme*	*object category*
equational	identity-91	*theme*	*equated referent*

Table 1: Nonverbal clause predicates

3   The road map

Section 2 covered solutions to typological issues that are raised by the inclusion of low- and no-resource languages in semantic annotation efforts. This section puts forth a "road map" approach to annotation, which synthesizes the typological solutions with practical solutions for the inclusion of languages with few existing computational or documentary resources.

	Stage 0	**Stage 1**
Annotation targets	treat derivational morphology as single word, separate inflectional morphology	indicate derivational morphological relations in lexicon
Aspect	coarse-grained categories on lattice	fine-grained categories on lattice
Modal strength	annotate with only MODSTR and placeholder values; no conceivers	use modal lexicon with modal strengths, fill in remaining unspecified modal strengths
Participant roles	general semantic roles	lexicalized roles, annotate implicit roles

Table 2: Road map annotation stages

The road map approach both ensures comparability across diverse languages, and allows for flexibility in the annotation of any one language. The road map specifies a starting point for languages with few resources (Stage 0), the end point for fully specified annotation (Stage 1), and a process for moving between these, defined for each annotation category. These are not discrete annotation stages, and languages will move gradually from the Stage 0 to Stage 1 annotation. Where a language begins on the road map for each annotation category is determined by the typological features of its grammar, its state of documentation, and the computational resources developed thus far.

The road map allows for flexibility across languages and annotation categories. Languages with a paucity of linguistic or computational resources can still begin annotation efforts. Languages with typological features that complicate the annotation of certain semantic categories can still be annotated for those categories, albeit at a less detailed level. Within a language, different annotation categories may be annotated at different stages, depending on the language's typological features and existing resources.

The road map approach also ensures comparability across languages, even when languages are at different stages, because annotation values retain their meaning across the road map stages. This also ensures that different-stage annotations for the same language are compatible. As annotation and documentation efforts continue, the annotation of a language may progress along the road map. But, the annotations done at the beginning stages are still accessible and comparable to the later stage annotations. For languages that have limited resources in terms of time investment by speakers and/or field linguists, having this type of compatibility built into the annotation scheme is critical.

The remainder of this section will demonstrate how the road map approach functions with regard to a number of annotation categories: annotation targets, participant roles, aspect, and modal strength and polarity. The road map for these categories is summarized in Table 2.

3.1 Annotation targets

The main cross-linguistic issues with the identification of annotation targets (i.e., predicates and arguments) are the types of multiconcept words covered in §2. The annotation of multiconcept words is the same throughout the stages of the road map; however, their representation in the lexicon builds up in complexity. For example, verbs with derivational morphology are first treated as different words than their non-derived counterparts in the lexicon. As the understanding of the language progresses, multiconcept words are morphologically decomposed and morphological relations are added to the lexicon.

The identification of a span of text for each annotation target is determined by the language experts for each language, since what is considered the 'citation form' of a word differs across languages. Fusional morphology, such as that for pronominal indexation in Arapaho (see 3, 5, 6 above), cannot be split apart at any stage of the road map and therefore a span of text is not indicated for those arguments.

3.2 Aspect

Aside from the multiconcept word issues with regard to aspectual morphology discussed above, the main issue with aspect annotations cross-linguistically is that languages differ widely in terms of which aspectual distinctions are conventionalized in their grammar. In order to resolve these differences, we utilize the aspectual lattice from Van Gysel et al. (2019), shown in the supplementary material. It ranges from the most coarse-grained categories of IMPERFECTIVE and PROGRESSIVE, to ATELIC PROCESS and PERFECTIVE, to the 'basic' level of STATE, ACTIVITY, ENDEAVOR, and PERFORMANCE, and finally, very fine-grained categories, such as POINT STATE or DIRECTED IRREVERSIBLE ACHIEVEMENT.

For a language at an earlier stage of linguistic analysis, it may not be clear to the annotator which of the more fine-grained aspect values should apply. Therefore, annotators may select a more coarse-grained category on the lattice. For example, the linguistic analysis of aspect in Sanapaná, in 9, is still under way. The aspectual implications of the suffixal morphology (specifically, the passive *-akp* which also functions as a reciprocal, and the subjunctive *-o*), are not yet fully understood. Therefore, the more coarse-grained ATELIC PROCESS value is used, instead of an ACTIVITY or ENDEAVOR value.

(9)   tenyo
      then
      apk-ehl-pa'met-kes-**akp-o**=hla
      2/3M-DISTR-talk-APPL-**PAS.M-SUBJ**=INF
      ap-yavokhoho.
      2/3M-all
      'Then they were all talking to each other.'

    (p / ehlpa'metkesamma'ap 'speak to each other'
    :Actor (a / apyavokhoho 'all')
    :Recipient (a / apyavokhoho 'all')
    :aspect Atelic Process
    :modstr Aff)

Stage 2 of the aspect annotation uses the more fine-grained categories on the aspect lattice. Example 5 above from Arapaho expresses an event that is aspectually similar to 9. Since Arapaho has a longer history of linguistic study, the more fine-grained annotation of ENDEAVOR can be applied.

3.3 Modal strength and polarity

We follow Vigus et al. (2019) in representing modal strength and polarity as a dependency structure. The nodes are events or conceivers (i.e., a source, an entity whose perspective on an event is modeled in the text). The edges in the dependency structure correspond to epistemic strength and polarity values; event nodes are the children of either conceivers or other events on whom they depend for their modal value.

Like aspect, languages differ in the modal strength distinctions that are conventionalized in their grammar and therefore we use a typological lattice, shown in the supplementary materials. This lattice is based around a FULL vs. PARTIAL vs. NEUTRAL modal strength distinction; the coarse-grained categories are NON-FULL and NON-NEUTRAL; the finer-grained categories include WEAK PARTIAL, STRONG NEUTRAL, etc. These combine with an AFFIRMATIVE/NEGATIVE polarity distinction.[5]

The Stage 0 annotation involves the underspecification of some parts of the modal dependency structure. Events are annotated for their modal strength (MODSTR) using the lattice, but conceivers are unspecified. Some event types receive special annotations; two of these are events under the scope of a modal predicate, and events under the scope of a reporting/speech predicate.[6] A placeholder MODAL value is used for modal predicates; and a QUOT value is used for reporting predicates. Events under the scope of modals don't receive a MODSTR value; reported events do receive a MODSTR value in the same way as other predicates. This way, events under the scope of other predicates in the modal dependency receive a consistent annotation, while annotators avoid the complexity of annotating the full dependency structure. This annotation for modal predicates is shown above in the English translation of 3.

The MODAL and QUOT values can be automatically converted into an underspecified dependency structure; the participant role annotation can also be leveraged to specify conceivers (e.g., the EXPERIENCER of a modal predicate is its conceiver). The modal strength imparted by modal predicates is unspecified in the dependency structure at Stage 0. Stage 1 involves adding this information to the lexicon entries for modal predicates (e.g., *want* imparts a NEUT strength on its complement) and filling in other unspecified values to reach a fully specified modal dependency structure.

3.4 Participant roles

Semantic role annotation is one category where issues related to typological differences and resource disparities intersect. As has been noted in the verbal semantic literature (Croft, 2012; Hartmann et al., 2014), semantic roles, such as AGENT or PATIENT are difficult to apply consistently across languages.[7]

---

[5] In this paper, we use the default level annotations to yield six modal strength values: full affirmative AFF, partial affirmative PARTAFF, neutral affirmative NEUTAFF, neutral negative NEUTNEG, partial negative PARTNEG, and full negative NEG.

[6] Conditionals and purpose clauses also receive special placeholder annotation values, COND and PURP respectively.

[7] For example, transfer constructions can realize either the giver as subject (*I gave the cat some wet food*), or the recipient as subject (*the cat received her wet food*). This varies both within and across languages, making it unclear which participant should receive the AGENT semantic role.

Central roles	Actor, Undergoer, Theme, Recipient, Force, Causer, Experiencer, Stimulus
Peripheral roles	Instrument, Companion, Material/Source, Place, Start, Goal, Affectee
Roles for entities and events	Cause, Manner, Reason, Purpose, Temporal, Extent

Table 3: UMR non-lexicalized roles

Therefore, both typological research (Hartmann, 2013; Malchukov and Comrie, 2015) and semantic annotation (e.g., PropBank) have moved away from general semantic roles and towards microroles, or lexicalized semantic roles. Roles are defined for each verb (e.g., *eat* has an EATER and FOOD); this allows for valid cross-linguistic comparison in typology and consistency in semantic annotation.

The major drawback of this approach is that it requires an existing lexicon complete with lexicalized roles for the verbs in a language. For languages that do not have this, the creation of such a resource is a rather large hurdle to overcome in order to begin annotation. Therefore, the road map moves from more general semantic roles at Stage 0 to lexicalized microroles at Stage 1. For languages that have PropBank-style frame files created, annotation can begin at Stage 1. For languages that do not, annotation begins with general semantic roles at Stage 0, while simultaneously building up a lexicon of frame files.

Stage 0 of the road map involves selecting a label for each participant from a set of general (i.e., non-lexicalized) semantic roles, shown in Table 3. This inventory is largely an extension of the AMR inventory of non-core roles, with roles added for core arguments such as STIMULUS. These additions are based upon the cross-linguistic argument realization patterns in the ValPaL database (Hartmann, 2013); this ensures that the labels reflect distinctions that are common in the grammatical systems of the world's languages. At Stage 0, implicit (i.e., unexpressed) participants are not annotated; this is shown in the Arapaho example in 3 above, where the goal participant is not annotated, as it is not overly expressed.

In order for a language to progress along the road map with regard to participant roles, Stage 0 also involves beginning to set up a lexicon with frame files. Within each frame file, the mapping between a lexicalized semantic role and its non-lexicalized counterpart is indicated. This way, annotations at different stages of the road map will be comparable with each other. As frame files are created, annotators use the lexicalized roles for verbs that have them; for other verbs, the general semantic roles are used. At Stage 1, the lexicalized roles are used; this is shown below for example 3 in §2.1. In Arapaho, the existing lexical description with argument structure information can be leveraged in annotation to create frame files like the one shown below. Stage 2 also involves the annotation of implicit roles, based on the frame files; therefore, the goal (ARG2) participant for example 3 is annotated.

predicate: BEETWON3EIIN
arguments:
    ARG0: putter → ACTOR
    ARG1: put thing → THEME
    ARG2: putting goal → GOAL

(n / beetwon3eiin 'want to go and put s.t. inside a place'
    :ARG0 (a / '3S')
    :ARG1 (t / '2S')
    :ARG2 (g / 'jail')
    :aspect Habitual
    :modstr Neut)

4 Conclusion

This paper recognizes issues not previously dealt with in the annotation of cross-linguistic semantic information: multiconcept words and no-resource languages. As multiconcept words are more common in languages with a smaller speech community, they have not been dealt with in past annotation schemes. We present solutions for extending AMR across languages, including the annotation of multiconcept words; these depend on the semantic category of the concept. We have also outlined a road map approach to beginning annotation on very low or no-resource languages, ensuring that the annotation is truly cross-linguistic in terms not only of typological diversity but of resource availability as well.

5 Credits

We gratefully acknowledge the support of the National Science Foundation Award Nos. 1764091 to the University of New Mexico and 1764048 to the University of Colorado (Collaborative Research: Building a Uniform Meaning Representation for Natural Language Processing).

References

Lasha Abzianidze, Rik van Noord, Hessel Haagsma, and Johan Bos. 2020. The first shared task on discourse representation structure parsing. *arXiv preprint arXiv:2005.13399*.

Laura Banarescu, Claire Bonial, Shu Cai, Madalina Georgescu, Kira Griffitt, Ulf Hermjakob, Kevin Knight, Philipp Koehn, Martha Palmer, and Nathan Schneider. 2013. Abstract meaning representation for sembanking. In *Proceedings of the 7th Linguistic Annotation Workshop and Interoperability with Discourse*, pages 178–186, Sofia, Bulgaria, August. Association for Computational Linguistics.

Balthasar Bickel and Johanna Nichols. 2013. Inflectional synthesis of the verb. In Matthew S. Dryer and Martin Haspelmath, editors, *The World Atlas of Language Structures Online*. Max Planck Institute for Evolutionary Anthropology, Leipzig.

Dwight Bolinger. 1963. The uniqueness of the word. *Lingua*, 12(2):113–136.

Johan Bos, Valerio Basile, Kilian Evang, Noortje J Venhuizen, and Johannes Bjerva. 2017. The groningen meaning bank. In *Handbook of linguistic annotation*, pages 463–496. Springer.

Greville G. Corbett. 2000. *Number*. Cambridge University Press.

Andrew Cowell and Alonzo Moss Sr. 2008. *The Arapaho language*. University Press of Colorado.

William Croft. 2012. *Verbs: Aspect and causal structure*. Oxford University Press, Oxford.

Marie-Catherine de Marneffe, Timothy Dozat, Natalia Silveira, Katri Haverinen, Filip Ginter, Joakim Nivre, and D. Manning, Christopher. 2014. Universal stanford dependencies: A cross-linguistic typology. In *Proceedings of the Ninth International Conference on Language Resources and Evaluation (LREC'14)*, pages 4585–4592. European Language Resources Association (ELRA).

Robert MW Dixon, Alexandra Y Aikhenvald, et al., 2002. *Word: A cross-linguistic typology*, chapter Word: a typological framework, pages 1–41.

David M Eberhard, Gary F. Simons, and Charles D. Fennig. 2020. Ethnologue: Languages of the world. twenty-third edition. http://www.ethnologue.com.

Antonio Almir Silva Gomes. 2013. *Sanapaná uma lingua maskoy: Aspectos gramaticais*. Ph.D. thesis, Universidade Estadual de Campinas.

Iren Hartmann, Martin Haspelmath, and Michael Cysouw. 2014. Identifying semantic role clusters and alignment types via microrole coexpression tendencies. *Studies in Language. International Journal sponsored by the Foundation "Foundations of Language"*, 38(3):463–484.

Martin Taylor Bradley (eds.) Hartmann, Iren Haspelmath, editor. 2013. *Valency Patterns Leipzig*. Max Planck Institute for Evolutionary Anthropology, Leipzig.

Bernd Heine. 1997. *Possession: Cognitive sources, forces, and grammaticalization*. Cambridge Studies in Linguistics. 83. Cambridge University Press, Cambridge.

Hans Kamp and Uwe Reyle. 2013. *From discourse to logic. Introduction to modeltheoretic semantics of natural language, formal logic and discourse representation theory*, volume 42. Springer Science & Business Media.

Knud Lambrecht. 1994. *Information structure and sentence form: Topic, focus, and the mental representations of discourse referents*. Cambridge studies in linguistics: 71. Cambridge University Press.

Gary Lupyan and Rick Dale. 2010. Language structure is partly determined by social structure. *PloS one*, 5(1):e8559.

Andrej Malchukov and Bernard Comrie. 2015. *Valency classes in the world's languages*. Walter de Gruyter, Berlin/Boston.

Jonathan May and Jay Priyadarshi. 2017. Semeval-2017 task 9: Abstract meaning representation parsing and generation. In *Proceedings of the 11th International Workshop on Semantic Evaluation (SemEval-2017)*, pages 536–545.

Marianne Mithun. 1984. The evolution of noun incorporation. *Language*, 60:847–94.

Martha Palmer, Daniel Gildea, and Paul Kingsbury. 2005. The proposition bank: An annotated corpus of semantic roles. *Computational linguistics*, 31(1):71–106.

Leon Stassen. 1997. *Intransitive predication*. Clarendon Press, Oxford.

Leon Stassen. 2009. *Predicative Possession*. Oxford University Press, Oxford, UK.

Rosa Vallejos and Rosa Amías. 2015. Diccionario kukama-kukamiria castellano. *Iquitos: AIDESEP: ISEPL: FORMABIAP*.

Rosa Vallejos. 2014. The kukama-kukamiria documentation project. https://elar.soas.ac.uk/Collection/MPI971108 (accessed: 4 August 2020).

Rosa Vallejos. 2016. *A Grammar of Kukama-Kukamiria: A language from the Amazon*. Brill.

Jens E. L. Van Gysel, Meagan Vigus, Pavlina Kalm, Sook-kyung Lee, Michael Regan, and William Croft. 2019. Cross-linguistic semantic annotation: Reconciling the language-specific and the universal. In *Proceedings of the First International Workshop on Designing Meaning Representations*, pages 1–14, Florence, Italy, August. Association for Computational Linguistics.

Jens E. L. Van Gysel. 2017. Temporal predicative particles in Sanapaná and the Enlhet-Enenlhet language family (Paraguay): A descriptive and comparative study. MA Thesis, Universiteit Leiden.

Jens E. L. Van Gysel. 2020. A documentation of historical narratives amongst the Sanapaná (Enlhet-Enenlhet) of the Paraguayan Chaco. https://elar.soas.ac.uk/Collection/MPI1234837 (accessed: 31 October 2020).

Meagan Vigus, Jens E. L. Van Gysel, and William Croft. 2019. A dependency structure annotation for modality. In *Proceedings of the First International Workshop on Designing Meaning Representations*, pages 182–198.

Tim Zingler. 2020. *Wordhood issues: typology and grammaticalization*. Ph.D. thesis, University of New Mexico.

Refining Implicit Argument Annotation for UCCA

Ruixiang Cui and **Daniel Hershcovich**
Department of Computer Science
University of Copenhagen
{rc, dh}@di.ku.dk

Abstract

Predicate-argument structure analysis is a central component in meaning representations of text. The fact that some arguments are not explicitly mentioned in a sentence gives rise to ambiguity in language understanding, and renders it difficult for machines to interpret text correctly. However, only few resources represent implicit roles for NLU, and existing studies in NLP only make coarse distinctions between categories of arguments omitted from linguistic form. This paper proposes a typology for fine-grained implicit argument annotation on top of Universal Conceptual Cognitive Annotation's foundational layer. The proposed implicit argument categorisation is driven by theories of implicit role interpretation and consists of six types: Deictic, Generic, Genre-based, Type-identifiable, Non-specific, and Iterated-set. We exemplify our design by revisiting part of the UCCA EWT corpus, providing a new dataset annotated with the refinement layer, and making a comparative analysis with other schemes.

1 Introduction

Semantic representation frameworks have been a major medium to understanding the nature of languages for NLP. Through these frameworks, researchers have been exploring linguistic phenomena such as quantification (Pustejovsky et al., 2019), coreference (Prange et al., 2019), and word sense (Schneider et al., 2018). However, most efforts were put into studying linguistic complexity superficially, rather than the more latent, implicit omission of arguments in an event. For instance, in the sentence "Just take the money!", the addressee who should "take the money" is left out. Such omission cannot be recovered directly from the text in the way of gapping or ellipsis, but require a higher level of understanding and inference from the context. Traditional studies approach argument omission from different aspects, namely syntactically, semantically, or pragmatically. The interpretation of implicit roles varies to a great extent, from phonological deleted role during production (Perlmutter, 1968; Mittwoch, 1971; Pérez-Leroux et al., 2018) to timecourse reference omission from a psycholinguistic aspect (Garrod and Terras, 2000). However, few studies have explored the implicit role phenomenon in NLP.

In this paper, we propose a fine-grained cross-linguistically applicable implicit argument annotation typology as a refinement for Universal Conceptual Cognitive Annotation (Abend and Rappoport, 2013, UCCA) categories. The typology follows UCCA's design concept, focusing on the semantic notion of Scene rather than linguistic form phenomena. The proposed implicit argument set contains six categories: Deictic, Generic, Genre-based, Type-identifiable, Non-specific, and Iterated-set. We refine the existing UCCA relation labels and add information to them, while keeping all categories from the underlying annotation. Our studies move UCCA, a semantic representation framework, to have less syntactic definitions of implicit arguments.

Based on the proposed typology, we conduct a pilot annotation study, including revisit and refinement of the UCCA EWT dataset,[1] and subsequently make a comparative analysis with the only other existing fine-grained implicit role annotation scheme, Fine-grained Annotations of Referential Interpretation Types (O'Gorman, 2019, FiGref).

---

[1] https://github.com/ruixiangcui/UCCA-Refined-Implicit-EWT_English

Proceedings of the 2nd International Workshop on Designing Meaning Representations, pages 41–52
Barcelona, Spain (Online), December 13, 2020

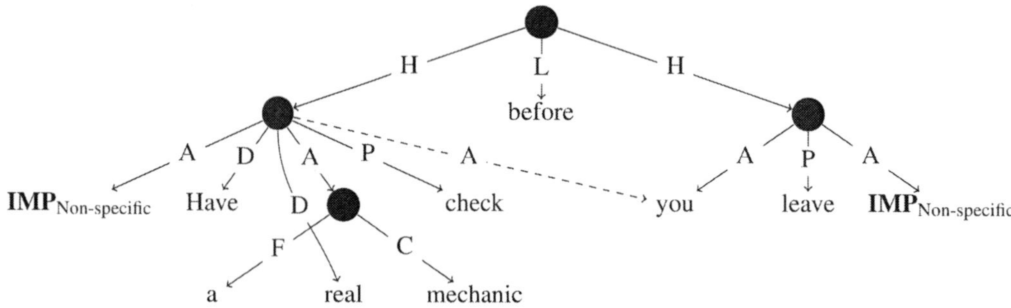

Figure 1: Example of UCCA graph: "Have a real mechanic check before you leave.". Abbreviation of UCCA edge labels is explained in Table 1. The dashed line stands for *Remote* edge. In this case it is a coreference "you". An **IMP** represents an *Implicit* argument denoting a null-instantiated core element in its corresponding Scene.

A few studies have explored the possibilities to parse implicit arguments. Both Gerber and Chai (2012) and Cheng and Erk (2019) have developed parsers to recover implicit arguments for nominal predicates; Bender et al. (2011) parses against some linguistic constructions, two of which could license implicit arguments, that is, tough adjectives and verbal gerund; Elazar and Goldberg (2019) focus on resolving missing numeric fused-heads, which are implicit Centers in UCCA.

Providing the most up-to-date and fine-grained annotation of implicit arguments, our studies can potentially enhance natural language understanding if supplied with an adequate parser. For example, when companies conduct satisfaction analyses through web reviews, customers often express themselves colloquially in these reviews. Examples include "Serves bad ice cream, Joe's is better" and "Near a nice district, bad service and expensive." If these reviews are annotated with Genre-based implicit arguments, referring to the conventional omission of reviewees, algorithms can study which part of the reviews really refers to the companies rather than other entities, and make better predictions, despite the omission of subjects and non-standard language.

2 Universal Conceptual Cognitive Annotation

Universal Conceptual Cognitive Annotation is a semantic representation scheme whose design concept comes from the Basic Linguistic Theory typological framework (Dixon, 2010a; Dixon, 2010b; Dixon, 2012) and Cognitive Linguistics literature (Croft and Cruse, 2004). Abstracting away from syntactic forms, it aims at representing the main semantic phenomena in text while maintaining a low learning cost and rapid annotation by non-experts (Abend et al., 2017). Already providing datasets in English, French, and German, UCCA has demonstrated its cross-linguistic applicability in several languages and has become a popular target framework in multiple pars-

Participant	A	Linker	L
Center	C	Connector	N
Adverbial	D	Process	P
Elaborator	E	Quantifier	Q
Function	F	Relator	R
Ground	G	State	S
Parellel Scene	H	Time	T

Table 1: Legend of UCCA edge categories (Hershcovich et al., 2019a)

ing tasks (Hershcovich et al., 2019b; Oepen et al., 2019). Abend et al. (2017) have also developed an open-source web-based annotation system, UCCAApp, which supports fast annotation for linguistic representations. The effectiveness and efficiency in annotating and refining UCCA have been proven by several studies (Shalev et al., 2019; Prange et al., 2019).

UCCA presents the meaning of a sentence with a directed acyclic graph (DAG) whose terminal nodes correspond either to surface lexical tokens or extra units representing implicit arguments. Non-terminal nodes correspond to semantic units that participate in some super-ordinate relation. Edges are labeled with the role of a child node related to its parent node. The basic notion in UCCA is Scene, describing a state, action, movement, or some other relation that evolves in time. Each Scene involves one main relation (Process or State), and one or more Participants, including locations, abstract entities and sub-Scenes serving as arguments.

Furthermore, UCCA distinguishes *primary* edges, appearing explicitly in one relation, from *remote* edges, allowing a Scene to indicate its arguments by linking from another Scene. *Primary* edges form a tree while *Remote* edges allow reentrancy, forming a DAG. In some cases, an entity of importance in the interpretation of a Scene does not explicitly exist in the text. Hence, UCCA introduces the notion of *Implicit* Units to represent such kind of entity.

For instance, the sentence "Have a real mechanic check before you leave" in Figure 1 contains two Scenes, evoked by "check" and "leave". The individual Scenes are annotated as follows:

1. "$(You)_A$ have$_D$[a$_F$ real$_D$ mechanic$_C$]$_A$ check$_P$ IMP_{1A}"

2. "You$_A$ leave$_P$ IMP_{2A}"

"A mechanic" is a Participant in the first Scene, while "You" is Participant in both Scenes, as *Remote* constituting reentrancy in the first one (shown in dashed line), but explicit in the latter super-ordinate relations. In the first Scene, "Check" is the main Process used in the causative construction, requiring three Participants. While "You" refers to the customer making a request and "a real mechanic" is the service provider who should check something, the object that needs to be "checked" is missing. Therefore, we introduce an IMP A node to symbolize it. In the second Scene, "leave" is the Process meaning someone moves away from a source location. Although we state our little concern for non-core elements like location in this study in §3.2, the case is different for the "leaving" Scene since the source location is vital to the understanding of the departing action. For this reason, we add an IMP A to represent the place that is being left.

In UCCA's foundational layer, only limited cases of implicit arguments have been annotated. The main focus is on omission licensed by certain grammatical structures,[2] whose notion is similar to *Constructional Null Instantiation* in FrameNet (Ruppenhofer et al., 2006). Two typical examples of such constructions are imperatives (forced omission of subjects) and passives (agent omission) in English:

1. Imperative: IMP_A Do$_F$ n't$_D$ bother$_P$.

2. Passive: [The$_F$ doctor$_C$]$_A$ has$_F$ already$_T$ been$_F$ paid$_P$ IMP_A.

Several other kinds of constructions are mentioned in UCCA foundation layer guidelines, such as infinitive clause, gerund, and *thank* construction.

3. Infinitive clause: Is$_F$ there$_F$ [no$_E$ other$_E$ Verizon$_C$]$_A$ IMP_A to$_F$ go$_P$ to$_R$ [around$_R$ downtown$_C$]$_A$?

4. Gerund: How$_D$ addicting$_S$ IMP_A going$_P$ [to$_R$ Fitness Unlimited$_C$]$_A$ can$_F$D be$_F$!"

5. "*Thank*" construction: IMP_A Thanks$_F$, John$_A$!

The annotation of implicit arguments in UCCA's foundation layer is restricted to specific linguistic constructions, which is coarse, language-specific, incomplete, and unlike other distinctions in UCCA, is based on criteria of form rather than meaning. We are faced with the challenge of maintaining UCCA's idiosyncrasy of differentiating *Remote* and *Implicit* while extending its boundary to include a rather refined categorisation for implicit roles.

---

[2] https://github.com/UniversalConceptualCognitiveAnnotation/docs/blob/master/guidelines.pdf

3 Implicit Roles In Meaning Representations

3.1 Background and Motivation

FrameNet (Ruppenhofer et al., 2006) is a source of inspiration for UCCA and Scenes can be seen as frame evocations. FrameNet developed Fillmore (1986)'s notion of null-instantiation into three types—Constructional Null Instantiation (CNI), licensed by grammatical constructions, Definite Null Instantiation (DNI), equivalent to core Frame Elements mentioned previously in text or inferrable from the discourse, and Indefinite Null Instantiation (INI), an element that is unknown and nowhere to be retrieved.

Nevertheless, this trichotomy treats unfavourably many cases where implicit roles occur, such as Free Null Instantiation (Fillmore and Kay, 1993, FNI;) and Identity of Sense Null Anaphora (Kay, 2004, ISNA;). FNI is neither restricted to definite nor indefinite null arguments, and ISNA is null instantiation within noun phrases. Lyngfelt (2012) even argues that the unclear definition of FNI leads to much false categorisation—some FNIs are unspecified, some are generic, and some should be considered DNI.

UCCA's foundational layer mainly focuses on CNI, that is, the current annotated datasets only include grammatically licensed implicit arguments. So far, only a few corpora for implicit role labelling have been proposed, such as SemEval-2010 Task 10 (Ruppenhofer et al., 2009), Beyond NomBank (Gerber and Chai, 2010; Gerber and Chai, 2012), and Multi-sentence AMR (O'Gorman et al., 2018). But none of them is based on a more comprehensive fine grained implicit role characterisation theory aside from FiGref, refined on three corpora mentioned above for recoverability studies.

Although FiGref is not available to the public, O'Gorman (2019) has counterbalanced previous studies on implicit role description and synthesized an inventory of eleven interpretation types for implicit roles distinguished by their referential behaviours. They are Script-inferrable pragmatic, Salient/recent, Deictic, Remembered Roles of Event Reference, Implicit "Sloppy anaphora" and Bridging, Genre-based Default, Type-identifiable, Generic ("People in General"), Cataphoric, Low-information, and Iterated Events Implicit Roles.

Recoverable implicit roles fall into the category of *Remote* Participants in UCCA, which typically calls for coreference resolution (Prange et al., 2019). We discern the eleven types of implicit roles mentioned above, recoverable or not, and extract those types where only true *Implicit* arguments occur, that is, the argument cannot be explicitly recovered from text, but inference and non-specificity are allowed as they are aligned with the definition of implicit arguments of UCCA. In the following section, we will analyze these implicit role types and argue the appropriateness of the set of categories we choose.

For the sake of operability and consistency, we only focus on core arguments in Scenes where these arguments are essential to the meaning of corresponding predicates (Jackendoff, 1992; Jackendoff, 1997; Goldberg, 1992; Grimshaw, 1993). Elements such as location, time, and manner are of little interest in this study whilst they are able to appear as foundational units or *Remote* Participant in UCCA.

As UCCA distinguishes *Remote* edges from *Implicit* units, it is natural to take advantage of this property to account for argument recoverability. The definition of implicit arguments in UCCA, particularly for its strong emphasis on the inability of explicit recovering from text, is not strictly corresponding with the eleven implicit role types.

3.2 Forming UCCA Implicit Argument Typology

Table 2 shows the comparison of the primary eleven implicit role types and UCCA's implicit argument set. Among these types of implicit roles in his inventory, four are definite implicit role constructions, viz. Salient/recent, Remember Roles, Script-inferrable, and Deictic. Only the last one of four, Deictic, we would consider a candidate category for UCCA's *Implicit* arguments. Salient/recent roles, which can be directly found in the recent prior discourse, is the quintessential type of DNI, and they can be easily replaced by pronouns. Remember Roles and Script-inferrable roles, however, require a cognitive and reasoning process, as the referents can be understood through a common ground in the text shared between the speaker and the addressee, or are reflecting a different facet of the same or a subordinate event. Deictic roles, albeit explicit reference to the speaker or addressee, is an extra-linguistic and cannot

O'Gorman 2019	Definite	Indefinite	Edge Cases	UCCA's Implicit Refinement
Salient/recent	✓			✗
Remember Roles	✓			✗
Script-inferrable	✓			✗
Deictic	✓			Deictic
Cataphoric		✓		✗
Low-information		✓		Non-specific
Iterated Events		✓		Iterated-set
Bridging			✓	✗
Genre-based			✓	Genre-based
Generic			✓	Generic
Type-Identifiable			✓	Type-Identifiable

Table 2: The 11 implicit role types in O'Gorman 2019 and the set for UCCA's implicit refinement.

be annotated as *Remote* Participant, since we are unable to retrieve them explicitly in the text. Therefore, we incorporate it in our set of *Implicit* arguments categories.

Three out of eleven implicit roles are marked as clearly indefinite arguments, namely Cataphoric, Low-information Arbitrary role, and Iterated Events Implicit Roles. Cataphoric, which Bhatia et al. (2014) define as "pragmatically specific indefinite", is the only type we do not include in UCCA's typology since it relies heavily on the interpretation of the discourse whether it will be referred to again. We would annotate it as *Remote* Participant if the role is mentioned in a later text, or Non-specific type if not so as not to complicate the reasoning process.

The other four, Bridging implicit roles, Genre-based Default, Generic and Type Identifiable, are regarded as edge cases. Once again, we will only admit the latter three in our typology. As far as we are concerned, bridging in ellipsis situations might not refer to the same referent conceptually. Nonetheless, it can be clearly resolved in the text. Therefore, it will be annotated as a *Remote* edge in UCCA.

We will focus on referents that do not appear anywhere in the text. Therefore, we follow the philosophy of UCCA and propose six categories of *implicit argument*, that is, Deictic, Generic, Genre-based, Type-identifiable, Non-specific and Iterated-set. In the next section, we will present and exemplify each one of them.

3.3 Categorisation Set for UCCA Implicit Arguments

3.3.1 Deictic

Deictic implicit arguments specifically refer to the speaker or the addressee in a sentence. In example 1, the second-person subject is exhorted to take a certain action, and such imperative construction allows the subject not to appear in the text explicitly. Shown in example 2, Deictic can also occur with certain interjections, where the subject as the speaker is habitually implicit.

(1) Just$_D$ ask$_P$ them$_A$ exactly$_E$ what$_C$ [you$_A$ want$_S$ (*what*)$_A$]$_E$ *IMP*$_{Deictic}$.

(2) [Thank you]$_P$ guys$_{G/A}$ *IMP*$_{Deictic}$.

It should be mentioned that only in certain languages is imperative likely to induce implicit arguments. In Romance languages such as Spanish, deictic information tends to be encoded morphologically due to person agreement (Ingram, 1971).

3.3.2 Generic

Generic implicit arguments denote "people in general" (Lambrecht and Lemoine, 2005). In example 3, the agent who "understands how this place has survived the earthquake" is not explicitly mentioned in the text, but it can be understood as it is the set of people in general. Example 4 can be construed as a gerund construction. "I" recommend taking a certain action. While the patient would not be specific, it conveys the message that "people in general" should follow such advice.

(3) It$_F$'s$_F$ impossible$_D$ to$_F$ understand$_P$ [how$_C$ [[this$_E$ place$_C$]$_A$ has$_F$ survived$_P$ [the$_F$ earthquake$_C$]$_A$]$_E$]$_A$ *IMP*$_{Generic}$.

(4) I$_A$ would$_F$ recommend$_P$ [not$_D$ using$_P$ [this$_E$ company$_C$]$_A$ *IMP*$_{Generic}$]$_A$.

3.3.3 Genre-based

Ruppenhofer and Michaelis (2010) found certain text genres, namely instructional imperatives, *labelese*, diary style, match report, and judgment-expressing quotative verbs, are closely linked with conventional omission. UCCA EWT corpus is based on online reviews of businesses and services by individuals. The review genre is so prominent acoss all dataset that it forms a pattern where the reviewers do not bother to mention the reviewees explicitly. In example 5 and 6, the review genre licenses the omission of the deliverer of the action "deliver" and server of the action "serve", as they refer to the reviewees by default, because in both contexts it is the restaurants that are being reviewed.

(5) Delivery$_P$ is$_F$ [lightning$_E$ fast$_C$]$_D$ *IMP*$_{Genre-based}$ *IMP*$_{Non-specific}$!

(6) [Great$_D$ service$_P$ *IMP*$_{Genre-based}$ *IMP*$_{Generic}$]$_H$ and$_L$ [awesome$_S$ prices$_A$]$_H$.

3.3.4 Type-identifiable

There exist some predicates allowing listeners to naturally think they "know" the omitted referents because of their high predictability. In example 7, the vague referent of "eat" can be understood from an inherent understanding of the listeners as "some kind of food". In example 8, the thing that "I drive" is not mentioned. Instead, it comes from common sense that the referent should be a kind of vehicle. Whatever kind it is, the lack of explicit mention barely affects the understanding of the text.

(7) It$_A$ is$_F$ my$_A$ favourite$_S$ [place$_C$ [(my)$_A$ to$_F$ eat$_P$ *IMP*$_{Type-identifiable}$]$_E$]$_A$.

(8) I$_A$ 'll$_F$ drive$_P$ [an$_Q$ hour$_C$]$_T$ [just$_E$ for$_R$ [their$_S$ (volcano)$_A$]$_E$ volcano$_C$]$_A$ *IMP*$_{Type-identifiable}$.

3.3.5 Non-specific

Non-specific implicit arguments refer to the kind of referents that cannot be inferred or understood at all. Such required information absent from the context attributes to the low interpretability of the implicit arguments, leaving them non-specific. As in example 9 and 10, it is impossible to infer what is "delivered" or who "charged me" neither from common knowledge nor given context. Such kind of implicit arguments are commonly found in nominalization and passive because there are high possibilities that not all agents/patients are always mentioned despite the fact that they might be core frame elements.

(9) There$_F$ is$_F$ no$_D$ delivery$_P$ *IMP*$_{Genre-based}$ *IMP*$_{Non-specific}$.

(10) I$_A$ don$_F$ 't$_D$ think$_P$ [I$_A$ have$_F$ ever$_T$ been$_F$ charged$_P$ before$_T$ *IMP*$_{Non-specific}$]$_A$.

3.3.6 Iterated-set

Iterated-set implicit arguments refer to a heterogeneous set of entities when the predicates are often an action that happens repeatedly, either iteratively or generically (Goldberg, 2001). For example, in sentence 11, the predicate "wait" implies high repetition, and the set of patients of "what/who I am waiting for" is so general that it does not hold any meaning beyond the context. As in example 12, the action " steal" designates a Scene where anything could be stolen, but "I" do not and will never steal. Unlike §3.3.4 Type-identifiable referring to a specific type of referents, the set of "things" in Iterated-set points to a vague set of entities to fill a role in a more functional way.

(11) I$_A$ never$_T$ wait$_P$ [in$_R$ the$_F$ waiting$_E$ room$_C$]$_A$ [[more$_C$ [than$_R$ two$_C$]$_C$]$_Q$ minutes$_C$]$_T$ *IMP*$_{Iterated-set}$.

(12) I$_A$ don$_F$ 't$_D$ steal$_P$ *IMP*$_{Iterated-set}$.

3.4 Inherent Ambiguity and "Continuum" of Coreness

3.4.1 Category Priority

There are a few cases when it is difficult to choose between two categories. Since UCCA does not aspire to annotate all possible interpretations (Abend and Rappoport, 2013), the annotator should make a best guess and choose one option. The first one is between Deictic and Generic, shown in example 13. The second one is between Genre-based and Non-specific, as in example 14. To keep the annotation consistent and maintain as much information as possible, we always choose Deictic over Generic, and Genre-based over Non-specific if available.

(13) [The$_F$ experience$_C$]$_A$ [with$_R$ every$_Q$ department$_C$]$_A$ has$_F$ been$_F$ great$_D$ *IMP*$_{Deictic}$.

(14) I$_A$ will$_F$ definitely$_D$ refer$_P$ [[my$_A$ friends$_{A/S}$]$_C$ and$_N$ [(my)$_A$ family$_{A/S}$]$_C$]$_A$ *IMP*$_{Genre-Based}$.

3.4.2 Nominalization As Occupation

It is a judgment call whether the patient of Process instantiated by a profession should be annotated at all. Even so it remains debatable which category such kind of implicit argument belongs to. In the current version of corpus, we will always annotate it as Type-identifiable. As in example 15, the patients of whom has been taught is unclear but neither require clarification. The Scene of teacher/teaching is annotated with a Type-identifiable implicit argument denoting a type of people recieving education.

(15) They$_A$ are$_F$ [very$_E$ good$_C$]$_D$ teachers$_{A/P}$ *IMP*$_{Type-identifiable}$.

4 Refined Implicit Corpus

In furtherance of investigating the characteristics of UCCA's implicit arguments, we piloted a study to revisit and refine part of English Web Treebank[3] annotated with the UCCA foundational layer.[4] 200 passages were randomly selected for experiment from the total 723 passages comprising the UCCA EWT dataset.

We use UCCAApp to carry out annotation. The process is divided into two stages. Firstly, we create passage-level review tasks to check the existing annotation whether they contain implicit arguments, and add missing arguments if necessary. Secondly, we split passages into sentences, create tasks with refinement layer and then annotate with corresponding fine-grained implicit categories. Since all the annotation works were undertaken by one single annotator, the dataset preferably serves as a demonstration of concept, and thus further measurement of inter-annotator agreement would be desired to establish a sounder dataset.

4.1 Revisiting Original EWT UCCA Dataset

The original implicit argument annotation in EWT UCCA corpus is restricted only to put concern on constructional null instantiations, and when a unit lacks a Center or a Process/State, which is out of the scope of this study. We only regard implicit argument whose category is Participant in UCCA as valid implicit in this research. Therefore, it is necessary to modify or add missing implicit arguments in the dataset. Considering the original corpus was annotated on passage-level, whereas our new dataset will be done on sentence-level, *Remote* edges across sentences will be treated by adding a new *Implicit* node under its origin Scene.

Table 3 shows the statistics before and after reviewing and refining according to the new UCCA Implicit Argument Typology. It can be seen that in the refined dataset, 116 out of 200 passages contain implicit arguments, 13 more passages than the original dataset, in which only 103 passages contain implicit arguments. Yielding an increase of 255%, the review process added 250 more valid implicit arguments in the corpus.

---

[3] https://catalog.ldc.upenn.edu/LDC2012T13
[4] https://github.com/UniversalConceptualCognitiveAnnotation/UCCA_English-EWT

	# Passages	# Passages w/ Implicit	# Sentences	# Sentences w/ Implicit	# Implicit (Valid)
Original	200 (out of 723)	103	306	111	153 (98)
Refined	200	116	393	221	**415 (385)**

Table 3: Statistics of the UCCA EWT dataset sampled passages before and after reviewing. The additional implicit arguments result from both reviewing original UCCA EWT and conducting new annotation according to out fine-grained typology. Implicit (Valid) denotes implicit argument whose role is Participant in UCCA.

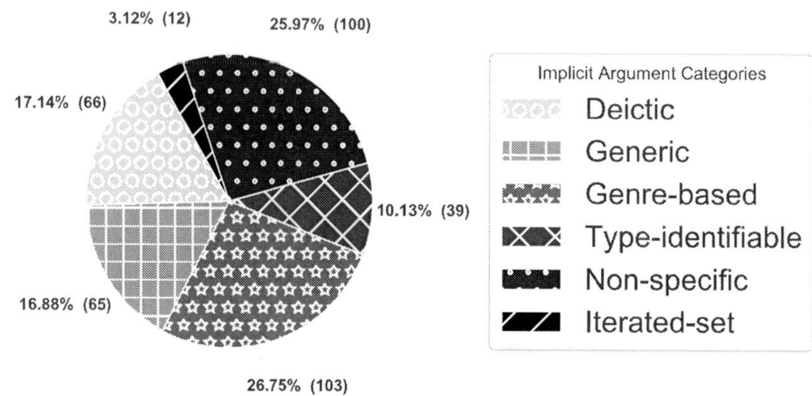

Figure 2: Statistics of pilot UCCA implicit dataset.

4.2 Statistics

Tokenized and split according to the Universal Dependencies English Web Treebank (Silveira et al., 2014; Hershcovich et al., 2019a), this pilot corpus consists of 3702 tokens, 1411 nodes, and 4759 edges over 393 sentences. In total, 385 valid implicit arguments are found and annotated on 221 sentences. Figure 2 demonstrates each implicit argument category with its corresponding number in the pilot refined implicit corpus, and illustrates the percentage of each implicit category in the dataset. One can see that Genre-based and Non-specific are the two most frequent categories, both of which have more than 100 instances in the dataset, making up approximately 52% combined. They are followed by Generic and Deictic, and each occupies about 17%. Type-identifiable comes penultimate with 39 instances, while Iterated-set is the least frequent type, which merely has 12 instances, accounting for 3.12% of the whole corpus.

4.3 Comparisons to FiGref Annotation

	Type-Identifiable	Deictic	Generic	Non-specific	Genre-based	Iterated-set	Script-inferrable	Other	Invalid
Ours	9.79%	17.29%	17.29%	25.93%	25.93%	2.59%	\	\	\
FiGref	7%	5%	10%	4%	\	\	9%	12%	53%

Table 4: Relative frequency of annotated implicit types in UCCA's refinement layer and FiGref's annoation for non-recoverable roles in Multi-sentence AMR. The first four types are shared by both annotation corpora. The following two are exclusive to UCCA's refinement layer. The last three are additonally introduced into FiGref's set of interpretation types.

FiGref is annotated over Multi-sentence AMR training data, SemEval-2010 Task 10 training data, and Beyond NomBank. It contains 856 implicit roles classified into 14 types, which includes all 11 proposed interpretation types except Genre-based, and four more kinds of invalid roles to account for those implicit roles of low importance or deal with tricky occasions (Local-mention, Contextually-invalid, Non-predictive and Low-importance). However, FiGref has a relatively low Cohen's κ score (Cohen, 1960) of 55.2. With 14 types to distinguish, FiGref has a relatively high annotation complexity and ambiguity.

Comparatively, we do not annotate genuinely invalid implicit role such as these four low importance kinds, since we consider they are simply not core elements of event. As UCCA differs *Implicit* units from *Remote* edges, it naturally reduces the annotation complexity. Therefore, we do not have to distinguish and annotate these five types in O'Gorman 2019, viz.: Saient/recent, Remember Roles, Script-inferrable, Cataphoric and Bridging. We consdier them belong to *Remote* in UCCA. We only need to attend to essential and unrecoverable implicit arguments within the set of six types we propose in §3.3.

Owing to the distinct annotation design and lack of statistics provided by FiGref, it is difficult to perform a comparative quantitative study between UCCA's implicit refinement layer and FiGref. However, we are able to look into the relative frequency of annotated implicit types in UCCA and FiGref's annotation for non-recoverable roles in Multi-sentence AMR shown in Table 4.

The distribution distinction can be possibly explained by the different domains of the corpora and their annotation methodology. We keep Genre-based type to account for the particular "review" genre in EWT dataset. Among the three types FiGref has introduced, We can see that invalid roles dominate the FiGref annotation with 53%. This is because a large amount of non-important interpretations of null-instantiation are taken into account in FiGref, whereas the implicit refinement annotation designed for UCCA is limited to essential important implicit arguments so as to lower annotation complexity and ambiguity.

5 Conclusion and Future Work

We proposed a novel typology for different implicit arguments in UCCA, which allows annotation with a relatively low cognitive load. Then we reviewed and refined part of the existing UCCA English Web Treebank dataset and piloted annotation of our guidelines with a refinement layer of fine-grained implicit arguments. It is currently the only published dataset with this kind of information.

Our work addresses a deep linguistic problem in implicit role interpretation, impossible to deal with current machine learning approaches, and provides an example for conducting research about it. It has the potential to benefit natural language understanding, especially in genre-specific context, e.g., social media and customer reviews. In this work we only use the existing definitions from O'Gorman (2019), testing their compatiblity with the UCCA guidelines and their applicability to an UCCA annotated corpus. In future work we would also like to reason about and possibly redesign the criteria based on semantic and pragmatic considerations (Lyngfelt, 2012). We will also consider the usefulness of the refined scheme for practical NLP tasks, and possibly discard some of the categories, such as Iterated-set, which is the least frequent category in our corpus.

It is anticipated that our study will inspire tailored design of implicit role annotation in other meaning representation frameworks. Downstream tasks such as coreference resolution and human-robot interaction are also likely to benefit from reducing ambiguity and increase contextual understanding by explicitly modelling implicit arguments.

While the pilot design is promising, existing parsers that tackle implicit arguments only attend to certain aspect of linguistic phenomena. Therefore, for a rather comprehensive implicit argument annotation the like of UCCA, it is crucial to develop a parser that can emit implicit nodes dynamically and label them with fair accuracy.

Finally, work on reviewing the corpus by a second annotator is underway to validate the annotation quality by providing an inter-annotator agreement measurement. Future work will also expand the corpus and extend it to multiple languages.

Acknowledgements

We would like to thank the anonymous reviewers, Omri Abend and Dotan Dvir for their helpful feedback.

References

Omri Abend and Ari Rappoport. 2013. Universal Conceptual Cognitive Annotation (UCCA). In *Proceedings of the 51st Annual Meeting of the Association for Computational Linguistics (Volume 1: Long Papers)*, pages 228–238, Sofia, Bulgaria, August. Association for Computational Linguistics.

Omri Abend, Shai Yerushalmi, and Ari Rappoport. 2017. UCCAApp: Web-application for syntactic and semantic phrase-based annotation. In *Proceedings of ACL 2017, System Demonstrations*, pages 109–114, Vancouver, Canada, July. Association for Computational Linguistics.

Emily M. Bender, Dan Flickinger, Stephan Oepen, and Yi Zhang. 2011. Parser evaluation over local and non-local deep dependencies in a large corpus. In *Proceedings of the 2011 Conference on Empirical Methods in Natural Language Processing*, pages 397–408, Edinburgh, Scotland, UK., July. Association for Computational Linguistics.

Archna Bhatia, Mandy Simons, Lori Levin, Yulia Tsvetkov, Chris Dyer, and Jordan Bender. 2014. A unified annotation scheme for the semantic/pragmatic components of definiteness. In *Proceedings of the Ninth International Conference on Language Resources and Evaluation (LREC'14)*, pages 910–916, Reykjavik, Iceland, May. European Language Resources Association (ELRA).

Pengxiang Cheng and Katrin Erk. 2019. Implicit argument prediction as reading comprehension. In *Proceedings of the AAAI Conference on Artificial Intelligence*, volume 33, pages 6284–6291.

Jacob Cohen. 1960. A coefficient of agreement for nominal scales. *Educational and Psychological Measurement*, 20(1):37–46.

William Croft and D Alan Cruse. 2004. *Cognitive linguistics*. Cambridge University Press.

Robert MW Dixon. 2010a. *Basic linguistic theory Volume 1: Methodology*, volume 1. Oxford University Press.

Robert MW Dixon. 2010b. *Basic linguistic theory Volume 2: Grammatical topics*. Oxford-New York, Oxford University Press.

Rober MW Dixon. 2012. *Basic linguistic theory: Further grammatical topics, Vol. 3*. Oxford: Oxford University Press.

Yanai Elazar and Yoav Goldberg. 2019. Wheres my head? definition, data set, and models for numeric fused-head identification and resolution. *Transactions of the Association for Computational Linguistics*, 7:519–535.

Charles John Fillmore and Paul Kay. 1993. *Construction grammar coursebook: Chapters 1 thru 11*. University of California.

Charles J Fillmore. 1986. Pragmatically controlled zero anaphora. In *Annual Meeting of the Berkeley Linguistics Society*, volume 12, pages 95–107.

Simon Garrod and Melody Terras. 2000. The contribution of lexical and situational knowledge to resolving discourse roles: Bonding and resolution. *Journal of memory and language*, 42(4):526–544.

Matthew Gerber and Joyce Chai. 2010. Beyond NomBank: A study of implicit arguments for nominal predicates. In *Proceedings of the 48th Annual Meeting of the Association for Computational Linguistics*, pages 1583–1592, Uppsala, Sweden, July. Association for Computational Linguistics.

Matthew Gerber and Joyce Y. Chai. 2012. Semantic role labeling of implicit arguments for nominal predicates. *Computational Linguistics*, 38(4):755–798.

Adele E. Goldberg. 1992. The inherent semantics of argument structure: The case of the english ditransitive construction. *Cognitive Linguistics*, 3(1):37–74, January.

Adele E Goldberg. 2001. Patient arguments of causative verbs can be omitted: The role of information structure in argument distribution. *Language sciences*, 23(4-5):503–524.

Jane Barbara Grimshaw. 1993. *Semantic structure and semantic content in lexical representation*. Rutgers University.

Daniel Hershcovich, Omri Abend, and Ari Rappoport. 2019a. Content differences in syntactic and semantic representation. In *Proceedings of the 2019 Conference of the North American Chapter of the Association for Computational Linguistics: Human Language Technologies, Volume 1 (Long and Short Papers)*, pages 478–488, Minneapolis, Minnesota, June. Association for Computational Linguistics.

Daniel Hershcovich, Leshem Choshen, Elior Sulem, Zohar Aizenbud, Ari Rappoport, and Omri Abend. 2019b. SemEval 2019 task 1: Cross-lingual semantic parsing with UCCA. In *Proc. of SemEval*.

David Ingram. 1971. Toward a theory of person deixis. *Research on Language & Social Interaction*, 4(1):37–53.

Ray Jackendoff. 1992. *Semantic structures*, volume 18. MIT press.

Ray Jackendoff. 1997. Twistin'the night away. *Language*, pages 534–559.

Paul Kay. 2004. Null instantiation of nominal complements. *Unpublished ms., University of California, Department of Linguistics, Berkeley*.

Knud Lambrecht and Kevin Lemoine. 2005. Definite null objects in (spoken) french. *Grammatical constructions: Back to the roots*, 4:13.

Benjamin Lyngfelt. 2012. Re-thinking fni: On null instantiation and control in construction grammar. *Constructions and frames*, 4(1):1–23.

Anita Mittwoch. 1971. Idioms and unspecified np deletion. *Linguistic Inquiry*, 2(2):255–259.

Stephan Oepen, Omri Abend, Jan Hajic, Daniel Hershcovich, Marco Kuhlmann, Tim O'Gorman, Nianwen Xue, Jayeol Chun, Milan Straka, and Zdenka Uresova. 2019. MRP 2019: Cross-framework meaning representation parsing. In *Proceedings of the Shared Task on Cross-Framework Meaning Representation Parsing at the 2019 Conference on Natural Language Learning*, pages 1–27, Hong Kong, November. Association for Computational Linguistics.

Tim O'Gorman, Michael Regan, Kira Griffitt, Ulf Hermjakob, Kevin Knight, and Martha Palmer. 2018. AMR beyond the sentence: the multi-sentence AMR corpus. In *Proceedings of the 27th International Conference on Computational Linguistics*, pages 3693–3702, Santa Fe, New Mexico, USA, August. Association for Computational Linguistics.

Timothy J O'Gorman. 2019. *Bringing Together Computational and Linguistic Models of Implicit Role Interpretation*. Ph.D. thesis, University of Colorado at Boulder.

David M Perlmutter. 1968. *Deep and surface structure constraints in syntax*. Ph.D. thesis, Massachusetts Institute of Technology.

Jakob Prange, Nathan Schneider, and Omri Abend. 2019. Semantically constrained multilayer annotation: The case of coreference. In *Proceedings of the First International Workshop on Designing Meaning Representations*, pages 164–176, Florence, Italy, August. Association for Computational Linguistics.

James Pustejovsky, Ken Lai, and Nianwen Xue. 2019. Modeling quantification and scope in Abstract Meaning Representations. In *Proceedings of the First International Workshop on Designing Meaning Representations*, pages 28–33, Florence, Italy, August. Association for Computational Linguistics.

Ana Teresa Pérez-Leroux, Mihaela Pirvulescu, and Yves Roberge. 2018. *Direct Objects and Language Acquisition*. Cambridge Studies in Linguistics. Cambridge University Press.

Josef Ruppenhofer and Laura A Michaelis. 2010. A constructional account of genre-based argument omissions. *Constructions and Frames*, 2(2):158–184.

Josef Ruppenhofer, Michael Ellsworth, Myriam Schwarzer-Petruck, Christopher R Johnson, and Jan Scheffczyk. 2006. Framenet ii: Extended theory and practice.

Josef Ruppenhofer, Caroline Sporleder, Roser Morante, Collin Baker, and Martha Palmer. 2009. SemEval-2010 task 10: Linking events and their participants in discourse. In *Proceedings of the Workshop on Semantic Evaluations: Recent Achievements and Future Directions (SEW 2009)*, pages 106–111, Boulder, Colorado, June. Association for Computational Linguistics.

Nathan Schneider, Jena D. Hwang, Vivek Srikumar, Jakob Prange, Austin Blodgett, Sarah R. Moeller, Aviram Stern, Adi Bitan, and Omri Abend. 2018. Comprehensive supersense disambiguation of English prepositions and possessives. In *Proceedings of the 56th Annual Meeting of the Association for Computational Linguistics (Volume 1: Long Papers)*, pages 185–196, Melbourne, Australia, July. Association for Computational Linguistics.

Adi Shalev, Jena D. Hwang, Nathan Schneider, Vivek Srikumar, Omri Abend, and Ari Rappoport. 2019. Preparing SNACS for subjects and objects. In *Proceedings of the First International Workshop on Designing Meaning Representations*, pages 141–147, Florence, Italy, August. Association for Computational Linguistics.

Natalia Silveira, Timothy Dozat, Marie-Catherine de Marneffe, Samuel Bowman, Miriam Connor, John Bauer, and Chris Manning. 2014. A gold standard dependency corpus for English. In *Proceedings of the Ninth International Conference on Language Resources and Evaluation (LREC'14)*, pages 2897–2904, Reykjavik, Iceland, May. European Language Resources Association (ELRA).

K-SNACS: Annotating Korean Adposition Semantics

Jena D. Hwang
Allen Institute for AI
jenah@allenai.org

Hanwool Choe
Georgetown University
hc563@georgetown.edu

Na-Rae Han
University of Pittsburgh
naraehan@pitt.edu

Nathan Schneider
Georgetown University
nathan.schneider@georgetown.edu

Abstract

While many languages use *adpositions* to encode semantic relationships between content words in a sentence (e.g., agentivity or temporality), the details of how adpositions work vary widely across languages with respect to both form and meaning. In this paper, we empirically adapt the SNACS framework (Schneider et al., 2018) to Korean, a language that is typologically distant from English—the language SNACS was originally designed upon. We apply the SNACS framework to annotate the highly popular novella *The Little Prince* with semantic supersense labels over all Korean postpositions. Thus, we introduce the first broad-coverage corpus annotated with Korean postposition semantics and provide a detailed analysis of the corpus with an apples-to-apples comparison between Korean and English annotations.

1 Introduction

Korean has a grammaticalized category of **postpositions** that includes highly polysemous morphemes that mediate semantic relationships between content words. On their own, they represent humble grammatical markers on nominals, but they play a whale of a role in piecing together the meaning of a sentence. Much like English **prepositions** (or collectively **adpositions**), the semantic relations that they encode range from thematic relationships like agentivity and instrumentality to relative circumstantial information like time, location, or purpose.

In this work we develop a Korean adaptation of an existing annotation schema, SNACS (§2.3), which is specifically geared towards adpositional semantics. The expanded schema details 54 semantic and pragmatic categories called **supersenses** that resolve major ambiguities and generalize across adpositional types. Although the SNACS framework was built based on English preposition senses, the authors claim that the semantically coarse-grained and lexically-agnostic characteristics of the supersenses are well-suited to their adoption for other languages (Hwang et al., 2017). The schema has been so far applied successfully to Mandarin Chinese (Peng et al., 2020). We now apply it to Korean in order to further test claims of cross linguistic extensibility. Notably, SNACS has yet to be tested on a highly agglutinative language like Korean, whose adpositions (*josa*, §2.1) are bound morphemes suffixed on nominals, rather than independent lexical items like in English and Chinese. Korean adpositions are also peculiar in that some participate in case marking; we annotate postpositional nominative and accusative markers within the purview of SNACS.

Our contributions are three-fold: (1) we show that SNACS can be applied to Korean by adapting the SNACS hierarchy and guidelines to cover language-specific phenomena (§3); (2) we produce a broad-coverage corpus of Korean SNACS annotations and provide a corpus analysis of the Korean data (§4); and (3) we provide in-depth comparison between parallel Korean and English SNACS for purposes of our own study and for basis of comparison for future application of SNACS (§5).[1] Our work represents the first application of SNACS to an agglutinative language where adpositions are bound morphemes. Additionally, it represents a first Korean supersense corpus that was specifically produced for Korean postpositions.

---

[1] Korean SNACS guidelines and corpora are available at https://github.com/jdch00/k-snacs.

Proceedings of the 2nd International Workshop on Designing Meaning Representations, pages 53–66
Barcelona, Spain (Online), December 13, 2020

2 Background

2.1 Korean Postpositions

We focus on the well-researched category of *josa* (Sohn, 2001), as postpositions are known in Korean linguistics, as a target of our annotation. Characteristic of agglutinative languages, josa are bound morphemes that are suffixed on a nominal unit, though some pragmatically motivated postpositions may also attach to non-nominal units such as predicates and adverbs. As noted earlier, while many of them can be thought of as rough counterparts to English prepositions and hence act primarily as encoders of semantic relations, the functions carried out by josa run a broader gamut: some are case markers (nominative, accusative and genitive), while others supply pragmatic or contextual information.

In terms of syntactic distribution, josa have two noteworthy traits. First, some may be show up stacked, as exemplified in 1.[2] Such stacking is strictly governed by morphosyntatic rules. Another is that the case-marking josa are not mandatory: the nominative and accusative markers may be absent, leaving bare nominals in place (example 2a)—which is especially common in a spoken context where there is no ambiguity—or they may be superseded by another, pragmatically motivated, josa (2b).

(1)   나에게-만-이   아니라 우리 모두에게...
       me-**DAT-FOC-NOM** not-but us   all-DAT
       "Not just to me but to all of us..."

(2)   a.   빌이   점심(을) 먹었다   b.   빌은   점심(을)   먹었다
           Bill-**NOM** lunch(-**ACC**) ate   Bill-**TOP** lunch(-**ACC**) ate
           "Bill ate lunch"   "Bill ate lunch"

2.2 Related Work

Josa have received considerable theoretical attention within Korean linguistics. Much of the work has focused on investigating their syntactic function and patterns of grammaticalization, and enumerating prototypical semantics of specific groups of postpositions (e.g., Kang, 2012; Hwang, 2012; Sohn, 2001; Choi-Jonin, 2008; Rhee, 2004). Within semantics, postpositions have been investigated within semantic domains such as spatial configuration (e.g., Kang, 2012; Choi and Choi, 2018; Lee and Kabata, 2006). Little attention has been paid to establishing broader semantic categories of meaning that generalize over specific postposition types. While the morphosyntactic literature traditionally recognizes a dozen different grammatical categories (e.g., Nominative, Accusative, Dative, Genitive, Locative, Allative) for postpositions (e.g., Sohn, 2001), these josa categories, as this paper will show, are only partially adequate in the face of the full range of semantic behaviors we observe in the data. Semantically adequate and comprehensive annotation requires a richer palette of semantic labels that can apply broadly across the postpositional types, for which we turn to SNACS.

Computational approaches and resource creation projects have also attempted to classify Korean postpositions, with a focus on morphosyntax (in morphological tagging and syntactic parsing) (Choi and Palmer, 2011; Hong, 2009; Han, 2005). The Penn Korean Treebank (Han et al., 2001), for example, recognizes four part-of-speech (POS) categories (case, adverbial, conjunctive, and auxiliary) to cover all postpositional morphemes, and the 21st Century Sejong Project (Park and Tyers, 2019; Kim, 2006) retains a slightly larger inventory of nine POS tags, generally corresponding to the grammatical categories found in the traditional literature. More recently, the Korean Universal Dependency project guidelines do not directly address the individual postpositions since Korean postpositions are considered sub-lexical units. Instead, the POS category of NOUN is assigned to the full (noun + postposition) lexical unit (Oh et al., 2020; Chun et al., 2018).

The status of postpositions as functional categories also plays into the lack of specific attention in computational semantic resources. For example, while the labeling of Korean PropBank (Palmer et al., 2006) arguments is to some extent guided by the semantics of the postposition (e.g., a nominative marker might suggest ARG0 and a locative marker, ARGM-LOC), the labels are annotated at the lexical and phrasal level centering on nominal elements. In the case of Korean AMR (Choe et al., 2019), postpositions

---

[2] Here is a list of gloss abbreviations used in this paper: accusative (ACC), dative (DAT), focus (FOC), genitive (GEN), nominative (NOM), question (Q), speculation mood (SPEC) and information topic (TOP).

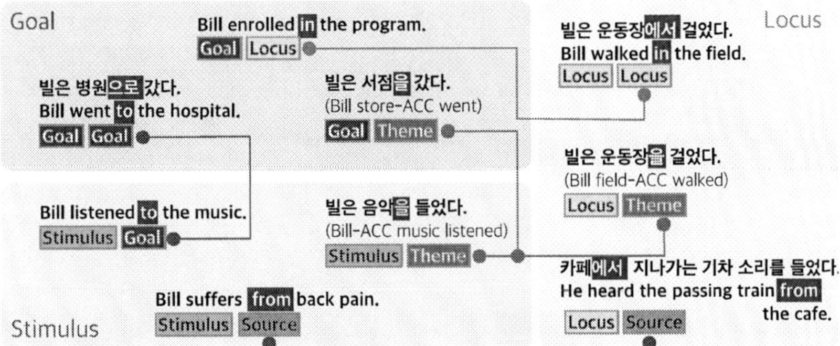

Figure 1: Conceptual diagram illustrating selected adposition usages and how they are related via construal within the SNACS framework. The light boxes cluster adpositional use by their scene roles. The lines indicate the connections various construals have via function labels—what the adposition lexically encodes. Some of these construals are found in both languages, others only in one or the other.

are omitted from the annotation entirely (as prepositions solely marking roles are omitted from English AMR; Banarescu et al., 2013).

SNACS is thus the most promising basis for a semantic framework with which to annotate Korean adpositions. The goal is to pave way for a full-scope, comprehensive treatment of the major semantic dimension of Korean postpositions. To the best of our knowledge, this work is the first to annotate a Korean corpus specifically targeting postpositions. Moreover, this work represents the first Korean application of a lexically-agnostic semantic analysis which cross-cuts adpositional types.

2.3 SNACS Framework

The Semantic Network of Adposition and Case Supersenses (SNACS; Schneider et al., 2018, 2020) is a framework for annotating adpositions with coarse-grained semantic classes called supersenses that broadly capture prepositional semantics without particular reference to any lexicon. The current version of the scheme defines 50 such supersenses for event participant roles (inspired by traditional thematic roles: AGENT, THEME, RECIPIENT, etc.), circumstantial roles (e.g. TIME, MANNER), and roles describing relationships between entities (e.g. POSSESSOR, WHOLE, QUANTITYVALUE). Annotating adposition uses in context serves to disambiguate them—e.g. "the wheel **of** the car" (WHOLE) versus "the destruction **of** the city" (THEME). Unlike dictionary senses (cf. Litkowski and Hargraves, 2005; Litkowski, 2014), the supersenses transcend lexical types in order to group together different adpositions with related meanings: thus WHOLE applies to both "the wheel **of** the car" and "the paint **on** the car". While the semantic criteria aim to be language-agnostic, the details of how to apply these labels to disambiguate adposition tokens in text—including specific criteria for which tokens to annotate, and how to deal with various language-specific constructions—need to be developed on a per-language basis. Extensive guidelines and multiple annotated corpora (web reviews; *The Little Prince*) are available for English. The Mandarin translation of *The Little Prince* has been fully annotated as well (Peng et al., 2020).

A distinctive aspect of SNACS is the so-called *construal analysis*, by which some tokens receive not one but two supersenses to reflect different facets of the usage: the **scene role** with respect to a larger situation (typically denoted by a predicate), and the **function** or primary lexical contribution of the adposition itself. These diverge in cases like "the paint **on** the car", where on the one hand the relationship between paint and car is one of part-whole; and on the other hand, the use of **on** frames it as a locational relationship. With the construal analysis this token would receive a scene role of WHOLE and function of LOCUS (WHOLE↝LOCUS for short). By default, if the role and function are congruent, a single label is given.

3 Applying SNACS to Korean

We apply the SNACS supersenses to explicit mentions of Korean postpositions, and we find that the labels are generally applicable to Korean postpositional semantics. In this section, we discuss a few of the language-specific challenges we faced in applying SNACS to Korean.

Nominative and Accusative Cases One of the earliest challenges in adapting SNACS to Korean postposition semantics was deciding how to consistently label the nominative (NOM) and accusative (ACC) case markings. NOM and ACC case markings are postpositions that attach to the subject and object of a sentence, respectively. Because these are identified in English via word order, there was no existing annotation scheme to follow in SNACS.

We adopt the view that the predicate's syntactic assignment of case marking such as NOM and ACC (as well as ergatives and absolutives) generally aligns with agentivity of the participant with respect to the verb given a transitive event (Grimm, 2011; Fillmore, 1968). Thus, for the function labels, we link the NOM and ACC labels to proto-agent and proto-patient roles (Dowty, 1991), respectively, in a transitive event: NOM (이/-i)[3] receives CAUSER or AGENT function label and ACC (을/-ul) receives the function of either THEME (i.e., general undergoer) or its subtype TOPIC (see example 3). In an intransitive event, where the NOM marks the patient argument, the function label of THEME is assigned (4).

For cases where the predicate assigns to NOM and ACC semantics that is different to that of their prototypical use, we represent the semantics assigned by the predicate as the scene role (e.g., ORIGINATOR of a communication event in 5 and LOCUS of an action in 6), while the function is the role associated most directly with the case marking (e.g. THEME for ACC). Our decisions are fully compatible with the treatment of English subjects and objects proposed in Shalev et al. (2019) (though available English SNACS corpora do not yet contain such annotations).

(3) 빌이/AGENT 사과를/THEME 먹었다
     Bill-**NOM**   apple-**ACC**   ate
     "Bill ate an apple"

(4) 해가/THEME 일찍 떴다
     sun-**NOM**   early rose
     "the sun rose early"

(5) 빌이/ORIGINATOR↝AGENT 대답했다
     Bill-**NOM**   answered
     "Bill answered"

(6) 빌이/AGENT 공원을/LOCUS↝THEME 걸었다
     Bill-**NOM**   park-**ACC**   walked
     "Bill took a walk in the park"

Contextual Postpositions. English SNACS has strictly focused on the annotation of semantic relations, excluding discourse connectives like "**according_to** him" or "**as_for** me" from annotation. We extend this treatment to two Korean discourse markers: vocative marker 야/-ya and politeness marker 요/-yo.

The pragmatic category in Korean, however, extends beyond these two markers. Korean also includes a category of frequently used pragmatic postpositions, whose role in a sentence is to evoke a particular set of contextual information regarding the entities to which they attach, thereby altering overall reading of the sentence. To address such usages, we introduce a new supertype CONTEXT as a fourth branch of SNACS hierarchy and add to it two new supersenses, TOPICAL and FOCUS.

We assign TOPICAL to postposition 은/-un that marks the information topic (TOP) in a sentence providing a contrast to a contextually available referent (7). FOCUS label is for postpositions that indicate the focus of a sentence (FOC), contributing information such as contrastiveness, likelihood, or value judgements (8 and 9).[4] There are a total of 10 identified postpositions that fall within the FOCUS category. In the example below, the three sentences have the same propositional value (i.e., "Bill did a good job"), but the postpositions situate the entity they mark within varying context.

(7) Bill은/TOPICAL 일을 잘 했다
     Bill-**TOP** work-ACC well did
     As for Bill, he did a good job.

(8) Bill만/FOCUS 일을 잘 했다
     Bill-**only** work-ACC well did
     Only Bill (and no one else) did
     a good job.

(9) Bill까지/FOCUS 일을 잘 했다
     Bill-**even** work-ACC well did
     Even Bill, the least likely candidate, did a good job.

Quotative Postpositions The Korean postposition inventory includes half a dozen markers that identify direct and indirect quotes in a sentence. The scene role that they play ranges from TOPIC (10), IDENTITY (11), to COMPARISONREF depending on the role assigned by the head verb. We propose a new supersense label QUOTE, a subcategory of THEME, to cover these at the function level.

(10) 오늘 도착한다고/TOPIC↝QUOTE 했다
      today arrive-**quote**   say
      "[They] said he'd arrive today."

(11) 지나를   천사라고/IDENT.↝QUOTE 생각한다
      Gina-ACC angel-**quote**   thinks
      "[They] thinks of Gina as an angel"

---

[3]NOM marker 가/-ka is an allomorphic variant of morpheme 이/-i, and ACC marker 를/-lul is an allomorph of the morpheme 을/-ul. A morpheme and its allomorphs are treated as a single postposition. Other morpheme-allophone pairs in this paper include: TOP marker 은/-un & 는/-nun, and goal/instrument marker 으로/-ulo & 로/-lo.

[4]We identify 7 sub-categories of FOCUS: contrast (translates roughly to *at the very least*), additive focus (*also*), exclusive focus (*only* in 8), negative polarity focus (*not even*), inclusive focus (*among others*), and two types of scalar focus (*merely, even* in 9). Since each postposition only maps to only one of these functions, we do not subdivide FOCUS according to use.

	Count		Count		Count
Documents (chapters)	27	Annotated P Targets	4166	Unique SNACS labels	42
Sentence	168	Unique Ps	39	Scene roles	41
Tokens	10939	Nominative & Accusative Ps	1676	Functions	32
Tokens w/explicit Ps	4020	Topical & Focus Ps	1319	Unique Construal pairs	108
		Construal Pairs: Scene = Function	3161	Scene = Function	31

Table 1: Statistics of the Korean *Little Prince* corpus.

The placement of the postposition under the THEME label was in recognition that these are participant arguments of verbs of communication (e.g., saying, telling) and cogitation (e.g., thinking, considering). What sets this usages apart from TOPIC is that by virtue of being marked by a QUOTE postposition, the sentence specifies that the information was heard or evidenced by the speaker/writer. Korean quotatives have also been widely studied as an evidential marker, which is not fully captured by its placement under the THEME. This is a topic of continued investigation.

Functionally Bleached Postposition 에/-ey   Scholars have noted 에/-ey marks inanimate entities for spatial, temporal and goal type relations (Kang, 2012; Choi-Jonin, 2008; Rhee, 2004). The postposition, however, is a highly bleached one: its meaning is largely dependent on the sense assigned by the predicate. On its own, it simply serves to specify that the nominal is in a certain circumstantial relationship with the predicate. For this reason, we specify CIRCUMSTANCE at the function level, and let the scene role to disambiguate the relationship between predicate and the nominal[5].

(12) 깊숙한 곳에/LOCUS↝CIRCUMSTANCE 보물을 감추고있는...
      deep   place-**ey**   treasure hide
      "a treasure hidden **in** a deep place"

(13) 나는 동이   틀   무렵에/TIME↝CIRCUMSTANCE 우물을   발견했다
      I-NOM sun-NOM rising cusp-**ey**   well-ACC discovered
      "I discovered a well **at** around the time of sun rise."

(14) 마음에/BENEFICIARY↝CIRCUMSTANCE 좋은 말
      heart-**ey**   good words
      "words that are good **for** the heart."

Postposition Stacking   Because of the agglutinative nature of Korean grammar, postpositional markers can productively stack on top of each other as exemplified by (1). Postposition stacking is governed by grammatical rules and exhibits varying levels of grammaticalization (Schütze, 2001; Sohn, 2001). For SNACS, we consider only six stacked postpositions as a single unit: 에게서/-eykeyse, 한테서/-hantheyse, 에게로/-eykeylo, 에다(가)/-eyta(ka), 에서부터/ eyseputhe, and 으로부터/-uloputhe. These six have acquired noncompositional meanings. Otherwise, the stacked postpositions (as in example 1) are considered compositional and annotated as separate targets.

4   The Korean *Little Prince* Corpus

4.1   Data & Annotation

We annotate the Korean translation of Antoine de Saint-Exupéry's novella *The Little Prince* (어린 왕자),[6] which is available in various languages and has previously received attention from AMR annotation (Banarescu et al., 2013) and SNACS efforts for English and Chinese (Peng et al., 2020; Schneider et al., 2018). This corpus consists of 27 chapters with 10,939 tokens (table 1).

---

[5]Unlike other macrolabels like PARTICIPANT, CONFIGURATION, and CONTEXT (see figure 3 that are not directly used for annotation, CIRCUMSTANCE is used directly to annotate adpositions that contextualize a background setting or occasions for an event (e.g. "We drink eggnog **for** Christmas." Christmas is not so much *why* one might drink eggnog, rather the cirucumstance in which one might drink eggnog). By analogy, we are claiming here that 에/-ey sets the scene for the relationship between the verb and the marked nominal, and the nominal further specifies what that relationship is.

[6]The translation we use can be found at http://cezz.com/blog/category/15. This particular translation has been made freely available online by various sites for over a decade now. Unfortunately, the translator is unknown.

| | All | | | Only | | | Excluding | | |
| | Postpositional Types | | | NOM, ACC, TOP, FOC | | | NOM, ACC, TOP, FOC | | |
	# Target	Scene	Function	# Target	Scene	Function	# Target	Scene	Function
Phase 1	1149	80.4%	87.2%	807	87.2%	90.5%	342	64.3%	79.5%
Phase 2	2465	83.8%	91.6%	1788	89.6%	93.4%	677	68.4%	87.0%
Overall	3614	82.7%	90.2%	2595	88.9%	92.5%	1019	67.0%	84.5%

Table 2: Inter-annotator agreement on the annotation of The Little Prince chapters 3,5-27.

Identifying postposition targets. We obtain automatic tokenization and morphological analysis via the KOMA tagger (Lee and Rim, 2009), which uses the morphological tagset from the Sejong Treebank (Hong, 2009). Postpositions are not treated as separate tokens. For each token the tagger analyzes internal morphological structure (e.g., the word token 영국의 is analyzed as 영국/NNP+의/JKG "England+GEN"). Target postpositions are identified by a subword morphological tag starting with J. In the case of stacking, a nominal can have more than one such postposition (e.g., 너/NP + 에게/JKB + 는/JX), in which case they are considered separate annotation targets.

Guidelines. In order to establish language-specific guidelines for Korean discussed in §3, we first selected the first three largest chapters in within the first chapters of the novella (1, 2, 4). The three chapters were double annotated by two linguists—an expert in Korean linguistics and a native Korean speaker, using the original SNACS guidelines established English. Standards for Korean SNACS (§3) were reached via analysis of disagreements during weekly discussions.

Annotation. Once the general guidelines were established, the remaining chapters (3, 5–27) were annotated by two linguists—the native Korean speaker who codeveloped the guidelines and a newly trained native speaker. The annotation was divided into two phases. In the first phase, the two annotators met on a weekly basis to discuss disagreements and tricky annotation cases. In the second phase, the annotators were given further independence to annotate without weekly discussions, and disagreements were tackled in two sessions: once at half-way point and once again at the end. All instances were double annotated this way and gold labels were adjudicated by consensus. Guidelines were also updated based on issues raised during the discussions.

4.2 Interannotator Agreement

Table 2 shows inter-annotator agreement rates for Chapters 3 and 5–27. On average, we observe rates of 82.7% on the scene role and 90.2% on the function label (first set of columns in table 2). Digging a little deeper, we uncover that the annotation of NOM, ACC, TOP and FOC markers (second set of columns in table 2; these vastly outnumber the other types) is much easier than the rest of the postpositional types (third set of columns in table 2). We expect that higher agreement is due the fact that there are only a limited number of supersenses available for these four postpositional types, especially for TOP, which categorically maps to the supersense TOPICAL. This also tells us that pragmatic uses, i.e., FOCUS, are clearly distinguishable for the native speakers.

Overall, agreement on function is higher than the scene agreement. This is expected as the assignment of scene depends more on the context of the postposition when compared with function, rather than the internal semantics of the postposition. It is also worth noting that despite the higher annotation targets and decreased discussion sessions, the agreements are higher in Phase 2, which suggests increased familiarity with the guidelines improves agreement.

4.3 Corpus Analysis

The Korean *Little Prince* corpus contains 4,020 tokens with one or more postpositions for a total of 4,166 postpositional targets. There are 42 unique SNACS labels and 108 unique construals represented in the data. Table 1 shows the full statistics of the annotated corpus.

NOM, ACC, FOC, TOP Postpositions. NOM, ACC, FOC, and TOP type postpositions account for over 70% of all annotation targets (table 1). The information topic postposition (은/-eun) is unambiguously

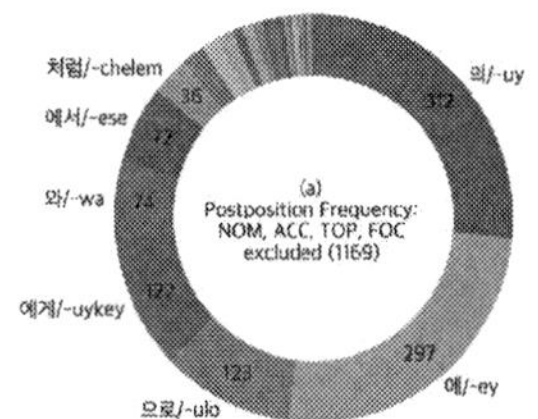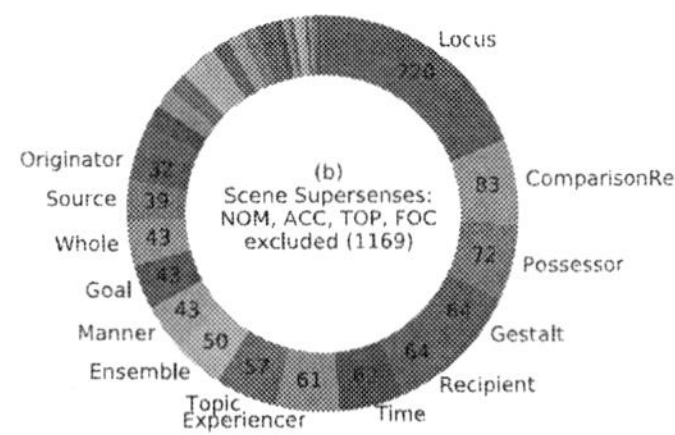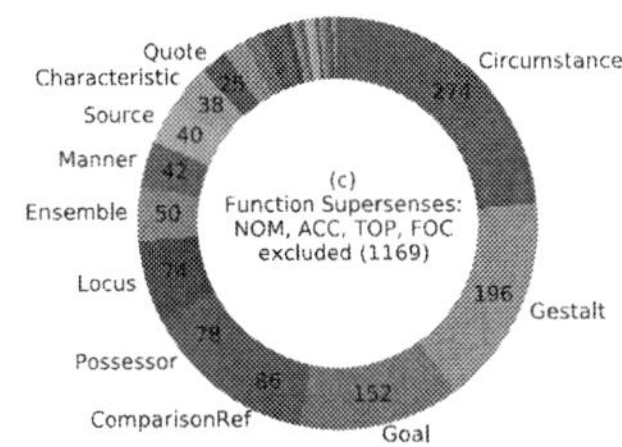

Figure 2: Distribution of postpositions and supersenses with nominative, accusative, information topic and focus postpositions are excluded. Distribution of the Korean postposition types in the corpus is in (a). Distributions of postposition supersenses at the scene role and function levels are shown in (b) and (c), respectively.

TOPICAL for both the scene role and the function, and all focus usages of postpositions (e.g., 도/-to, 만/-man) are labeled FOCUS. The most common supersenses for the NOM postposition (이/-i) are THEME (48.6%), AGENT (22.6%) and ORIGINATOR (19.5%) for the scene role, and THEME (52.0%) and AGENT (44.1%) for function. The majority of ACC supersenses are, unsurprisingly, THEME or its subtype TOPIC at both the scene role (83.1%) and function (82.2%) levels. We leave these four postpositional types out of the discussion for the remainder of §4.3.

Supersenses. Figures 2b and 2c shows the supersense label distributions for scene role and function. Out of the 42 unique SNACS labels, 15 labels are subtypes of CIRCUMSTANCE, 13 are CONFIGURATION subtypes, 11 are from PARTICIPANT, and 2 are from the new top-level category CONTEXT.

Eight supersenses in our inventory never appear in the annotated corpus. Four—INTERVAL, ORGROLE, SPECIES and STUFF—could be expressed postpositionally, though this never happened in the corpus. PURPOSE, APPROXIMATOR and COST are expressed through other grammatical categories such as verbal endings and nominal affixation,[7] which we do not currently annotate. The narrow set of usages listed in the English guidelines as TEMPORAL (as opposed to TIME, FREQUENCY, etc.) do not appear to correspond to any Korean postpositional usages, either.

Postposition Types. The frequency of Korean postpositions in the corpus is shown in figure 2a. What is interesting is that, in line with Croft (2000) and Dryer (1997), general linguistic categories assigned to Korean adpositions only partially describe their actual use. For example, 의/-uy, the most frequent postposition, is considered a genitive case marker in grammar texts (e.g., 빌의 집 "Bill's house"), but it also exhibits a CHARACTERISTIC function that does not align with the genitive use like in 바둑판 무늬의 옷 "checkered-patterned-**uy** clothing" and a QUANTITYVALUE use exemplified by 세개의 화산 "three-**uy** volcanoes." In fact, it retains 18 distinct scene roles, which outnumbers the 16 unique scene roles for the bleached postposition 에/-ey (see §3), which we expected to be highly polysemous.[8]

The postpostion 으로/-ulo is another such case. It is primarily thought to mark DIRECTION (동쪽으로 가다 "go **towards** east"), INSTRUMENT (망치로 치다 "hit **with** a hammer"), and IDENTITY (바보로 여기다 "consider **as** dumb") (Kang, 2012; Choi-Jonin, 2008; Rhee, 2004). However, the data points to a wider variety of functions including MANNER (큰 소리로 떠들다 "make ruckus **in** a loud manner"), GOAL (학교로 가다 "go **to** school"), and MEANS (울음으로 깨웠다 "woke [me] up **by** (the means of) a loud cry"). In fact, 으로/-ulo is highly polysemous at 15 unique scene and 12 unique function labels.

5 Korean vs. English: An Inter-Annotation Discussion

We chose to annotate *The Little Prince* as it has been widely translated, and already annotated (partially) for SNACS in English (Schneider et al., 2018). In this section we compare chapters 1–7 of Korean and English *Little Prince* annotations.

---

[7]For example, the verbal ending 려고/-lyeko marks purpose in a sentential complement like 내가 먹으려고 샀다 "I bought it *for* eating", and the nominal suffix (distinct category from postpositions) 쯤/-ccum marks approximate time in 1시쯤 "*about* 1 o'clock". These are currently under investigation for potential future addition to SNACS annotation.

[8]By way of comparison, Blodgett and Schneider (2018) applied SNACS to English possessives in online reviews. They report 15 supersenses as being attested for possessive pronouns/'**s**.

(a)

Korean targets: 1144 (447)	Uniq Ps: 29 (27)	Uniq scene: 36 (32)	Uniq functions: 27 (24)	Uniq construals: 75 (60)
English targets: 591	Uniq Ps: 60	Uniq scene: 45	Uniq functions: 39	Uniq construals: 97

(b)

Scene Roles				Functions				Construals			
KO		EN		KO		EN		KO		EN	
val	%	val	%	val	%	val	%	val	%	val	%
Theme	24.4	**Locus**	8.3	Theme	25.2	**Gestalt**	13.2	Topical↝Topical	24.2	**Topic↝Topic**	7.7
Topical	24.2	**Topic**	8.3	Topical	24.2	**Goal**	9.0	Theme↝Theme	24.1	**Locus↝Locus****	6.5
Focus	9.4	**CompRef**	5.4	Focus	9.4	Locus	9.0	Focus↝Focus	9.4	**Recipient↝Goal**	4.7
Locus	4.9	**Time**	5.1	Circums.	6.7	**Topic**	8.5	Agent↝Agent	4.4	Time↝Time	4.7
Topic	4.5	Recipient	4.9	Agent	5.9	**Possessor**	6.4	Stimulus↝Topic	3.1	Possessor↝Possessor	4.3
Agent	4.4	Manner	4.7	Topic	5.7	Source	6.3	**Locus↝Circums.****	2.8	Gestalt↝Gestalt	4.2
Stimulus	3.2	Whole	4.7	**Gestalt**	5.4	Time	5.1	**Topic↝Topic**	2.5	**CompRef↝CompRef**	4.2
CompRef	2.3	Gestalt	4.6	**Goal**	2.9	**CompRef**	4.9	**CompRef↝CompRef**	2.3	Source↝Source	4.0
Orig.	2.2	Possessor	4.4	**CompRef**	2.3	Identity	4.9	**Manner↝Manner**	1.6	Whole↝Gestalt	3.0
Time	2.0	Source	4.1	**Possessor**	2.2	Direction	3.6	**Recipient↝Goal**	1.6	**Manner↝Manner**	2.8

Table 3: (a) Distribution of adposition targets, supersenses and construal. For Korean numbers in parentheses specify counts when the NOM, ACC, and TOP postpositions are excluded. (b) A comparison between top 10 most frequent Korean and English scene roles, function labels and construals as found in the first 7 chapters of *The Little Prince*. The commonalities are marked in **bold**, Korean-only labels are highlighted in light gray, labels whose counts are highly influenced by NOM and ACC markers are in dark gray, and construals that are approximate cognates are marked with **.

5.1 Adposition, Supersense and Construal Distributions

Table 3 provides statistics and shows a side-by-side comparison between the top 10 most frequent scene roles, function labels, and construals in Korean and in English.

More Tokens, Fewer Types. We observe that given the translation of the same text, Korean postpositional targets outnumber English prepositions by nearly 2:1 in token count but are dwarfed in unique postposition types, about two-thirds that of English. This is mainly due to NOM, ACC and TOP, which attach to either subjects or objects of a verb as AGENT, THEME or TOPICAL. These account for over 60% (697 of 1144) of all targets, and they do not currently have annotation counterparts in the English annotation. Although the English SNACS project began applying supersenses to subjects and objects (Shalev et al., 2019), *The Little Prince* chapters do not yet reflect this update. The high token counts may also be related to the postpositional expression of FOCUS, which is currently unique to Korean.

Consequently, AGENT, THEME, and TOPICAL and FOCUS are the most frequent in the data. We observe two more scene labels used frequently by the NOM and ACC markers: ORIGINATOR (the source of communication; e.g., "he {said | replied}") and STIMULUS in the construal STIMULUS↝TOPIC (the object perception; e.g., "he saw *a picture of a boa*"). Interestingly, EXPERIENCER↝AGENTs, the experiencing counterparts of STIMULUS↝TOPICs (i.e., "*he* saw a picture of a boa") are much further down the frequency list, in large part due to the fact that Korean allows for subjects to be dropped if recoverable from context.

While attested adposition type counts are significantly lower than in English, Korean postpositions are more *polysemous* both in terms of scene roles and functions. In fact, over half of all postpositions are associated with two or more supersenses, while in English only about a third of the targets are associated with multiple supersenses.

Comparable Scene Roles and Diverging Functions & Construals. Overall, the two languages share the most frequent supersenses for scene roles. Beyond the supersenses shown to be in common in table 3, all of the top 10 English scene roles can be located among the list of top 15 Korean scene roles.

Label correspondences are lower at the function level, where 7 out of 10 most frequent English functions number among the top 15 Korean function supersenses. At first glance, it is admittedly odd that postpositions whose function is to deal with basic meanings like LOCUS, TIME, or BENEFICIARY should not number among the most frequent in Korean. However, this gap is explained by 에/-ey, a postposition associated with one function label, CIRCUMSTANCE (ranking 4th for function in Table 3; see §3 for examples). With a single function label, it mediates 13 distinct scene roles in the first 7 chapters and 19 distinct scene roles in the whole of *Little Prince*.[9]

This agrees with what we saw earlier: Korean seemingly economizes on postposition types to express a variety of semantics. While at at the scene level Korean and English cover similar ground, English has a more diverse array of adposition choice. In order to gain a better understanding of the linguistic differences, we turn to an apples-to-apples comparison by aligning Korean and English annotations side-by-side to explore just how each language handles the same overall content.

5.2 Adposition Alignment Study

We pick the two chapters with the most English preposition targets, 2 and 7, to manually align the Korean and English annotations. Among 226 English and 410 Korean adpositions in these chapters, 81 were aligned based on the following criteria: firstly, the nominal to which Korean postposition is attached must refer to the same mention as the object of the English preposition, and secondly, the head [10] of the marked Korean nominal must refer to the same mention as the head of the English preposition. When possible, we align all markers including NOM and ACC markers (15), English possessives that internalize the object (i.e, my = of me) (16), and semantically approximate references like in 17 where "image" and "suggestion" are considered the same concept.

(15)   나를   바라보았다
me-**ACC** stare.
"[He] stared at me."
ALIGNED TO EN: He stared **at** me.

(16)   나는   얼마나   놀라웠겠는가
I-**TOP** just-how surprised-SPEC-Q
"Can you suppose just how surprised I was?"
ALIGNED TO EN: Imagine **my** amazement.

(17)   길 잃은   아이의   모습이   아니었다
way lost-TOP child-**GEN** image-NOM wasn't
"It wasn't an image of a lost child"
ALIGNED TO EN: Nothing about him gave any suggestion **of** a lost child

Among aligned adpositions, the two languages agree on scene role 66.7% of time and the function label agreement is 38.3%. While it is expected that the scene role should be higher in agreement than the function label as scene roles are assigned by the predicate or the verb, the numbers seem surprisingly low, especially for the function label. The intuition is, since two corpora represent parallel stories, we would expect the two languages to agree more at very least for the scene role. And this is not limited idiomatic usages that do not align like "I jumped to my feet" vs. "벌떡 일어섰다" (suddenly stood up) or partially align like in example 1 in table 4.

The best case disagreement scenario would be that of example 2 in table 4, where the same situation, thus same scene label, is mediated by differing postpositions according to the language-specific expectations (different functions); e.g., the STIMULUS of the staring event is realized with different adpositions in the two languages. These types of disagreement would account for low function label agreement, but this does not explain the scene roles.

What seems to be going on is that while Korean and English pairs do express parallel meaning via adpositions, the subject matter is handled in ways that the supersenses can't generalize. In some cases, the same semantics is conveyed from a different angle or point of view. For example, the third translation pair in table 4 is conceptually equal. But while English chooses to describe how long a flower has been producing thorns via DURATION semantics, Korean relays the same information by specifying STARTTIME of the event (which "The flowers have been making thorns **since** a million years ago"). We could possibly allow for SNACS to generalize the two sentences by stepping up the hierarchy to the TEMPORAL node. But there are other instances where generalization via hierarchy does not work so well.

Take for instance example 4, where English chooses MANNER, which is a part of CIRCUMSTANCE hierarchy and Korean chooses THEME from the PARTICIPANT tree. This difference is a direct result from

---

[9]Top 5 most frequent scenes for 에/-ey include LOCUS, TIME, GOAL, TOPIC and EXPLANATION in the full corpus.

[10]By "head" we mean the phrase to which the prepositional phrase (in English) or the marked nominal (in Korean) attaches in a constituency representation. In English, a head is most often a verb or a noun, and in Korean, most often the head is a verb (noun heads are possible but limited).

	English	Korean
1)	(surprised to see) a light <u>break</u> **over**/PATH the face [of the prince]	얼굴이/THEME 환하게 밝아지[다] *face-**NOM** brightly <u>brighten-up</u>*
2)	He <u>stared</u> **at**/STIMULUS↝DIRECTION me thunderstruck	그는 어리둥절해서 나를/STIMULUS↝THEME 바라보았다 *he-NOM puzzled me-**ACC** <u>stared</u>*
3)	The flowers have been <u>growing</u> thorns **for**/DURATION millions of years	수백만 년 전부터/STARTTIME 꽃들은 가시를 만들고 있어 *millions years prior-**since** flowers-TOP thorns-ACC <u>make</u> be*
4)	<u>swell</u> up **with**/MANNER pride	교만으로/THEME↝MANNER 가득 차 있다 *I-**TOP** just-how pride-**with** full <u>filled</u> be*
5)	I was <u>upset</u> **over**/STIMULUS↝TOPIC that bolt	나는 볼트 때문에/EXPLAN.↝CIRCUMS. 신경이 곤두[섰다] *I-**TOP** bolt reason-**ey** nerves <u>tensed-up</u>*

Table 4: Examples of most common cross-linguistic differences among aligned adpositions. The aligned adpositions are in **bold** and the heads are <u>underlined</u>.

verb choice ("swell up" vs. "be filled"), which alters the scene role (i.e., how is it swelled up? vs. what is it filled with?). In example 5, the semantics of the head predicate are parallel, but the difference comes from a collocational difference based on which adposition the verb prefers. In the example, English chooses to talk about the topic of the pilot's emotion STIMULUS↝TOPIC versus Korean's choice of an EXPLANATION modifier to describe the reason behind the pilot's mood (caused by the emotion).

These divergences are natural variations based on linguistic choice and are complicated by the fact that both English and Korean texts are translations of the original French novella. Bridging such translation divergences (Dorr, 1994; Deng and Xue, 2017) would require a richer modeling of causality and representations that will allow for deeper inferences about the divergent categories (Vyas et al., 2018; Hershcovich et al., 2019; Nikolaev et al., 2020; Briakou and Carpuat, 2020). We do not have a ready proposal to offer for bridging such differences through the SNACS framework. However, investigating further into nuanced semantics like casuality or force dynamics (Croft, 2015, 2012) that would aid generalizations certainly remains a compelling area of future research.

6 Conclusion & Future Work

In this work, we have presented the first annotated corpus of Korean preposition supersenses and included a detailed comparison of a subset of the data with a parallel English corpus. We find that, overall, Korean and English adpositions cover similar semantic ground, making English SNACS adaptable to typologically distant language like Korean. Still, applying the scheme to Korean required us to establish new supersenses for pragmatic usages not found in English adpositions, and to develop policies for case marking, among other innovations.

A number of directions remain for future work. One is an inquiry into supersenses that do not appear or appear infrequently in the annotated corpora (§4.3). We believe there may be certain language-specific phenomena at play (e.g., multi-word postpositions) meriting further investigation. The English-Korean parallel study also indicates a further need for investigating nuanced semantics like causality and force dynamics within the SNACS framework. Finally, as we have noted earlier, the SNACS framework has been recently applied to Mandarin Chinese (Peng et al., 2020). Preliminary adaptation efforts are also underway for Hindi (Arora and Schneider, 2020) and German (Jakob Prange and Nathan Schneider, personal communication). All three initiatives target *The Little Prince*. These efforts thus herald an auspicious opportunity for cross-linguistic comparison of adposition and case systems.

Acknowledgments

We thank Vivek Srikumar and Austin Blodgett for helpful discussions as we were formulating the details of Korean SNACS guidelines. We would also like to thank the anonymous reviewers for their insightful comments. This research was supported in part by NSF award IIS-1812778 and grant 2016375 from the United States–Israel Binational Science Foundation (BSF), Jerusalem, Israel.

References

Aryaman Arora and Nathan Schneider. 2020. SNACS annotation of case markers and adpositions in Hindi. Presented at SIGTYP 2020: The Second Workshop on Computational Research in Linguistic Typology.

Laura Banarescu, Claire Bonial, Shu Cai, Madalina Georgescu, Kira Griffitt, Ulf Hermjakob, Kevin Knight, Philipp Koehn, Martha Palmer, and Nathan Schneider. 2013. Abstract Meaning Representation for sembanking. In *Proc. of the 7th Linguistic Annotation Workshop and Interoperability with Discourse*, pages 178–186, Sofia, Bulgaria.

Austin Blodgett and Nathan Schneider. 2018. Semantic supersenses for English possessives. In *Proc. of LREC*, pages 1529–1534, Miyazaki, Japan.

Eleftheria Briakou and Marine Carpuat. 2020. Detecting fine-grained cross-lingual semantic divergences without supervision by learning to rank. *arXiv:2010.03662 [cs]*.

Hyonsu Choe, Jiyoon Han, Hyejin Park, and Hansaem Kim. 2019. Copula and case-stacking annotations for Korean AMR. In *Proc. of the First International Workshop on Designing Meaning Representations*, pages 128–135, Florence, Italy.

Hong-yeol Choi and Youn Choi. 2018. 조사 '에', '에서' 의 공간의미 연구 - 인지의미론적 접근을 통한 조사의 의미자질 설정 가능성 고찰. *Yongbong Journal of Humanities*, 53:253–275.

Jinho D. Choi and Martha Palmer. 2011. Statistical dependency parsing in Korean: from corpus generation to automatic parsing. In *Proc. of the Second Workshop on Statistical Parsing of Morphologically Rich Languages*, pages 1–11, Dublin, Ireland.

Injoo Choi-Jonin. 2008. Particles and postpositions in Korean. *Typological Studies in Language*, 74:133.

Jayeol Chun, Na-Rae Han, Jena D. Hwang, and Jinho D. Choi. 2018. Building Universal Dependency treebanks in Korean. In *Proc. of LREC*, pages 2194–2202, Miyazaki, Japan.

William Croft. 2000. Parts of speech as language universals and as language-particular categories. In Petra M. Vogel and Bernard Comrie, editors, *Approaches to the Typology of Word Classes*, number 23 in Empirical Approaches to Language Typology, pages 65–102. De Gruyter Mouton, Berlin.

William Croft. 2012. *Verbs: Aspect and Causal Structure*. Oxford University Press, Oxford, UK.

William Croft. 2015. Force dynamics and directed change in event lexicalization and argument realization. In Roberto G. de Almeida and Christina Manouilidou, editors, *Cognitive Science Perspectives on Verb Representation and Processing*, pages 103–129. Springer International Publishing, Cham, Switzerland.

Dun Deng and Nianwen Xue. 2017. Translation divergences in Chinese–English machine translation: an empirical investigation. *Computational Linguistics*, 43(3):521–565.

Bonnie J. Dorr. 1994. Machine translation divergences: a formal description and proposed solution. *Computational Linguistics*, 20(4).

David Dowty. 1991. Thematic proto-roles and argument selection. *Language*, 67(3):547–619.

Matthew S. Dryer. 1997. Are grammatical relations universal? In Joan L. Bybee, John Haiman, and Sandra A. Thompson, editors, *Essays on Language Function and Language Type: Dedicated to T. Givón*, pages 115–143. John Benjamins, Amsterdam.

Charles J. Fillmore. 1968. The case for case. In Emmon Bach and Robert Thomas Harms, editors, *Universals in Linguistic Theory*, pages 1–88. Holt, Rinehart, and Winston, New York.

Scott Grimm. 2011. Semantics of case. *Morphology*, 21(3-4):515–544.

Chung-hye Han, Na-Rae Han, Eon-Suk Ko, Martha Palmer, and Heejong Yi. 2001. Penn Korean Treebank: Development and evaluation. In *Proc. of the 16th Pacific Asia Conference on Language, Information and Computation*, pages 69–78.

Na-Rae Han. 2005. Klex: A finite-state transducer lexicon of Korean. In *International Workshop on Finite-State Methods and Natural Language Processing*, pages 67–77. Springer.

Daniel Hershcovich, Omri Abend, and Ari Rappoport. 2019. Content differences in syntactic and semantic representation. In *Proc. of NAACL-HLT*, pages 478–488, Minneapolis, Minnesota.

Yun-Pyo Hong. 2009. 21 세기 세종 계획 사업 성과 및 과제 [21st Century Sejong Project results and tasks]. *새국어생활 [New Korean Life]*, 19(1):0–0.

Hwa-Sang Hwang. 2012. *국어 조사 의 문법 [Grammar of Korean Postpositions]*. Knowledge and Culture [지식 과 교양].

Jena D. Hwang, Archna Bhatia, Na-Rae Han, Tim O'Gorman, Vivek Srikumar, and Nathan Schneider. 2017. Double trouble: the problem of construal in semantic annotation of adpositions. In *Proc. of *SEM*, pages 178–188, Vancouver, Canada.

Yunkyoung Kang. 2012. *Cognitive linguistics approach to semantics of spatial relations in Korean*. Ph.D. thesis, Georgetown University, Washington, DC.

Hansaem Kim. 2006. Korean National Corpus in the 21st Century Sejong Project. In *Proc. of the 13th NIJL International Symposium*, pages 49–54. National Institute for Japanese Language Tokyo.

Do-Gil Lee and Hae-Chang Rim. 2009. Probabilistic modeling of Korean morphology. *IEEE transactions on audio, speech, and language processing*, 17(5):945–955.

Jeong-Hwa Lee and Kaori Kabata. 2006. A comparative cognitive-semantic analysis of spatial postpositions in Korean and Japanese. *담화와인지 [Discourse and Cognition]*, 13(2):187–203.

Ken Litkowski. 2014. Pattern Dictionary of English Prepositions. In *Proc. of ACL*, pages 1274–1283, Baltimore, Maryland, USA.

Ken Litkowski and Orin Hargraves. 2005. The Preposition Project. In *Proc. of the Second ACL-SIGSEM Workshop on the Linguistic Dimensions of Prepositions and their Use in Computational Linguistics Formalisms and Applications*, pages 171–179, Colchester, Essex, UK.

Dmitry Nikolaev, Ofir Arviv, Taelin Karidi, Neta Kenneth, Veronika Mitnik, Lilja Maria Saeboe, and Omri Abend. 2020. Fine-grained analysis of cross-linguistic syntactic divergences. In *Proc. of ACL*, pages 1159–1176, Online.

Tae Hwan Oh, Ji Yoon Han, Hyonsu Choe, Seokwon Park, Han He, Jinho D. Choi, Na-Rae Han, Jena D. Hwang, and Hansaem Kim. 2020. Analysis of the Penn Korean Universal Dependency Treebank (PKT-UD): Manual revision to build robust parsing model in Korean. In *Proc. of IWPT*, pages 122–131, Online.

Martha Palmer, Shijong Ryu, Jinyoung Choi, Sinwon Yoon, and Yeongmi Jeon. 2006. Korean Propbank. Technical Report LDC2006T03, Linguistic Data Consortium, Philadelphia, PA.

Jungyeul Park and Francis Tyers. 2019. A new annotation scheme for the Sejong part-of-speech tagged corpus. In *Proc. of the 13th Linguistic Annotation Workshop*, pages 195–202, Florence, Italy.

Siyao Peng, Yang Liu, Yilun Zhu, Austin Blodgett, Yushi Zhao, and Nathan Schneider. 2020. A corpus of adpositional supersenses for Mandarin Chinese. In *Proc. of LREC*, pages 5988–5996, Marseille, France.

Seongha Rhee. 2004. Grammaticalization of spatio-temporal postpositions in Korean. *The Journal of Linguistic Science*, 31:169–188.

Nathan Schneider, Jena D. Hwang, Archna Bhatia, Vivek Srikumar, Na-Rae Han, Tim O'Gorman, Sarah R. Moeller, Omri Abend, Adi Shalev, Austin Blodgett, and Jakob Prange. 2020. Adposition and Case Supersenses v2.5: Guidelines for English. *arXiv:1704.02134v6 [cs]*.

Nathan Schneider, Jena D. Hwang, Vivek Srikumar, Jakob Prange, Austin Blodgett, Sarah R. Moeller, Aviram Stern, Adi Bitan, and Omri Abend. 2018. Comprehensive supersense disambiguation of English prepositions and possessives. In *Proc. of ACL*, pages 185–196, Melbourne, Australia.

Carson T. Schütze. 2001. On Korean case stacking: The varied functions of the particles *ka* and *lul*. *The Linguistic Review*, 18(3):193–232.

Adi Shalev, Jena D. Hwang, Nathan Schneider, Vivek Srikumar, Omri Abend, and Ari Rappoport. 2019. Preparing SNACS for subjects and objects. In *Proc. of the First International Workshop on Designing Meaning Representations*, pages 141–147, Florence, Italy.

Ho-Min Sohn. 2001. *The Korean Language*. Cambridge University Press.

Yogarshi Vyas, Xing Niu, and Marine Carpuat. 2018. Identifying semantic divergences in parallel text without annotations. In *Proc. of NAACL-HLT*, pages 1503–1515, New Orleans, Louisiana.

Additional Details

SNACS hierarchy. Figure 3 shows the hierarchy of 54 supersenses used for Korean SNACS annotation of *The Little Prince*. The pragmatic CONTEXT tree and its supertypes are new, as is the QUOTE under the PARTICIPANT tree. The scene role and function counts for each label in the corpus are shown in gray.

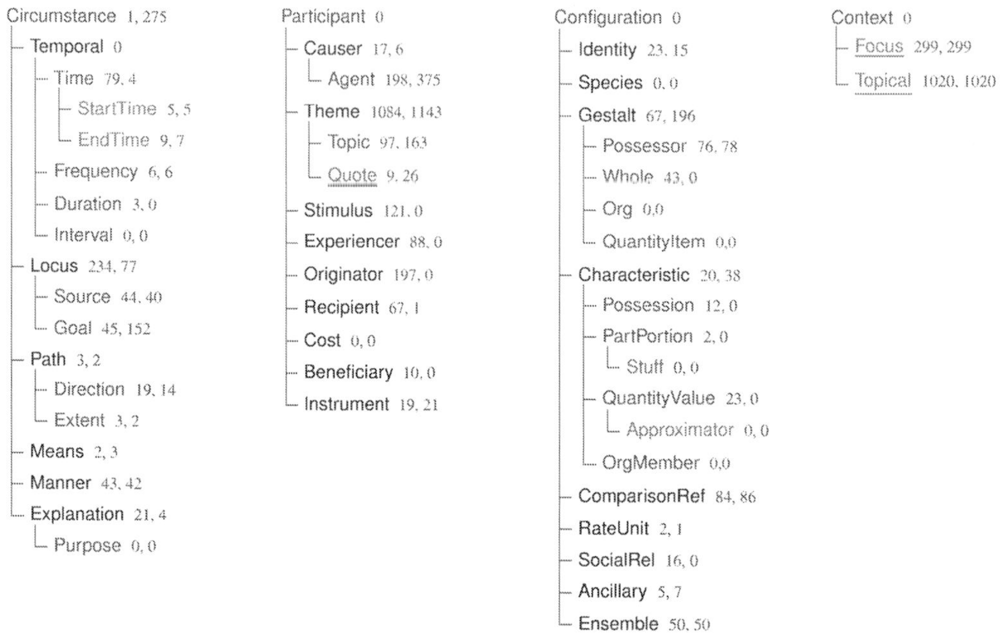

Figure 3: SNACS hierarchy of supersenses.

InfoForager: Leveraging Semantic Search with AMR
for COVID-19 Research

Claire Bonial, Stephanie M. Lukin, David C. Doughty, Steven C. Hill, Clare R. Voss
U.S. Army Research Lab
`claire.n.bonial.civ@mail.mil`

Abstract

This paper examines how Abstract Meaning Representation (AMR) can be utilized for finding answers to research questions in medical scientific documents, in particular, to advance the study of UV (ultraviolet) inactivation of the novel coronavirus that causes the disease COVID-19. We describe the development of a proof-of-concept prototype tool, InfoForager, which uses AMR to conduct a semantic search, targeting the *meaning* of the user question, and matching this to sentences in medical documents that may contain information to answer that question. This work was conducted as a sprint over a period of six weeks, and reveals both promising results and challenges in reducing the user search time relating to COVID-19 research, and in general, domain adaption of AMR for this task.

1 Introduction

UV light can inactivate viruses by making them unable to infect cells, thereby reducing the transmission of viral diseases. While a wealth of literature pertaining to UV inactivation of viruses exists, searching this literature for trustworthy and relevant information can be difficult and inefficient. This difficulty can be especially evident when focusing on diseases such as COVID-19 (caused by the novel coronavirus, SARS-CoV-2[1]), which can be transmitted via aerosols or droplets in a complex process spanning disciplines ranging from physiology to optics to fluid mechanics. There are many unknowns, poorly quantified parameters, and even confusions resulting from differing terminology used. Nonetheless, efficiently finding needed information may be critical in discovering improved methods, such as the use of germicidal UV,[2] to reduce the transmission of COVID-19 and other diseases.

This paper identifies an opportunity for NLP tools to aid in automatically sifting through this mass of documents to find relevant answers to specific and targeted questions from subject matter experts working in the space of UV inactivation of viruses. We introduce InfoForager, a proof-of-concept prototype tool that utilizes semantic understanding and search, going beyond the words in a user question to focus on its *meaning*. By employing a semantic search, we hypothesize that the user will more easily search through medical documents because they do not need to rephrase their questions (for example, into keywords) to conform to the system's search limitations and capabilities. InfoForager first parses a user research question into Abstract Meaning Representation (AMR) (Banarescu et al., 2013), then compares the resulting AMR query to a collection of medical research papers already parsed into AMR. All AMR query sentence pairs in each paper are scored for their semantic similarity, and InfoForager returns the highest-ranking answer sentence and the source document.

Given the urgent nature of this research, we allotted six weeks during which four NLP researchers worked with two UV inactivation researchers to perform a shallow pass through the semantic searching problem space. Additionally, we worked with test users to obtain an understanding of the system requirements

---

[1]SARS-CoV-2: Severe acute respiratory syndrome coronavirus 2, first identified in 2019.

[2]Germicidal UV: Also known as UVC, relating to the UV spectrum between 200 - 280 nm.

Proceedings of the 2nd International Workshop on Designing Meaning Representations, pages 67–77
Barcelona, Spain (Online), December 13, 2020

and developed a prototype framework to address those needs. Section 2 describes the UV inactivation problem space. Our semantic search approach is described in Section 3, and Section 4 details a Wizard-of-Oz prototyping user study of the framework and the initial development of the prototype system. An evaluation of the prototype and the results are discussed in Section 5.

2 Background: UV Inactivation Research

Virus particles (virions) can remain infectious on surfaces (e.g., walls, doorknobs, and masks), and may be contained within sneezed or coughed droplets of airway (e.g., mouth, nose, throat) fluids. Such virions can be inactivated by treating them and particles containing them with sufficient UV light (Sagripanti and Lytle, 2011); however, it remains unclear whether, and to what extent, the virions within dried droplets, or particles, are shielded from UV. Researchers need to know how the optical properties of a particle of such respiratory fluids affect the intensity of UV in a virion within that particle. If the particle of dried respiratory fluids actually protects virions within it from UV, then how much more intense does the UV source need to be to achieve adequate inactivation of the virions? Furthermore, what techniques could be used to increase the effectiveness of UV light for inactivation of SARS-CoV-2 in such particles? Given the tremendous variation in sizes, shapes, and compositions of dried respiratory particles, answering these questions by experimentation alone is far too expensive. Having a computational model to accurately represent intensities within UV-illuminated respiratory particles would be beneficial for testing multiple use-cases, and may be critical in discovering improved methods for using germicidal UV to reduce the transmission of COVID-19 and other diseases. Such modeling requires knowledge of the optical properties of airway fluids, which can be estimated from the concentrations and optical properties of the materials in these fluids. However, to date and to our knowledge, there are no medical papers or reports that include all the optically relevant materials in any airway fluids to create such a model.

We designed InfoForager with the aforementioned challenges in mind. The UV researchers and NLP researchers iteratively refined the general topic of UV inactivation of coronavirus into two main research questions of interest, which were used in developing and testing InfoForager:

Q_1 *Which (bodily) fluids have higher concentrations of SARS-CoV-2 particles?*

Q_2 *What is the range of sizes of respiratory droplets, specifically from coughing and sneezing?*

For the purposes of training participants in our Wizard-of-Oz user study, we introduced a basic question:

Q_t *What types of UV light are used in coronavirus research?*

The UV researchers made clear that they were not seeking a system that returned a single answer to their research questions, as there are often multiple, even conflicting answers in cutting-edge medical research. Instead, they desired a system that returns all relevant results and that also clearly points to where the relevant content is in the document, allowing them to quickly assess where the information they are searching for is discussed in the approach, background, or results section of a paper.

This approach stands in contrast to search systems that the UV researchers have become accustomed to and use primarily for building their initial pool of medical documents, or abstracts when the documents are behind paywalls. For example, PubMed is as an extensive, publicly available, online, searchable database of medical and life sciences research abstracts.[3] In this study, we rely on it as a benchmark resource, given its broad and updating coverage of research papers, and make use of its keyword search, wherein terms from the user query are matched against subject designations for articles, the title, abstract, and author names. If no matches are made, the search terms are broken apart and the search process is repeated with the individual terms. This, indirectly, has led researchers away from posing natural language questions. When backing off to break such questions into keywords, PubMed may return either too many results for very general keywords or no results for more targeted combinations. For example, Q_1 yields zero results, and subsequent alterations of the question, e.g., *Which fluids higher SARS-CoV-2 particles* and *Which fluids higher concentration particles*, yield 1 and 1,157 individual research papers respectively. This approach places the burden on the user to determine which terms in the query are the most important for the system to function.

---

[3] `https://pubmed.ncbi.nlm.nih.gov`

3 InfoForager Approach: Semantic Parse and Search

InfoForager was designed with the UV researchers' goals, criteria, and the current tool limitations in mind. Given that they expect to conduct an iterative search process (to "forage"), where they may find partial information, including different and possibly discrepant values (especially as new findings emerge), we start with the following working hypothesis: an AMR-based approach can assist in identifying such partial information based on where their questions share semantics with sentences within the documents in their collection. Thus, we aim to create a system that accepts natural language questions, interprets their underlying meaning as AMR, detects a range of answers, and finally points to where that information was found in research papers. Our semantic search interaction is presented in Figure 1. First, a user provides a question, which is semantically parsed into AMR (left panel of Figure 1). Second, a semantic search is conducted that matches the parsed query against a collection of medical research papers that had also been semantically parsed (center panel). Finally, the results are scored and ranked, and the top responses along with the source papers are returned (right panel). The remainder of this section describes the parsing, and search and rank processes.

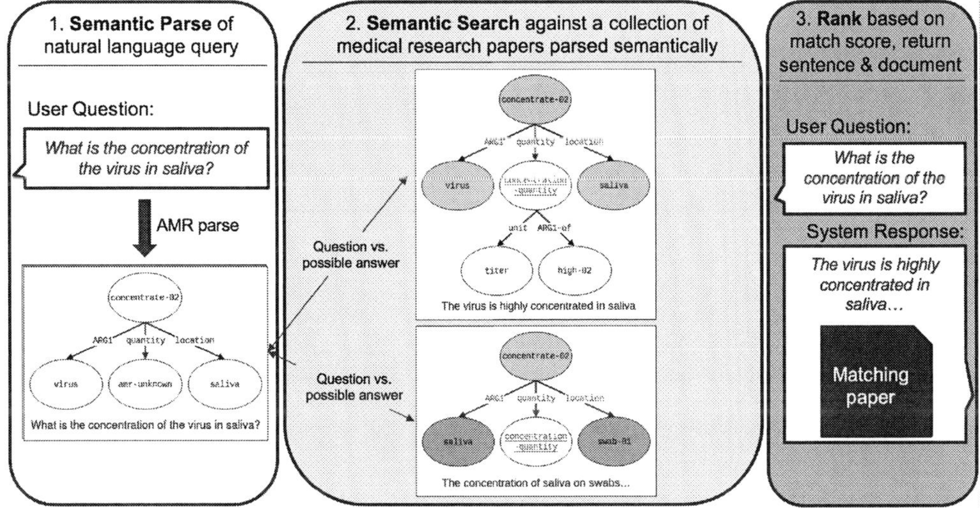

Figure 1: InfoForager overview—(1) User question is automatically parsed into AMR (parsed-query); (2) Parsed-query is compared to a collection of research papers already parsed into AMR (parsed-answers); (3) Matches are ranked and highest ranking sentence is returned with its source document.

3.1 Semantic Parse Using AMR

AMR is a directed, acyclic graph (DAG) representation of the meaning of a sentence, in which nodes map to words in the sentence, and edges map to the relations between them. Figure 2 shows the AMR in the text-based Penman notation (a) and the graph notation (b). There is a relatively large and active body of research surrounding AMR, such that there are a variety of parsers for automatically converting natural language text into AMR, including our own work to retrain and adapt various AMR parsers for dialogue systems (Bonial et al., 2019, Bonial et al., 2020). AMR has demonstrated value in biomedical NLP applications in the past (see Section 6), so we elected to explore the use of AMR in the development of a research framework that has the potential to match not only the concepts within a research AMR query, but also the relations between those concepts for more efficient "semantic search."

To obtain AMR parses of our user questions and the medical research document collection, we leverage the parser from Lindemann et al. (2019) based on its high performance after retraining within a new domain in previous research. The parser was retrained on the Linguistic Data Consortium's AMR 3.0 corpora (LDC2020T02) and the freely available Bio-AMR corpus,[4] as well as our own manually annotated dataset of approximately 1,000 AMRs drawn from the Dial-AMR corpus (Bonial et al., 2020).

---

[4]https://amr.isi.edu/download/2018-01-25/amr-release-bio-v3.0.txt

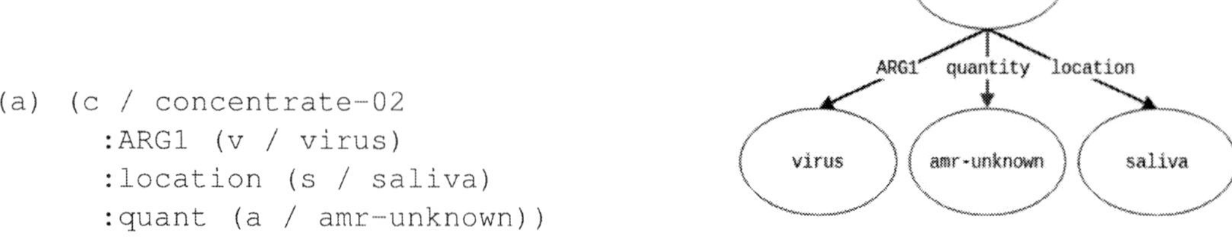


```
(a)  (c / concentrate-02
        :ARG1 (v / virus)
        :location (s / saliva)
        :quant (a / amr-unknown))
```

(a) AMR in Penman notation   (b) AMR in directed, a-cyclic graph notation

Figure 2: The utterance *What is the concentration of the virus in saliva?* represented in (a) Penman notation and (b) its equivalent, in directed, a-cyclic graph notation.

Given time constraints of this six-week research effort, we opted to rely on our prior evaluations of several AMR parsers in selecting this parser and worked with a limited set of manual ground-truth AMRs for the project assessments.

Once the document collection was tokenized and segmented, we used the retrained parser to obtain a set of AMR graphs for each sentence of the collection. In addition, we parsed Q_t, Q_1, and Q_2, defined in Section 2, into AMR to have automatically-obtained AMRs of the questions. An experienced AMR annotator also provided gold standard, ground-truth AMRs for the questions and portions of the document collection with information relevant to answering the questions. This resulted in a collection of gold-standard AMR parses for the user questions and answers, as well as automatically-obtained AMR parses for the same user questions and answers, henceforth referred to as "gold-queries" and "gold-answers," and "parsed-queries" and "parsed-answers," respectively.

3.2   Semantic Search and Rank Using Graph Matching

To leverage the structured semantic information of AMR for determining if a document contains an answer to a question, we explored how adequately graph matching could serve to find a sentence that best addresses a particular question. We used the Smatch (semantic match) metric (Cai and Knight, 2013), which converts two input AMRs into two sets of node/edge triples, and measures the overlap between two resulting sets of triples. In our study applying Smatch, the AMR parsed-query was compared to all AMR parsed-answers in the document collection, then a list of the sentences ranked by Smatch scores was returned with IDs of documents containing those sentences for the top matches.[5]

To our knowledge, this is the first application of Smatch for semantic overlap of AMRs for a question and a sentence, as it was originally designed to find the closest match between AMRs for two sentences, one a ground-truth and the other a system output. We hypothesized that a strength of our novel application of Smatch would be in its ability to locate relevant information in other sentences that contain not only the same words and concepts as the original question, but also the same semantic relations between those concepts. However, a conceptual shortcoming is that Smatch is not necessarily finding *answers*, but finding the sentences with content most similar to that in the question, as it was designed to do. For example, were the question itself written out in a research paper, then it, and not an answer, would be returned as the best match.[6] Thus, we sought to identify the range or threshold of Smatch scores that would indicate when the AMRs of a question and document sentence were similar enough to capture shared semantics of a question-answer (Q-A) pair. For example, if we compare the parsed-query in Figure 1 for *What is the concentration of the virus in saliva?* to a parsed-answer (*The virus is highly concentrated in saliva*), this Q-A pair receives an Smatch F-score of 78%. Inspection of the Q-A graphs underscores this level of matching: the Q-A graphs are identical, with the exception of the amr-unknown node sitting in the position of the question word in the parsed-query; in the answer

---

[5]Smatch leverages smart initialization and 4 random restarts, where the highest overall score is reported as the final Smatch score. As a result, we observed some variation in Smatch scores when the same graphs are compared in multiple runs.

[6]Given that the UV researchers also track who is working on problems like theirs, even a question match is valuable: the document matched provides provenance to track the authors and institutions where relevant research is being conducted.

graph, it appears as a `concentration-quantity` node with additional modifiers. Thus, we argue that the graph-matching process is a suitable starting point for exploring the effectiveness of AMR in our semantic search framework, and describe in Section 7 other possible approaches.[7]

4   User Studies and Proof-of-Concept Development

Having developed the initial framework for semantic search to address the needs of UV researchers, we conducted a Wizard-of-Oz user study (Section 4.1) to explore how non-expert users interacted as research assistants with the system, while we developed the proof-of-concept prototype (Section 4.2).

4.1   Wizard-of-Oz User Studies

We conducted user studies of InfoForager's semantic search and PubMed, as noted in Section 2, for its keyword-based search. To put both systems on equal footing while InfoForager was under development and lacked a user interface, we deployed a simple chat interface and "Wizard-of-Oz" setup as the same front-end to both. Participants placed their search input in a text box, and a "Search Engine" (a human experimenter) retrieved a summary webpage listing the top five matching research papers from one of the search systems. The participant could then ask to view the individual results for further information in a listed research paper. Participants could remove or re-order words in the research question, but could not add or change words. In this way, for PubMed, we controlled for possible permutations of the research questions, enabling us to run the queries in advance, and return to participants actual PubMed results (as if run in real time). Results were displayed in a ranked list with the article title and authors displayed, along with a snippet of the abstract. This included returning no results when PubMed did not find a match. Similarly, for InfoForager, the "Search Engine" returned a summary webpage listing a ranked set of results with the title of the document, but also the relevant/matching text and what section of the document that text comes from (e.g., abstract, approach, results, etc.). When a user asks to see the source document for a particular summary result, the user is then shown only the abstract for the PubMed system (in keeping with actual follow-on phase in PubMed[8]), whereas for the prototype InfoForager, the user is shown the entire section that the result came from and the matching phrase is outlined in red.

Four subjects without a background in medicine or biology were recruited for the user study. They were told they would be assisting subject matter experts in answering research questions related to the coronavirus. Each participant underwent a training phase to become familiar with both search systems as well as the subject area using Q_t. During training, participants were given ten minutes to attempt to answer the question by searching a collection of medical literature using InfoForager, and then given another ten minutes to search for the answer to the same question using PubMed. Following that phase, there were two main trials, up to twenty minutes each, for answering Q_1 and Q_2. For the main trials, we alternated the order of which search engine was used first; two subjects started with InfoForager, while the others started with PubMed, and then their systems were swapped on the next question.

From the user studies, we observed that participants were able to find answers to their questions more quickly with the InfoForager framework—they felt more confident that they had looked through the collection as extensively as they needed to and therefore tended to declare their task complete at an earlier point. With InfoForager, participants could enter a natural language question, and the matches detected were similar not only in the words used, but also the semantic relationship between those words. In contrast, after discovering that they might receive no results for natural language questions with the PubMed system, participants would quickly turn to a keyword strategy, though this led, at times, to too many results that were not relevant. As a keyword search system, PubMed did not offer explicit indicators for where or why a match occurred. Overall, participants spent more time, in comparison to InfoForager, in reading through the entire returned abstract to determine if it was relevant, or trying different permutations of keywords to see if they could find the right combination to get their answer. Thus, the user studies established motivating evidence for a prototype tool with semantic search, described next.

---

[7]Several new AMR measures now also exist (Anchieta et al., 2019; Song and Gildea, 2019; Opitz et al., 2020).

[8]For some documents, users may be able click an additional link to access the full text.

4.2 Proof-of-Concept Prototype

After running user studies, we put the anticipated components together into an end-to-end, proof-of-concept system that we could begin to formally evaluate. Prior to any real-time user interaction, the medical document collection of papers are preprocessed, including conversion from PDF to text using the Poppler PDF[9] rendering library, and word tokenization and sentence segmentation using a toolkit developed internally within our team. The documents in our collection had very different formats (e.g., multiple columns or one) which could result in the conversion to text being out of order. Furthermore, the documents had a variety of abbreviations, parenthetical references to figures, and widespread use of footnotes and end notes, all of which could cause errors in the tokenization and sentence segmentation. Thus, it was necessary for us to make adjustments to these components for this medical domain. Then, the document collection was parsed into AMR parsed-answers and the triple formalism required by Smatch. This process is depicted in steps 1 - 6 in Figure 3. During real-time interaction, the user question is parsed into an AMR parsed-query, subsequently converted into a triple representation, and then compared against the triples of the preprocessed collection (steps 7 - 8 in Figure 3).

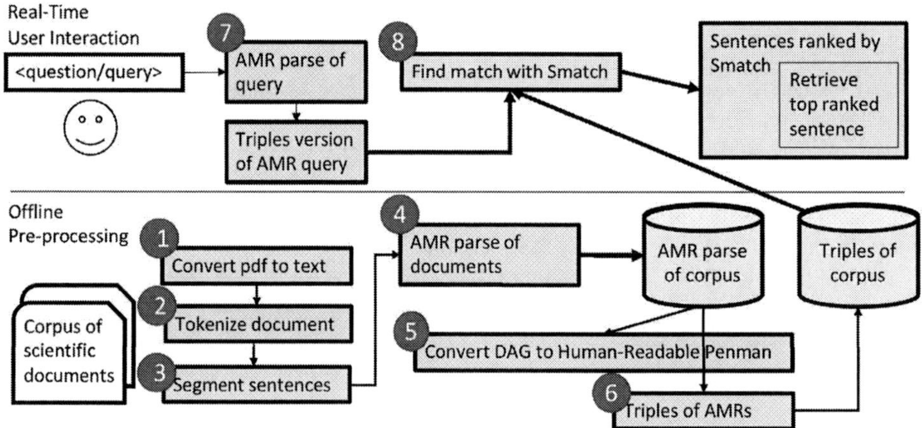

Figure 3: InfoForager Prototype Pipeline

5 Results and Discussion

To make an initial assessment of the validity of our approach, we evaluated the prototype system on the three research questions, for which we had manually identified documents and sentences that best answer the questions. Using these answers and documents as a ground truth, we compared the ranked list of sentences output by our system, thus determining the extent to which our methodology would highly rank and return the same answers as a human researcher.

To focus on the potential for this semantic search approach without introducing too much noise from automatic parsing of the *question* at this stage, we conducted the evaluation using the manually annotated AMR gold-queries, as opposed to the AMR parsed-queries. Note, however, that the target *answer* documents are all automatically parsed. In the subsequent analysis, we compute both 1) gold-query vs. parsed-answer, and 2) gold-query vs. gold-answer, to determine how effective the Smatch metric is in capturing the shared semantic content between query and answer with and without AMR parsing error.

Q_1 *Which fluids have higher concentrations of SARS-CoV-2 particles?*
As of June 2020, this research question was judged most urgent by the UV researchers and they found very little supporting literature on the subject—only a single document with several informative sentences in the results section, and one sentence summarizing the information sought:
A_1 *Overall, we found higher SARS-CoV-2 titers from saliva than nasopharyngeal swabs from hospital inpatients* (Wyllie et al., 2020).

---

[9]https://poppler.freedesktop.org/

We were encouraged to find that our system ranked this sentence as an answer third by Smatch F-measure (23%) and fifth by recall (17%). Notably, this sentence has similar phrasing to the question, and as a result, their AMR structures are more similar. The parsed-answer does have a variety of errors, most arising from problems with the `have-degree-91` argument assignment (this is the roleset used to express comparatives in AMR, including "higher"). As noted above, to test for the noise introduced by automatic parsing errors, we also scored the gold-query vs. gold-answer, shown in Figure 4. This gold pair actually receives a slightly lower Smatch F-measure, at 20% (compared to 23% on gold-query vs. parsed-answer). These results made clear that valid query-answer AMR pairs may vary widely in Smatch scores, ranging from 20% to just under 80%, as found for the simple pair in Figure 1.

```
Q1. Which fluids had higher concentrations of virus particles ?
    (h2 / have-degree-91
       :ARG1 (a / amr-unknown
             :domain (f / fluid))
       :ARG2 (h / high-02
             :ARG1 f
             :ARG2 (v2 / virus
                   :consist-of (p / particle
                         :mod (v / virus)
                         :ARG1-of (c / concentrate-02)))))
       :ARG3 (m2 / more))

A1. Overall , we found higher SARS-CoV-2 titers from saliva than nasopharyngeal swabs
    from hospital inpatients.
    (f / find-01
       :ARG0 (w / we)
       :ARG1 (h / have-degree-91
             :ARG1 (s3 / saliva
                   :source (i3 / inpatient
                         :location (h6 / hospital)))
             :ARG2 (h5 / high-02
                   :ARG1 s3
                   :ARG2 (v / virus :name (n2 / name :op1 "SARS-CoV-2")
                         :quant (v2 / concentration-quantity
                               :unit (t2 / titer))))
             :ARG3 (m / more)
             :ARG4 (s5 / swab-01
                   :ARG2 (n3 / nasopharynx
                         :part-of i3)))
       :mod (o / overall))
```

Figure 4: Gold-query Q_1 compared with gold-answer A_1

Q_2 *What is the range of sizes of respiratory droplets, specifically from coughing and sneezing?*
This question had two target documents with several answers that provided information on different aspects of this question. As discussed earlier, the expected InfoForager output need not be a single answer, but rather might include various types of relevant information, which the experts would examine further for source and approach used to obtain that data point. Answers to this question depend on, for example, the methods used to detect the sizes and numbers of droplets, and the location of measurement relative to the droplet source. Because definitions of "droplet" or "aerosol" can depend upon the user, it was expected InfoForager may not find all relevant answers. Answers here include:
A_{2a} And the geometric mean of droplet size of all the sneezes is 360.1 μm for unimodal distribution and 74.4 μm for bimodal distribution... (Han et al., 2013).
A_{2b} ...while sneezing produces a greater number of particles than coughing, particles from both activities are of a similar size (a sneeze produces 40,000 - 4,600 particles with 80% of these particles being smaller than 100 μm compared with coughing which produced up to few hundred particles sized between 20 and > 100 μm) (Gralton et al., 2011).
Although both answers mention "size," they are more complex and distinctly phrased than the question. As a result, our system rankings for this question were weak. For the first target document, two answer sentences ranked in 55th and 128th positions (by Smatch F-measure) out of 1,056 possible matches. For the second target document, one answer sentence ranked 156th of 850 possible matches, while the other received a 0 Smatch score, placing it in the lowest rank where all sentences received a 0 Smatch score.

Given that these low Smatch scores could reflect poor automatic parsing preventing a match, or that the Smatch algorithm does not capture the overlap seen in a Q-A pair, we again examine the gold pair (gold-query vs. gold-answer) for the two answers above (to compare against the gold-query vs parsed-answer). When scored against the gold-query, the gold-answer A_{2a} receives an Smatch f-score of 16%, whereas the parsed-answer A_1 scored significantly higher at 25.8%. For the far longer sentence A_{2b}, its gold-answer receives an Smatch score of 10%, due in large part to its length and complex structure relative to the question. Curiously, the parsed-answer A_{2b} fared far worse, receiving a score of 0. Thus, these A_{2a} and A_{2b} scores for the gold pairs are, in a rough sense, about as challenging to interpret as the A_{2a} and A_{2b} scores comparing the gold-query to their parsed-answers. Significantly more data will be needed to ascertain all the factors in the scoring, but we can see that noise alone from the automatic parse is not the primary cause of low Smatch scores.

Q_t *What types of UV light are used in coronavirus research?*
For this user-study training question, one target answer document and the following answer sentence were identified:
A_t *In conclusion, air disinfection using 254 nm UV-C may be an effective tool for inactivating viral aerosols* (Walker and Ko, 2007).
As with Q_2 above, the phrasing of Q_t leaves open a variety of different answer types, with very different phrasing from the question itself. Nonetheless, our system performed better with this Q-A pair, ranking this parsed answer at the 29th position (Smatch F-measure 24%) out of 406 possible matches, compared to the corresponding gold pair scoring an Smatch of 18%, indicating again, that noise alone from the automatic parse is not bringing down the Smatch score.

To recap, we have seen that this approach using AMR and Smatch can be effective when an answer sentence shares structured semantics with the question. However, when the question is more open-ended, searching for "ranges" and "types," the Smatch approach is much less likely to perform adequately. While these words may on occasion be present in document collections with answers that the UV researchers seek, we realize that InfoForager itself must be augmented to recognize such higher-order questions and, more like a dialogue system with an intelligent agent, potentially engage the user in reformulating their question.

6 Related Work

Previous research has leveraged AMR within the biomedical domain for applications that, like ours, entail natural language understanding, such as information extraction. Garg et al. (2016) use AMR in a graph kernel learning framework to extract biomolecular interactions and report that the use of AMR significantly improves accuracy on this task over surface and syntax-based features, with the best performance achieved by combining AMR and syntax-based features. Notably, this research also furnished the Bio-AMR dataset of 400 manually annotated and 3k automatically annotated AMRs from PubMed scientific articles, which were incorporated into retraining the AMR parser used in InfoForager. Rao et al. (2017) use AMR to identify molecular events/interactions in biomedical text. The authors first define biomedical events of interest as subgraphs within AMR graphs, and develop a neural network-based model that identifies such an event subgraph given an AMR. While the method shows promising results, the authors find that improvements in AMR parsing are needed for further improvement on the task. Wang et al. (2017) were the first to make use of AMR embeddings, in this case along with word and dependency embeddings, to mine for otherwise hidden reports of drug-drug interactions (DDI) in the textual biomedical literature. The best performance the authors report was obtained by combining these three types of embeddings. They also noted that AMR embeddings alone, leveraging the JAMR parser (Flanigan et al., 2014), did not perform adequately for this DDI task, and, like others, attributed this to poor parser performance due to limited medical terms and documents in its training dataset.

Other research that leverages AMR in tasks similar to ours has focused on question-answering. Mitra and Baral (2016) use AMR as an intermediate representation for question-answering tasks designed to test an agent's understanding. The authors find that the addition of a formal reasoning layer significantly increases the reasoning capability of an agent, and that AMR serves as an effective pivot from natural language to the Answer Set Programming language used for reasoning and inductive logic. AMR is leveraged for a machine reading comprehension (MRC) task for question-answering in Sachan and Xing (2016). Here, the authors first convert a Q-A pair into a single AMR "hypothesis" graph. Additionally, the authors create an AMR for an entire passage, as opposed to the standard single-sentence AMR, by combining at coreference points. With these two AMR graphs, the authors transform the MRC task to a graph containment problem. The authors use a max-margin approach for subgraph matching, reasoning that the hypothesis graph aligns to the passage graph where the question is best answered, not unlike the intuition in InfoForager of applying Smatch to find the best alignment of triples from the query AMR DAG to triples from sentence AMR DAGs in a searched document. The authors obtain competitive results and point out that this approach uniquely allows them to combine evidence from multiple sentences. Although they do not use the AMR formalism per se, Du and Cardie (2020) achieve state-of-the-art performance on the Automatic Content Extraction (ACE) 2005 benchmark event extraction task by making use of template-based questions within a BERT-based question-answering model, suggesting to us that an extension to AMR-based question templates might further improve their approach. The authors experimented with several template strategies for forming the questions targeting the event and its participants. Most relevant to our work, the authors found that the success of their approach was strongly influenced by different questioning strategies, ranging from posing a single keyword as the question to a multi-turn progression of structured questions, and conclude that more natural language questions lead to significantly better performance.

7 Conclusions & Future Work

Our six-week sprint brought together researchers of different backgrounds (UV inactivation and NLP) to identify research requirements, and design and test a prototype framework with software available from other projects. We also identified facts about COVID-19 now more widely known: testing saliva is more effective than nasopharyngeal swabs, given the concentration of the virus is higher in saliva.

We maintain our working hypothesis that the InfoForager framework is promising for facilitating a search system that allows for natural language questions, and in finding answers matching not only on keywords, but the semantic relations between those keywords. However, this process demonstrated that using Smatch for graph matching does not allow us to take full advantage of the semantic structure that AMR offers in this task—namely pinpointing the concept sought in an answer and its direct semantic relations to other concepts. One path we are exploring in the short-term is to have users input their hypotheses in lieu of queries. For example, for Q_1, a user might input a hypothesis like *Saliva has a higher concentration of coronavirus than nasopharyngeal fluid.* Prompting an expert user for a hypothesis could enable us to leverage Smatch more fruitfully to find other graphs more similar overall to the candidate answer, following insights from Sachan and Xing (2016). Although this approach may prove useful, it runs counter to our users' stated preference for posing natural language questions, and would bias the presentation of system results towards the hypothesis graph. This approach would also be inherently limiting for non-expert users with insufficient background to formulate initial hypotheses. The longer-term solution we are exploring follows the related work mentioned above more closely, searching for subgraphs within larger passage graphs that match the query graph (as opposed to scoring the triples of a full query graph against those of a full sentence graph), with supervision from ontological and lexical resources to determine the categories of words in general that could fill certain semantic slots, thereby augmenting what constitutes subgraph matches. For example, for Q_1, we would search for matching subgraph structures where the concepts in the graph could be filled with any phrase for bodily fluids in the relationship of comparison of virus concentrations. Thus, the query would be expanded to a variety of paraphrase alternates, similar to the use of HyTER networks in past AMR research (Dreyer and Marcu, 2012), supporting the full range of matching answer subgraphs. These avenues for future work, in combination with our own findings, encourage us to continue this exploration of semantic search for information foraging, and engage with users to rapidly adapt capabilities for such urgent and dynamically changing situations as the coronavirus pandemic.

References

Rafael T. Anchieta, Marco A. S. Cabezudo, and Thiago A. S. Pardo. 2019. SEMA: an extended semantic evaluation metric for AMR. *arXiv preprint arXiv:1905.12069*.

L. Banarescu, C. Bonial, S. Cai, M. Georgescu, K. Griffitt, U. Hermjakob, K. Knight, P. Koehn, M. Palmer, and N. Schneider. 2013. Abstract Meaning Representation for sembanking. In *Proc. LAW*, pages 178–186.

Claire N Bonial, Lucia Donatelli, Jessica Ervin, and Clare R Voss. 2019. Abstract Meaning Representation for human-robot dialogue. *Proceedings of the Society for Computation in Linguistics*, 2(1):236–246.

Claire Bonial, Lucia Donatelli, Mitchell Abrams, Stephanie M. Lukin, Stephen Tratz, Matthew Marge, Ron Artstein, David Traum, and Clare R. Voss. 2020. Dialogue-AMR: Abstract Meaning Representation for dialogue. In *LREC*.

Shu Cai and Kevin Knight. 2013. Smatch: an evaluation metric for semantic feature structures. In *Proceedings of the 51st Annual Meeting of the Association for Computational Linguistics (Volume 2: Short Papers)*, pages 748–752, Sofia, Bulgaria, August. Association for Computational Linguistics.

Markus Dreyer and Daniel Marcu. 2012. Hyter: Meaning-equivalent semantics for translation evaluation. In *Proceedings of the 2012 Conference of the North American Chapter of the Association for Computational Linguistics: Human Language Technologies*, pages 162–171.

Xinya Du and Claire Cardie. 2020. Event extraction by answering (almost) natural questions. *Empirical Methods in Natural Language Processing (EMNLP)*.

Jeffrey Flanigan, Sam Thomson, Jaime Carbonell, Chris Dyer, and Noah A. Smith. 2014. A discriminative graph-based parser for the Abstract Meaning Representation. In *Proceedings of the 52nd Annual Meeting of the Association for Computational Linguistics (Volume 1: Long Papers)*, pages 1426–1436, Baltimore, Maryland.

Sahil Garg, Aram Galstyan, Ulf Hermjakob, and Daniel Marcu. 2016. Extracting biomolecular interactions using semantic parsing of biomedical text. In Dale Schuurmans and Michael P. Wellman, editors, *Proceedings of the Thirtieth AAAI Conference on Artificial Intelligence, February 12-17, 2016, Phoenix, Arizona, USA*, pages 2718–2726. AAAI Press.

Jan Gralton, Euan Tovey, Mary-Louise McLaws, and William D Rawlinson. 2011. The role of particle size in aerosolised pathogen transmission: a review. *Journal of Infection*, 62(1):1–13.

ZY Han, WG Weng, and QY Huang. 2013. Characterizations of particle size distribution of the droplets exhaled by sneeze. *Journal of the Royal Society Interface*, 10(88):20130560.

M. Lindemann, J. Groschwitz, and A. Koller. 2019. Compositional semantic parsing across graphbanks. In *Proc. of ACL*, pages 4576–4585, July.

Arindam Mitra and Chitta Baral. 2016. Addressing a question answering challenge by combining statistical methods with inductive rule learning and reasoning. In *Proc. of AAAI*, pages 2779–2785.

Juri Opitz, Anette Frank, and Letitia Parcalabescu. 2020. AMR similarity metrics from principles. *Trans. Assoc. Comput. Linguistics*, 8:522–538.

Sudha Rao, Daniel Marcu, Kevin Knight, and Hal Daumé III. 2017. Biomedical event extraction using Abstract Meaning Representation. In *Proc. of ACL*, pages 126–135, Vancouver, Canada.

Mrinmaya Sachan and Eric Xing. 2016. Machine comprehension using rich semantic representations. In *Proceedings of the 54th Annual Meeting of the Association for Computational Linguistics (Volume 2: Short Papers)*, pages 486–492.

Jose-Luis Sagripanti and C David Lytle. 2011. Sensitivity to ultraviolet radiation of lassa, vaccinia, and ebola viruses dried on surfaces. *Archives of virology*, 156(3):489–494.

Linfeng Song and Daniel Gildea. 2019. SemBleu: A robust metric for AMR parsing evaluation. In *Proceedings of the 57th Annual Meeting of the Association for Computational Linguistics*, pages 4547–4552, Florence, Italy, July. Association for Computational Linguistics.

Christopher M Walker and GwangPyo Ko. 2007. Effect of ultraviolet germicidal irradiation on viral aerosols. *Environmental science & technology*, 41(15):5460–5465.

Yanshan Wang, Sijia Liu, Majid Rastegar-Mojarad, Liwei Wang, Feichen Shen, Fei Liu, and Hongfang Liu. 2017. Dependency and AMR embeddings for drug-drug interaction extraction from biomedical literature. In *Proc. of ACM-BCB*, pages 36–43, New York, NY, USA.

Anne L Wyllie, John Fournier, Arnau Casanovas-Massana, Melissa Campbell, Maria Tokuyama, Pavithra Vijayakumar, Joshua L Warren, Bertie Geng, M Catherine Muenker, Adam J Moore, et al. 2020. Saliva or nasopharyngeal swab specimens for detection of sars-cov-2. *New England Journal of Medicine*, 383(13):1283–1286.

Semantic parsing with fuzzy meaning representations

Pavlo Kapustin
University of Bergen
pavlo.kapustin@uib.no

Michael Kapustin
Moscow Institute of Physics and Technology
michael.kapustin@gmail.com

Abstract

We propose an approach and a software framework for semantic parsing of natural language sentences to discourse representation structures with use of fuzzy meaning representations such as fuzzy sets and compatibility intervals. We explain the motivation for using fuzzy meaning representations in semantic parsing and describe the design of the proposed approach and the software framework, discussing various examples. We argue that the use of fuzzy meaning representations have potential to improve understanding and reasoning capabilities of systems working with natural language.

1 Introduction

The meaning representation based on fuzzy sets was first proposed by Lotfi Zadeh (Zadeh, 1971; Zadeh, 1972). One of the very interesting properties of this representation is allowing to quantitatively describe relations between different concepts (e.g. "young"/"age", "common"/"surprisingness", "seldom"/"frequency"), as well as represent vagueness and imprecision that are so common to natural language. We recently proposed a related meaning representation, compatibility intervals, that, instead of using membership functions, describes similar relations using several intervals on a certain scale (Kapustin and Kapustin, 2019a).

Fuzzy meaning representations are relatively little known among linguists, and little used in natural language processing (Carvalho et al., 2012; Novák, 2017). We believe that this is well explained by the fact that these rich interpretations are generally not easy to learn from data, compared to the representations like word embeddings that can be derived from text. However, we believe that due to their expressiveness these representations have a huge potential when it comes to understanding and reasoning capabilities of the systems working with natural language. They allow to quantitatively express differences between similar language constructs (synonyms/antonyms, stronger/weaker constructs, wider/narrower constructs, etc.), making this knowledge available to the systems. In addition, compared to more opaque representations like word embeddings, they are also linguistically interpretable, potentially allowing to build the systems whose behaviour can be easier analyzed and explained.

We would like to contribute to the knowledge of using fuzzy meaning representations in natural language understanding, in particular, in semantic parsing. In this introductory paper we describe an approach and a software framework for semantic parsing of natural language sentences to discourse representation structures (DRS) with the use of fuzzy meaning representations.

First, we use these representations to enrich the resulting DRS with certain types of semantic information that can be helpful for downstream applications. In particular, both meaning similarity and vagueness can in many cases be directly represented in the DRS with the use of fuzzy meaning representations. For example, in the suggested approach, the constructs "this was not completely expected" and "this was fairly surprising" should lead to similar parses, expressing the meaning of the words "expected" and "surprising" in terms of the same underlying properties. Constructs "not completely" and "fairly" are modeled as modifiers acting on the words "expected" and "surprising" and transforming their

Proceedings of the 2nd International Workshop on Designing Meaning Representations, pages 78–89
Barcelona, Spain (Online), December 13, 2020

underlying representations (either the fuzzy sets or the compatibility intervals). This allows the systems to analyze the similarity of the constructs computationally.

Second, fuzzy meaning representations also play a key role during the semantic parsing, as they are used for the assessment of the understanding level and scoring of the different interpretations.

2 Related work

2.1 Fuzzy meaning representations

In his early works, Lotfi Zadeh suggests modeling meaning of certain types of adjectives (e.g. "small", "medium", "large") as fuzzy sets, and some lingustic hedges (e.g. "very", "slightly" — as operators, acting on these fuzzy sets (Zadeh, 1971; Zadeh, 1972). He introduces the concept of a linguistic variable (a variable whose values are words or expressions in a natural language) and suggests that values of membership function can be seen as degrees of compatibility between the value of the function argument and the construct the membership function is describing (Zadeh, 1975; Zadeh, 1978). Novák (2017) describes Fuzzy Natural Logic, a mathematical theory attempting to model the semantics of natural language, including Theory of Evaluative Linguistic Expressions (Novák, 2008), and further studies the concept of the linguistic variable (Novák, 2020).

Hersh and Caramazza (1976) introduce logical and linguistic interpretations of membership functions. We discuss these interpretations and other issues related to modeling natural language constructs with fuzzy sets (Kapustin and Kapustin, 2019b) and introduce another another fuzzy meaning representation, compatibility intervals (Kapustin and Kapustin, 2019a), also conducting a small-scale experiment that relates some language constructs to compatibility intervals (Kapustin and Kapustin, 2020).

There is some work aiming to make fuzzy sets easier to learn from data. Runkler (2016) describes an approach for generation of linguistically meaningful membership functions from word vectors. We believe that compatibility intervals (Kapustin and Kapustin, 2019a), a somewhat simpler representation than the fuzzy sets, may also be easier to learn from data.

Earlier we described a theoretical framework (Kapustin and Kapustin, 2015) for computational interpreting of natural language fragments, suggesting modeling meaning of words as operators. Some of the ideas of this framework are tested in a simplified setting in Kapustin (2015). Our approach and software framework also draw upon many of the ideas from that work.

2.2 Semantic parsing

There has been a growing body of research in semantic parsing with use of different meaning representations, including Minimal Recursion Semantics (Copestake et al., 2005), Discourse Representation Theory (Kamp and Reyle, 2013), Abstract Meaning Representation (Banarescu et al., 2013), Broad-Coverage Semantic Dependencies (Oepen et al., 2014; Oepen et al., 2015), Universal Conceptual Cognitive Annotation (Abend and Rappoport, 2013) and Universal Decompositional Semantics (White et al., 2016).

Abzianidze et al. (2019) describe a highly expressive scoped meaning representation based on Discourse Representation Theory (Kamp and Reyle, 2013) that combines logical (negation, quantification and modals), pragmatic (presuppositions) and lexical (word senses and thematic roles) aspects of semantics. The Parallel Meaning Bank (Abzianidze et al., 2017) uses this representation to annotate a corpus of translations including over 11 million words in four different languages. In the Parallel Meaning Bank concepts, states and events are annotated by the word senses from WordNet (Fellbaum, 1998), relations are modeled with thematic roles from VerbNet (Bonial et al., 2011) and optionally annotated with semantic roles from FrameNet (Baker et al., 1998). In addition to CCG categories (Steedman, 2000), the Parallel Meaning Bank annotates the words with semantic tags (Abzianidze and Bos, 2017). In our work, we loosely follow Abzianidze et al. (2019), extending it with fuzzy meaning representations.

3 Background

3.1 Fuzzy meaning representations

Using fuzzy sets, one may model meaning of language constructs by relating them to a certain property that is described by these constructs (e.g. "age", "time", "frequency", etc.). Then, the language construct is represented as a fuzzy set, and the membership function of this set models compatibility of the construct with different values that the property may take. For example, earlier we suggested how one could relate the meaning of depicted words to properties "surprisingness" and "frequency" by using one-dimensional *projections*, see figs. 1 and 2 (Kapustin and Kapustin, 2019b).

Note that on fig. 2 $\mu_{\text{seldom}}(0)$ and $\mu_{\text{often}}(1)$ are significantly lower, than 1. This corresponds to the *linguistic interpretation* (Hersh and Caramazza, 1976; Kapustin and Kapustin, 2019b) that is related to scalar implicatures and models the fact that stronger words like "never" and "always" are more likely to be used near the ends of the scale, than words like "seldom" and "often".

We recently proposed compatibility intervals, a meaning representation closely related to fuzzy sets (Kapustin and Kapustin, 2019a). Compatibility interval is an interval of property values on some scale that are compatible with a given language construct. Compatibility intervals consist of the main subinterval with high compatibility, and optional left ("increasing") and right ("decreasing") subintervals adjacent to the main subinterval. The following invariants are maintained: all the values in the main subinterval have equal (high) compatibility, and the closer the values are to the main subinterval the higher their compatibility is.

Consider an example of how one could define compatibility intervals for different age groups (which is, of course, entirely subjective). We use double hyphens between the start and the end of the main subinterval, and single hyphens between the start and the end of the left and the right subintervals).

```
child: [0 -- 15-20]
young1: [0 -- 30-50]
young2: [0-18 -- 30-50]
adult: [15-20 -- 100]
middle-aged: [40-45 -- 65-70]
old: [70-80 -- 100]
```

Note that construct $young_1$ corresponds to the *logical interpretation*, modeling the fact that newborns and infants are as young as one can be, while construct $young_2$ corresponds to the linguistic interpretation, modeling the fact that when someone refers to a person as "young", we usually do not imagine a newborn or an infant.

Let's consider how one could approximately translate figs. 1 and 2 to compatibility intervals:

```
expected: [0 -- 0.1-0.2]
common: [0-0.1 -- 0.2-0.3]
possible: [0-0.2 -- 0.5-0.6]
extraordinary: [0.6-0.9 -- 1]
```

```
seldom: [0-0.1 -- 0.2-0.3]
occasionally: [0-0.2 -- 0.4-0.8]
regularly: [0-0.4 -- 0.7-1]
often: [0.6-0.8 -- 0.9-1]
```

As long as both fuzzy sets and compatibility intervals model compatibility between a language construct and different values a property may take, and they both directly represent vagueness, we refer to both as fuzzy meaning representations and consider them somewhat interchangeable for the purposes of the paper. Although, there are some differences. While compatibility intervals is a simpler representation that may be easier to work with (Kapustin and Kapustin, 2019a) and may also be easier to learn from data, we consider fuzzy sets to be a more general, and in some sense, more powerful representation. For example, one cannot use compatibility intervals to model situations that use multi-dimensional membership functions (Kapustin and Kapustin, 2019b).

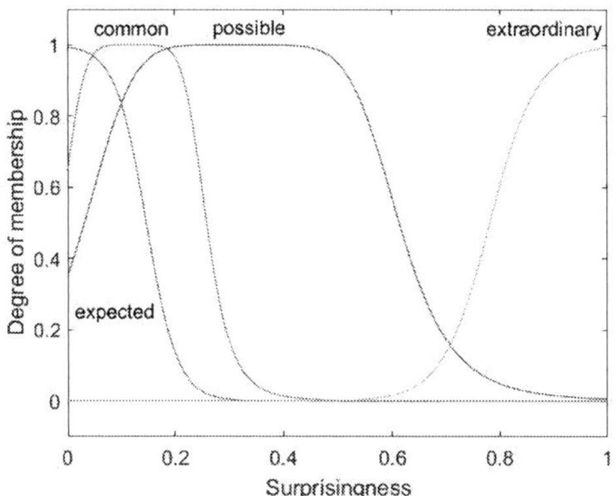

Figure 1: Depicted constructs related to "surprising-ness". Surprisingness values are in the range between 0 ("completely expected") and 1 ("completely unex-pected").

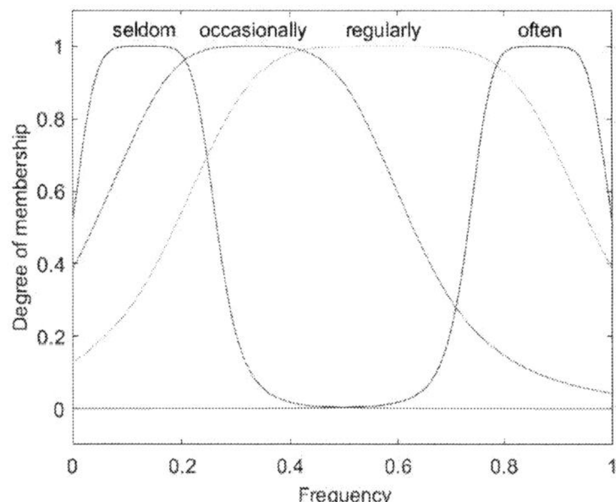

Figure 2: Depicted constructs related to event fre-quency. Frequency values are in the range between 0 ("never") and 1 ("as often as it can be").

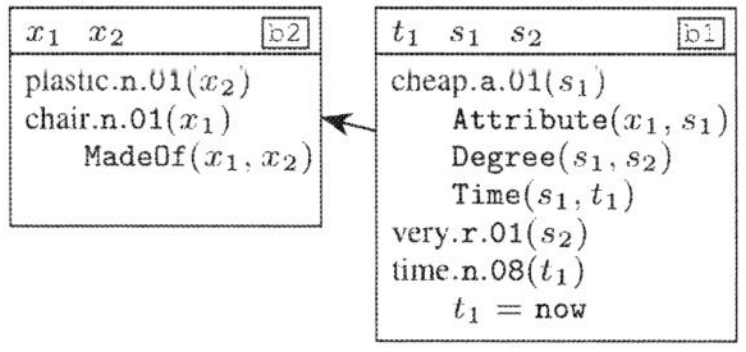

Figure 3: Example 81/2996. "This plastic chair is very cheap".

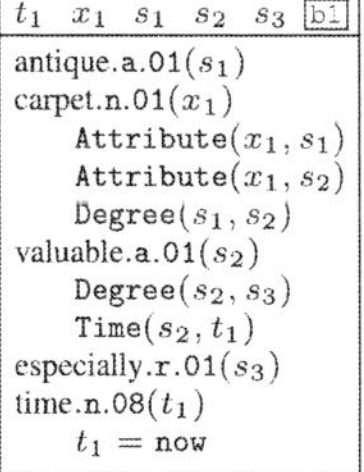

Figure 4: Example 20/0810. "Antique carpets are espe-cially valuable".

3.2 Semantic parsing

Semantic parsing attempts to map natural language to meaning representations. DRS parsing is a type of semantic parsing that targets Discourse Representation Structures (Kamp and Reyle, 2013), consisting of discourse referents and discourse conditions optionally organized into scopes (see Abzianidze et al. (2019) for an introduction to the scoped DRS representation).

Consider examples 81/2996 and 20/0810 from the Parallel Meaning Bank (Abzianidze et al., 2017), see figs. 3 and 4. While this representation is semantically very rich, it has limitations when it comes to the reasoning it may facilitate. For example, while there is clearly a relation between the meaning of the constructs "very cheap" and "especially valuable" (in terms of "price"), it is not easy to explore this relation. Indeed, the meaning of the words "cheap" and "valuable" is only defined by references to WordNet meanings, and while it is specified that both "very" and "especially" are degree modifiers, the effect of these modifiers is also only defined by references to WordNet.

One of the goals of our approach is attempting to be able to look "inside" the concepts, allowing to enable such reasoning. In this example this would mean relating both "cheap" and "valuable" to "price" using fuzzy meaning representations and defining "very" and "especially" as modifiers that transform those representations. In this way, the resulting DRS structures may express the meanings of the con-structs in terms of the same underlying properties, facilitating additional types of reasoning.

4 Approach

The presented approach and the framework are largely based on the idea of exploring what various language constructs (e.g. "often") tell us about possible values of different properties (e.g. "frequency"). We don't know about a general way of deriving such knowledge from texts, however, see e.g. Runkler (2016). For this reason, our approach is dependent on having a predefined lexicon containing rather rich semantic information. Currently, the lexicon is defined manually. While we are planning to work on obtaining some parts of this lexicon in an automated way and making the framework work with a broader lexicon, we consider it to be a different research topic. Our main interest is studying whether such information may improve understanding and reasoning capabilities of natural language understanding systems in general and semantic parsing systems in particular.

Relying on a rich semantic lexicon has other important implications on the design of the system. We are trying to make use of this information in the best possible way, as it may help to guide all the tasks that are part of the semantic parsing (e.g. syntactic parsing, handling multi-word expressions, choosing relevant word meaning, etc.). Also, we believe that any decision made during the natural language understanding process may need to be reversed as a result of the information obtained later in the process. For example, first we may parse "a few" as a multi-word expression, but later we may have to reconsider it, because we cannot arrive at any satisfactory interpretations that are based on that decision. For these reasons, rather than viewing the system as a pipeline that makes use of standard components working with different tasks, we design it as a single process that may take input from other specialized systems. Currently, the framework does not yet integrate with other systems, handling main tasks of the semantic parsing internally.

Given a lexicon, the framework parses natural language sentences to a variant of scoped DRS representation, loosely following Abzianidze et al. (2019). We extend the DRS to represent fuzziness by using *regions*, see also Kapustin and Kapustin (2015). Regions define which values of a certain property (e.g. "age", "surprisingness", "frequency") are compatible with a certain word or utterance by the means of either fuzzy sets or compatibility intervals. Composition of meaning in a sentence is modeled by the application of word-operators to words-operands, and whether a word-operator may accept a particular word as an operand is based on various syntactic and semantic tags. The framework processes words in the order they appear in the input sentence, performing a series of transitions corresponding to the decisions made during the semantic parsing. As several alternative transitions are often possible, transitions form a search tree. Paths in this tree correspond to different interpretations of the sentence, and each parse is assigned a score. Finally, to find the best interpretation of the sentence, we traverse the tree, taking the scores into account.

The framework is written in Haskell and is under active development. While it is not open source software at the moment, we encourage everyone interested in the framework to contact the authors.

In this paper we describe our approach in general, and the framework in its current state. First, we briefly describe the main components of the framework, and then discuss the role that fuzzy meaning representations play in the framework.

4.1 Operator application

We model composition of meaning in a sentence by application of word-operators to words-operands, somewhat similar to predicate-argument structure. Such applications give rise to new *meaning elements* (meaning composition units within a sentence). Whether a word-operator may accept another word as an operand is based on various syntactic and semantic tags, see also Abzianidze and Bos (2017). The tags may be defined in the lexicon, and in some cases calculated (for example, modeling transfer of some properties from an individual word to a compound). In the future, we plan to add support for tag expression levels, capability of inferring of tags (for example, in case of coercion), and also using both external sources and machine learning techniques to obtain the tags for the words that are not in the lexicon.

We use the following data type to represent a particular state in the semantic parsing that we call *application data*. This data type contains:

- The list of all *active operators* (word-operators awaiting their arguments).
- *Available operands* (seen words and meaning elements not yet assigned to any active operator).
- New meaning elements (created as a result of previous applications).
- Unprocessed sentence words.

- Current DRS.

- Current score of the interpretation.

Consider a somewhat shortened example, representing a state in the semantic parsing.

```
1   Application data:
2     ActiveOperators: [
3       Definition:
4         Description: after,
5         Operands: [
6           Name: ReferenceTime, Needed tags: [TimeMoment], Core: False},
7           Name: TimeInterval, Needed tags: [TimeInterval], Core: False}
8         ],
9         MatchCriteria:
10          OneOf: [ReferenceTime, TimeInterval],
11        Location: (5, 5),
12        OperandMatches: [
13          Definition:
14            Name: TimeInterval,
15            Needed tags: [TimeInterval],
16            Core: False
17          MatchData:
18            Description: just (a few (minutes)),
19            Tags: [Quantity, TimeInterval],
20            Location: (1, 4),
21            DrsReferentName: x1
22        ],
23        AvailableOperands: [],
24        MeaningElements: [
25          Description: starting,
26          Tags: [TimeMoment],
27          Location: (6, 6),
28          DrsReferentName: x2
29        ],
30        RemainingWords: []
```

According to the example, there is one active operator "after". The operator's definition (lines 3-10) says that it may accept two operands referred to as "ReferenceTime" and "TimeInterval", and that both of them are optional. To be accepted as the operands, the candidate words or meaning elements need to have tags "TimeMoment" and "TimeInterval", respectively. The operator is considered sufficiently matched if at least one of these operands is matched (line 10).

Lines 12-22 say that one of these operands, "TimeInterval", is currently matched with the meaning element corresponding to the construct "just a few minutes". This meaning element has tags "Quantity" and "TimeInterval", originates from the words 1-4 in the sentence and corresponds to the discourse referent x_1 in the output DRS.

Lines 24-29 say that the next meaning element to consider is "starting". It has tag "TimeMoment", originates from word 6 in the sentence and corresponds to the discourse referent x_2 in the output DRS. Based on the tags, this meaning element can be matched with the "ReferenceTime" operand of the operator "after".

4.2 DRS

Ultimately, all operator applications result in the modification of the output DRS. Consider the result of the semantic parsing of the construct "just a few minutes after starting".

```
1    Ref x1 <- just (a few (minutes))
2    Quantity (x1)
3    Object (x1, "minutes")
4    Value (x1, "Countable": [0.10-0.20 -- 0.50-0.70])
5    Perceived (x1, "Perceived quantity": [0.10-0.20 -- 0.30-0.40])
6    Ref x2 <- starting
7    TimeMoment (x2)
8    Ref x3 <- starting
9    Process (x3)
10   StartTime (x3, x2)
```

```
11    Ref x4 <- after (starting, just (a few (minutes)))
12    TimeMoment (x4)
13    ReferenceTime (x4, x2)
14    Value (x4, "Time": [0.00-0.10 -- 0.50-0.80])
```

Lines 1-5 define a discourse referent x_1 corresponding to the result of applying operator "just" to the meaning element "a few minutes", along with several discourse conditions related to that referent. Predicate "Quantity" defines the type of the referent x_1. Relation "Object" defines the unit of measure which is "minutes". Relation "Value" defines the value of the quantity, given by the compatibility interval `[0.10-0.20 -- 0.50-0.70]` over the property "countable". Relation "Perceived value" defines the quantity's perceived value, given by the compatibility interval `[0.10-0.20 -- 0.30-0.40]` over the property "perceived quantity". Both of the compatibility intervals come from the definitions of the operators for the words "a few" and "just".

Lines 6-10 define discourse referents x_2 and x_3, both created during the *standalone application* (application without arguments) of the operator "starting". x_2 corresponds to the process, and x_3 — to the starting moment of the process.

Lines 11-14 define discourse referent x_4, corresponding to the time moment defined by the operator "after", applied to "just a few minutes" and "starting". This time moment is defined with regards to the time moment x_2, and its value is given by the time interval `[0-0.1 -- 0.5-0.8]` that comes from the definition of the operator for the word "after".

4.3 Tree search

As previously mentioned, we model the task of finding the best interpretation of the sentence as a tree search task. Each branch in the tree corresponds to a certain decision in the semantic parsing process, from more syntactic (e.g. treating two words as a multi-word expression to more semantic (exploring a certain meaning of a word, applying an operator to arguments, etc.). Each search path in the tree corresponds to a potential interpretation of the sentence, and all the interpretations are scored. Some examples of the scores include:

- Ratio between the number of the matched operands and the numbers of the operands supported by the operator (optionally considering their importance).

- Distance between the operator and the operands in the sentence (reflecting that placement of various modifiers and function words relative to the word they specify varies between languages, and how strict the placement needs to be followed also depends on the words and the language).

- Different heuristics (see section 4.5).

Various types of scores are currently under development.

In addition to the automatic search mode, the framework supports an interactive mode where the user may choose which search path to explore next. In this mode, all paths in the tree are written to files that are updated as the search proceeds. The files contain various information about the search paths, in particular its status, scores, current output DRS, current application data and the steps the path consists of. Consider a somewhat shortened example of a search path to the semantic parsing of the construct "just a few minutes after starting".

```
[ProcessLexeme("just"), ProcessMeaningElement("just"), NewActiveOperator("just"),
ProcessLexeme("a few"), ProcessMeaningElement("a few"), NewActiveOperator("a
few"), ProcessLexeme("minutes"), ProcessMeaningElement("minutes"), OperandMatches
("a few":"Countable"->"minutes"]), Apply("a few"), OperandMatches("just":
["Quantity"->"a few (minutes)"]), Apply("just"), NewAvailableOperand("just(a few
(minutes))"), ProcessLexeme("after"), ProcessMeaningElement ("after"),
AvailableOperandAllocation("after":["TimeInterval"->"just (a few (minutes))"]),
OperandMatches("after":["TimeInterval"->"just (a few (minutes))"]),ProcessLexeme(
"starting"),ProcessMeaningElement("starting"), ApplyStandalone("starting"),
OperandMatches("after":["ReferenceTime"->"starting"]),Apply("after"),
NewAvailableOperand("after(starting, just(a few (minutes)))")]
```

This shows how the semantic parsing is separated into smaller steps, from parsing new lexemes to matching operands and applying operators. All these steps form a path in a single search tree.

4.4 Lexicon

The lexicon is used to define all the words with special meaning for the framework, i.e. operators. While the system may handle words not present in the lexicon, this is currently quite limited (they are treated as strings). At the moment, all the semantic tags also have to be defined in the lexicon, and the words not present in the lexicon are treated as if they didn't have any tags. However, we plan to use external sources and machine learning techniques to obtain semantic tags for the words that are not in the lexicon.

Curently, the lexicon is described using an embedded domain specific language in Haskell, but we plan to use a configuration language in the future.

For example, consider this piece of configuration:

```
oneWord "just"
  & addOperands [quantityOperand]
  & addNewCondition
  (operandRef Operands.quantity)
  ( relation
      Roles.perceived
      (regionValue (IntervalRegion Properties.quantity Intervals.low)))
  & setResultReferent (operandRef Operands.quantity)
  & addTagAction (AddTagsFrom Operands.quantity)
```

This says the following:

- "just" is a single-word lexeme.
- In this meaning, it takes one mandatory operand that needs to have a tag "Quantity".
- When applied, "just" will add a new discourse condition "Perceived" to the discourse referent associated with this operand (here referred to as x_1). The value of this relation is set to the compatibility interval "Intervals.low" (e.g. `[0.1-0.2 -- 0.3-0.4]`).
- The result of the application of "just" to an operand gives rise to a new meaning element that will have the same tags as the argument.
- The resulting meaning element is associated with the discourse referent x_1.

4.5 The role of fuzzy meaning representations

Using fuzzy meaning representations, the framework allows us to express the meaning of words in terms of the same underlying properties. For example, "seldom", "occasionally", "regularly", "often" can all be related to frequency. This allows the system, in particular, to compare meanings of sentences containing related words.

The framework allows us to model the meaning of compound constructs in a compositional way, using operator application. In case of modifiers this means transformation of the original fuzzy set or compatibility interval by the modifier, and the result is again either a fuzzy set or a compatibility interval over the same underlying property. This means that the system can also compare meanings of sentences containing compound constructs, for example, "after", "soon after", "slightly after", "right after", "five minutes after".

Expressing meaning of the constructs in terms of underlying properties also means that the system can in some cases decompose the meaning of the constructs in several parts. Let's discuss several examples.

(1)   Just a few minutes after starting, it has already completed cleaning of the whole room

(2)   Only a few minutes after starting, it has already completed cleaning of the whole room.

(3)   ? Just an hour after the movie started, he realized it was a different title.

(4)   Only an hour after the movie started, he realized it was a different title.

Consider (1) and (2). While the words "a few" and "minutes" tell us about the actual duration of the process, the meaning of the words "just" and "only" in this context is different. Rather than describing the actual duration, they tell us how the duration is perceived (in this case "shorter, than expected"). This is also related to mirativity, or surprise, see e.g. Zeevat (2013), Zeevat (2009). In our approach, semantic parsing of "just a few minutes" results in two fuzzy sets or compatibility intervals, one defined over property "quantity" and one defined over property "perceived quantity". This allows the systems using these representations to analyze and compare the meanings of constructs like "just a few minutes" and "a couple of minutes") property by property.

It is interesting to note that "only" in a similar context may actually have opposite meanings, "shorter than expected" (2) and "longer than expected" (4). However, "just" in a similar context always means "less than expected", or "shorter than expected", and this essentially makes (3) either ironic or infelicitous. If a system has information about both communicated perceived and actual values, it may detect irony in case of their disagreement.

While detection of irony in practice would often require some extra domain-specific knowledge e.g. in (3) it is necessary to know that "one hour" is a long time in this domain, often analysis of fuzzy meaning representations defined over the same or related properties may help to assess text understanding level and detect contradictions, tautologies and other situations that may suggest an infelicitous sentence (or a misunderstanding of a sentence by the system). Let's discuss several examples.

(5)   ? This car is slow and very quick.

(6)   ? He is young but not too old.

(7)   ? The pizza is slightly medium.

(8)   ? I go there very always.

(9)   ? I will be there approximately in the evening.

(10)   Only a few people like sushi.

(11)   ? Only a great number of people like sushi.

Consider (5). Suppose "slow" and "quick" are defined by the compatibility intervals [0 -- 0.2-0.3] and [0.7-0.8 -- 1] over the property "speed". Their intersection is empty, indicating a contradiction as long as the use of "and" suggests that both "slow" and "quick" should be possible at the same time.

Consider (6). Suppose "young" and "old" are defined by the compatibility intervals [0-18 -- 30-50] and [70-80 -- 100] over the property "age" (see also section 3.1). Modifier "too" would shift "old" even more to the right edge of the scale. However, the use of "but not" assumes some non-empty intersection between "young" and "too old", which is not the case.

Consider (7). Suppose "medium" is defined by the compatibility interval [0.3-0.4 -- 0.6-0.7] over the property "size". Modifier "slightly" would normally shift the compatibility interval to the middle of the scale, making the construct less polar. However, the compatibility interval is already in the middle, and the shift has no effect.

Consider (8). Suppose "always" is defined by the compatibility interval [0.95-0.99 -- 1] over the property "frequency". Modifier "very" would normally shift the compatibility interval to the edge of the scale, making the construct more polar. However, the compatibility interval is already at the very edge, and the shift has virtually no effect.

Consider (9). Suppose "evening" is defined by the compatibility interval [0.5-0.6 -- 1] over the property "time" where "0.5" means 6PM and "1" means 12AM. Modifier "approximately" would normally expect a rather narrow compatibility interval and make it wider. However, the compatibility interval is already rather wide.

While (10), even if not true, is a valid sentence, (11), on the other hand, seems infelicitous, if not ungrammatical. Suppose that "only" is defined by the compatibility interval [0-0.2 -- 0.3-0.4] over the property "perceived quantity", and "a great number" is defined by the compatibility interval [0.7-0.8 -- 1] over the property "quantity". The use of "only" tells us that the quantity is perceived as small and presupposes that the quantity is indeed small, so the compatibility intervals should agree, but they do not.

With use of fuzzy meaning representations, many of these situations may be detected computationally, possibly meaning that the phrase is infelicitous, or, more likely, that the system's interpretation of the phrase is incorrect. We are currently working on development of similar heuristics in the framework, partly drawing upon some of the ideas from Kapustin and Kapustin (2015), and they are going take part in the scoring of the interpretations.

5   Discussion

One of the primary design goals for the approach and the framework is extensibility, as only a little part of the lexicon can be defined manually. Short-term, we are looking at using external sources and machine learning techniques to obtain semantic tags for the words not present in the lexicon. Long-term, we are planning to use various knowledge bases, synonym dictionaries and machine learning techniques to let the system learn more words.

At the same time, we would like to emphasize that our main research goal is exploring how natural language understanding systems in general and semantic parsers in particular may benefit from using rich quantitative meaning representations, focusing somewhat less on obtaining these representations automatically at this point. We know how to automatically learn some fuzzy sets, see e.g. Runkler (2016), and maybe we can find out how to learn more. We would like to study whether we should, and what understanding and reasoning capabilities this may facilitate, compared to what is supported by easily learnable but not easily linguistically interpretable representations like word embeddings.

As a reviewer pointed out, it is also interesting to compare fuzzy meaning representations to Universal Decompositional Semantics (White et al., 2016) in terms of the aspects of meaning they can express. Universal Decompositional Semantics is another quantitative representation and annotation scheme that uses continuous scales and is based on linguistic theory. While it is very different from fuzzy sets and compatibility intervals, we think it is worthwhile to explore how these representations could be used together to model different aspects of semantics.

We believe that fuzzy meaning representations may improve capabilities of the systems working with natural language as they provide linguistically interpretable projections (Kapustin and Kapustin, 2019b) of the construct meanings onto certain properties. These may allow natural language understanding systems to interpret meanings of the words in a quantitative way, allowing to analyze and compare them with higher "precision". For example, instead of just knowing that the words are similar, the system may analyze in details how they are similar or different, e.g which word is wider, which one is more polar, which situations can be described by both words and which — only by one of them.

Seeing whether natural language understanding systems can actually use some of the described ideas and techniques, and being able to evaluate this in practice will require more research, and we hope that our approach and the software framework can be a useful contribution to the study of this complex field.

Acknoweldgements

We thank Csaba Veres, Vadim Kimmelman, Rik van Noord, Costanza Marini and anonymous reviewers for helpful discussions, comments and feedback. We thank Rik van Noord and Lasha Abzianidze for their assistance with preparation of the illustrations for the paper.

References

Omri Abend and Ari Rappoport. 2013. Universal conceptual cognitive annotation (ucca). In *Proceedings of the 51st Annual Meeting of the Association for Computational Linguistics (Volume 1: Long Papers)*, pages 228–238.

Lasha Abzianidze and Johan Bos. 2017. Towards universal semantic tagging. In *IWCS 2017—12th International Conference on Computational Semantics—Short papers*.

Lasha Abzianidze, Johannes Bjerva, Kilian Evang, Hessel Haagsma, Rik van Noord, Pierre Ludmann, Duc-Duy Nguyen, and Johan Bos. 2017. The parallel meaning bank: Towards a multilingual corpus of translations annotated with compositional meaning representations. In *Proceedings of the 15th Conference of the European Chapter of the Association for Computational Linguistics: Volume 2, Short Papers*, pages 242–247.

Lasha Abzianidze, Rik van Noord, Hessel Haagsma, and Johan Bos. 2019. The first shared task on discourse representation structure parsing. In *Proceedings of the IWCS Shared Task on Semantic Parsing*, Gothenburg, Sweden, May. Association for Computational Linguistics.

Collin F Baker, Charles J Fillmore, and John B Lowe. 1998. The berkeley framenet project. In *Proceedings of the 17th international conference on Computational linguistics-Volume 1*, pages 86–90. Association for Computational Linguistics.

Laura Banarescu, Claire Bonial, Shu Cai, Madalina Georgescu, Kira Griffitt, Ulf Hermjakob, Kevin Knight, Philipp Koehn, Martha Palmer, and Nathan Schneider. 2013. Abstract meaning representation for sembanking. In *Proceedings of the 7th linguistic annotation workshop and interoperability with discourse*, pages 178–186.

Claire Bonial, William Corvey, Martha Palmer, Volha V Petukhova, and Harry Bunt. 2011. A hierarchical unification of lirics and verbnet semantic roles. In *2011 IEEE Fifth International Conference on Semantic Computing*, pages 483–489. IEEE.

Joao P Carvalho, Fernando Batista, and Luisa Coheur. 2012. A critical survey on the use of fuzzy sets in speech and natural language processing. In *Fuzzy Systems (FUZZ-IEEE), 2012 IEEE International Conference on*, pages 1–8. IEEE.

Ann Copestake, Dan Flickinger, Carl Pollard, and Ivan A Sag. 2005. Minimal recursion semantics: An introduction. *Research on language and computation*, 3(2-3):281–332.

Christiane Fellbaum, editor. 1998. *WordNet. An Electronic Lexical Database*. The MIT Press, Cambridge, Ma., USA.

Harry M Hersh and Alfonso Caramazza. 1976. A fuzzy set approach to modifiers and vagueness in natural language. *Journal of Experimental Psychology: General*, 105(3):254.

Hans Kamp and Uwe Reyle. 2013. *From discourse to logic: Introduction to modeltheoretic semantics of natural language, formal logic and discourse representation theory*, volume 42. Springer Science & Business Media.

Michael Kapustin and Pavlo Kapustin. 2015. Modeling meaning: computational interpreting and understanding of natural language fragments. *arXiv preprint arXiv:1505.08149*.

Pavlo Kapustin and Michael Kapustin. 2019a. Modeling language constructs with compatibility intervals. In *Proceedings of the IWCS 2019 Workshop on Computing Semantics with Types, Frames and Related Structures*, pages 49–54, Gothenburg, Sweden, June. Association for Computational Linguistics.

Pavlo Kapustin and Michael Kapustin. 2019b. Modeling language constructs with fuzzy sets: some approaches, examples and interpretations. In *Proceedings of the 13th International Conference on Computational Semantics - Student Papers*, pages 24–33, Gothenburg, Sweden, May. Association for Computational Linguistics.

Pavlo Kapustin and Michael Kapustin. 2020. Language constructs as compatibility intervals: a small-scale experiment. In *ExLing 2020: Proceedings of the 11th International Conference of Experimental Linguistics*. International Society of Experimental Linguistics. Accepted for publication.

Pavlo Kapustin. 2015. Computational comprehension of spatial directions expressed in natural language. Master's thesis, The University of Bergen.

Vilém Novák. 2008. A comprehensive theory of trichotomous evaluative linguistic expressions. *Fuzzy Sets and Systems*, 159(22):2939–2969.

Vilém Novák. 2017. Fuzzy logic in natural language processing. In *Fuzzy Systems (FUZZ-IEEE), 2017 IEEE International Conference on*, pages 1–6. IEEE.

Vilém Novák. 2020. The concept of linguistic variable revisited. In *Recent Developments in Fuzzy Logic and Fuzzy Sets*, pages 105–118. Springer.

Stephan Oepen, Marco Kuhlmann, Yusuke Miyao, Daniel Zeman, Dan Flickinger, Jan Hajic, Angelina Ivanova, and Yi Zhang. 2014. Semeval 2014 task 8: Broad-coverage semantic dependency parsing.

Stephan Oepen, Marco Kuhlmann, Yusuke Miyao, Daniel Zeman, Silvie Cinková, Dan Flickinger, Jan Hajic, and Zdenka Uresova. 2015. Semeval 2015 task 18: Broad-coverage semantic dependency parsing. In *Proceedings of the 9th International Workshop on Semantic Evaluation (SemEval 2015)*, pages 915–926.

Thomas A Runkler. 2016. Generation of linguistic membership functions from word vectors. In *Fuzzy Systems (FUZZ-IEEE), 2016 IEEE International Conference on*, pages 993–999. IEEE.

Mark Steedman. 2000. *The syntactic process*, volume 24. MIT press Cambridge, MA.

Aaron Steven White, Drew Reisinger, Keisuke Sakaguchi, Tim Vieira, Sheng Zhang, Rachel Rudinger, Kyle Rawlins, and Benjamin Van Durme. 2016. Universal decompositional semantics on universal dependencies. In *Proceedings of the 2016 Conference on Empirical Methods in Natural Language Processing*, pages 1713–1723.

Lotfi A Zadeh. 1971. Quantitative fuzzy semantics. *Information Sciences*, 3(2):159–176.

Lotfi A Zadeh. 1972. A fuzzy-set-theoretic interpretation of linguistic hedges. *Journal of Cybernetics*.

Lotfi Asker Zadeh. 1975. The concept of a linguistic variable and its application to approximate reasoning—i. *Information sciences*, 8(3):199–249.

Lotfi Asker Zadeh. 1978. Fuzzy sets as a basis for a theory of possibility. *Fuzzy sets and systems*, 1(1):3–28.

Henk Zeevat. 2009. "only" as a mirative particle.

Henk Zeevat. 2013. Expressing surprise by particles. In *Beyond Expressives: Explorations in Use-Conditional Meaning*, pages 297–320. Brill.

Representing constructional metaphors

Pavlina Kalm
Dept. of Linguistics
Univ. of New Mexico
pavlinap@unm.edu

Michael Regan
Dept. of Linguistics
Univ. of New Mexico
reganman@unm.edu

Sook-kyung Lee
Dept. of Linguistics
Univ. of New Mexico
sklee@unm.edu

Chris Peverada
Dept. of Linguistics
Univ. of New Mexico
peverada@unm.edu

William Croft
Dept. of Linguistics
Univ. of New Mexico
wcroft@unm.edu

Abstract

This paper introduces a representation and annotation scheme for argument structure constructions that are used metaphorically with verbs in different semantic domains. We aim to contribute to the study of constructional metaphors which has received little attention in theoretical and computational linguistics. The proposed representation consists of a systematic mapping between the constructional and verbal event structures in two domains. It reveals the semantic motivations that lead to constructions being metaphorically extended. We demonstrate this representation on argument structure constructions with Transfer of Possession verbs and test the viability of this scheme with an annotation exercise.

1 Introduction

Verbal semantics has received much attention in theoretical and computational linguistics. Representing the event structure evoked by verbs has been at the heart of recent theoretical and computational linguistic models (Fillmore et al., 2003; Banarescu et al., 2013; Hajič et al., 2012; Abend and Rappoport, 2013). Verb meaning is a crucial determinant of the syntactic realization of arguments and their semantic interpretation within events (Fillmore, 1985; Talmy, 1988; Levin, 1993). Conversely, argument structure constructions contribute much of the semantic structure of events (Goldberg, 1995; Croft, 2012).

Most event representations do not explicitly address metaphorical extensions across domains or metaphorical correspondences between constructional meanings. For example, the syntactic realization of arguments associated with certain verbs in the physical domain, e.g. *place* verbs (1a), *remove* verbs (2a), *cover* verbs (3a), or *uncover* verbs (4a) is also used with Transfer of Possession and Communication verbs in the social domain (the (b) and (c) sentences) (Jackendoff, 1972; Goldberg, 1995):

(1)   a. Linda taped the picture <u>to the wall.</u>

        b. Jerry loaned his skateboard <u>to his brother.</u>

        c. I told a bedtime story <u>to his son.</u>

(2)   a. Doug removed the smudges <u>from the table.</u>

        b. He stole money <u>from me.</u>

(3)   a. Leslie covered the bed <u>with blankets.</u>

        b. The Russians supplied Syrians <u>with firearms.</u>

        c. She called me <u>with the information.</u>

(4)   a. Doug cleaned the table <u>of dishes.</u>

        b. She robbed him <u>of his wallet.</u>

Transfer of Possession verbs use the same inventory of argument structure constructions as physical verbs to describe the semantic relations between participants. Communication verbs use only some of the

Proceedings of the 2nd International Workshop on Designing Meaning Representations, pages 90–100
Barcelona, Spain (Online), December 13, 2020

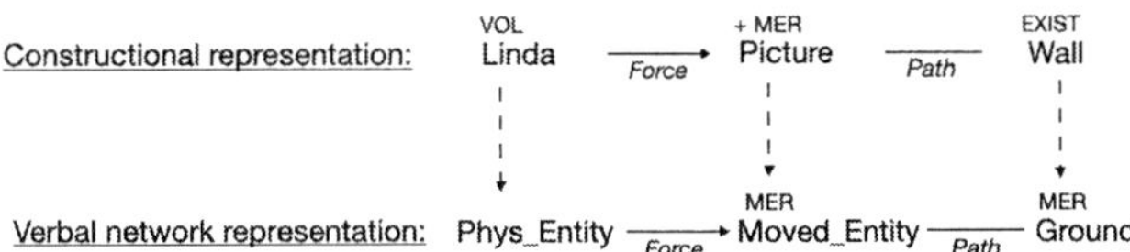

Figure 1: A mapping of a Place causal chain to the Application network

physical argument structure constructions[1]. As shown above, verbs of *giving* and *telling* use the physical placing argument structure construction (1), verbs of *taking* use the physical removal construction (2), verbs of *providing* use the physical covering construction (3), and verbs of *depriving* use the physical uncovering construction (4).[2]

Metaphorical cross-domain mappings of constructional patterns are not uncommon. The use of metaphor in language is pervasive (Lakoff and Johnson, 1980; Gibbs Jr. and Steen, 1997) and a structured representation for various types of figurative language is crucial to many NLP tasks (Bolognesi et al., 2019; Hwang et al., 2017). As the examples (1-4) show, there is a need for a systematic representation that makes metaphorical correspondences between argument structure constructions explicit. In this paper, we propose a model that captures shared semantic elements that lead to argument structure constructions being extended across semantic domains. We argue that allowing for metaphorical use of argument structure constructions will prevent a proliferation of distinct constructional semantic annotations.

2   Semantic representation of the source domain: Application events

The semantic representation adopted in this paper distinguishes verbal event structure from constructional semantics (Kalm et al., 2019). We follow Goldberg (1995) in recognizing the separate contributions of argument structure constructions and verbal semantics to the specification of event structure. Our representation builds on the notion of transmission of force and its relevance to argument realization (Talmy, 1988; Croft, 1991; Croft, 2012). We identify a limited set of force-dynamic relations between event participants (cf. Croft et al., 2016). The relations can be causal (Talmy, 1988), e.g. a FORCE relation between an Agent and a Theme in *She hit the ball*, or non-causal (Croft, 1991), e.g. a spatial PATH relation between two physical entities, as in *Italy borders France*. Force-dynamic relations are used to construct verbal semantic networks and constructional causal chains. The event structure representations also include information about the type of change that each participant undergoes over the course of the event.

Application events, which subsume removal as well as placement events, describe a spatial configuration relation between two entities. Unlike Motion events (e.g. *She rolled the ball down the hill*), which describe the path of motion, Application events describe the co-location, including attachment, of two entities. Application events proceed incrementally part by part – mereologically (Dowty, 1991) – while Motion events proceed incrementally along the path of motion (Dowty's "holistic theme").

Each physical example in (1-4) is represented by a distinct causal chain which specifies which participant is construed as the incremental theme in the argument structure construction. We illustrate the causal chain for the Place construal only, due to limitations of space.

The constructional representation for Place (see Figure 1) identifies a causal FORCE relation between the initiator *Linda* and the theme *picture* which undergoes motion. The theme is in a PATH relation with the Ground *wall*. Depending on the argument structure construction, either the Ground or the Moved_Entity is construed as the incremental theme. In the placing construal, example (1a), the incremental theme is the Moved_Entity because it is syntactically realized as the direct object. The Moved_Entity is labeled +MER to indicate that the path of motion is *to* the Ground. This notation con-

---

[1]Communication verbs do not occur in the *remove* (2) or *uncover* (4) construals.

[2]*Giving* and *telling* verbs also use a double object ("Transfer") argument structure construction; however, the semantics of this construction with Transfer of Possession verbs is not metaphorical. Its representation is therefore not a focus of this paper.

(a) Application network   (b) Constrain network

Figure 2: Verbal networks associated with Application and Constrain verbs

trasts with removal events, in which the incremental theme moves *away from* the Ground and is labeled -MER. The Ground in the placing construal is EXIST; it doesn't undergo any change in the event.

Placing and removal verbs share the same verbal event structure which is referred to as the Application network in this paper, see Figure 2a. The motivation for having a single network for these verbs is that they share the same force-dynamic relations between participants, and both construe the incremental theme as mereological. The Moved_Entity and the Ground are both labeled mereological (MER) in the verbal network. This label does not specify whether the verb describes a placing or removal event and allows for either constructional construal to map to the network. The type of change that the Phys_Entity undergoes in the verbal network is unspecified. Its specification is dependent on the volitionality of the initiator and is therefore determined contextually.

Some Application events describe a different type of event in which the figure's movement results in a co-location relation with the Agent (or a physical entity that initiates the Application event). Verbs such as *pick up* or *drop* describe this type of self-directed action, as shown in Figure 2b. The result state of such an event is a holding event expressed in English with verbs such as *hold*. Talmy (1988) refers to this type of force-dynamic relation as 'extended causation of rest' in contrast to other physical Application events. We describe this type of Application event as a Constrain event. The Constrain event structure evokes two participants: a Phys_Entity and Theme. In our analysis, we use a superordinate Force relation to describe the force-dynamic interaction between the Phys_Entity and the Theme. The argument realization of participants in Force and Constrain events is the same. Hence, there is no constructional motivation to distinguish these force-dynamic types from each other.

A complete representation of the event structure consists of a mapping between the verbal network and the constructional causal chain. When all participants are syntactically evoked, there is a nearly complete correspondence in the mapping from the constructional semantics to the verbal network. Figure 1 shows a mapping from the Place argument structure construction associated with the example in (1a) to the Application network. In the Place construal, the label MER on the incremental theme *picture* matches the label of the corresponding participant in the network. However, the label on the Ground in the verbal network is 'overridden' by the role that the Ground *wall* is assigned in the constructional semantics.

The following sections develop a model for representing the metaphorical extensions of the Application and Constrain argument structure constructions to verbs in the social domain.

3 Metaphorical analysis

The use of metaphor in language has been extensively discussed in theoretical linguistics (Lakoff and Johnson, 1980; Lakoff, 1993; Grady, 1997; Fauconnier and Turner, 2008; Evans, 2009). Various frameworks have been put forth in recent years with the aim of explaining underlying cognitive principles that lead to the use of figurative language. However, metaphorical extensions of argument structure constructions (which we refer to as "constructional metaphors") have not received much attention.

One of the most prominent theories of metaphor is the Conceptual Metaphor Theory (CMT) (Lakoff and Johnson, 1980; Lakoff, 1993). The CMT has primarily addressed metaphors that involve stable and systematic correspondences between two conceptual domains. Metaphorical mappings are analyzed as originating in a 'source' domain and being extended to a 'target' domain. For example, the conceptual metaphor TIME IS MONEY originates in our understanding of time as a valuable commodity that can be wasted, spent, or invested. This metaphor reflects a connection between concepts in two domains: time (in the target domain) and money (in the source domain).

Our discussion of metaphorical mappings that motivate the syntactic realization of participants with Transfer of Possession verbs is guided by CMT. We consider constructional metaphors to reflect knowl-

(a) Dynamic Possession network

(b) Transfer of Possession network

Figure 3: Verbal networks associated with Possession verbs

edge structures that are regular and follow conventional patterns of metaphorical conceptualization. The physical argument structure constructions with Application events are source domain representations. They are metaphorically extended to verbs in social domains which are the target domains.

The role of metaphor in constructions has been addressed in the linguistics literature to some extent but theoretical accounts of this phenomenon are fairly limited (Jackendoff, 1972; Goldberg, 1995; de Mendoza Ibáñez and Usén, 2007). Relevant descriptions lack depth and do not provide explanations for underlying semantic motivations that lead to metaphorical extensions. For example, Goldberg (1995) argues that there is a metaphor "that involves understanding possession as the 'possessed' being located next to the 'possessor,' transferring an entity to a recipient as causing the entity to move to that recipient, and transferring ownership away from a possessor as taking that entity away from the possessor." She uses Application argument structure constructions to provide evidence for her claim. Goldberg (1995) and other scholars provide only a verbal description of the phenomenon rather than a formal representation that would make explicit the semantic motivations that lead to metaphorical extensions.

3.1 Verbal event structure of Transfer of Possession verbs

Our semantic representation of social verbs expands on the notion of transmission of force by identifying schematic force-dynamic relations between participants in the social domain. Transmission of force in social interactions has been addressed in the literature (Talmy, 1988; Croft, 2012); however, an in-depth analysis of social force-dynamic relations has not yet been proposed. To develop a representation for metaphorical constructions with possession verbs, we first describe a force-dynamic analysis of relations between participants with these verbs.

Our social event representations employ the same set of categories used in the physical domain to describe the type of change that each participant undergoes in the event. These categories are defined as domain-independent semantic features. They describe abstract qualitative changes that are not associated with any particular force-dynamic relation in any given domain. For example, the MER label describes a mereologically incremental change that the participant undergoes in an event. This type of change is not specific to any particular domain. Force-dynamic relations between participants, on the other hand, are defined as domain-specific to capture the different types of interactions that physical, social, or mental entities engage in. Force-dynamic relations define the semantic content of the network structure that is specific to the verbal domain. Using domain-independent labels to define participants' internal changes and domain-specific force-dynamic relations between participants allows us to capture common structures across domains as well as distinguish the interactions between participants that are domain dependent.

We distinguish Transfer of Possession verbs ("Transfer verbs") from Dynamic Possession verbs ("Possession verbs"). Dynamic Possession verbs (e.g. *find, obtain, lose*, etc.) describe an event structure in which the Possessor either gains or loses control over the Possession, as shown in Figure 3a.[3] Transfer verbs (e.g. *give, take*, etc.) inherit and elaborate on the event structure of Possession verbs. As shown in Figure 3b, the event structure of Transfer verbs evokes an additional participant, a Possessor. With *giving* verbs, the Possessor is a recipient who comes to gain control over the Possession. With *taking* verbs, the Possessor is the original possessor who loses control over the Possession. On an abstract force-dynamic level, *giving* and *taking* verbs share the same event structure representation.

PERFORM describes a force-dynamic relation between the Agent and Possession. PERFORM is an asymmetrical causal interaction in which the initiator uses performative illocutionary force in the sense of

---

[3]We distinguish Dynamic Possession verbs from Static Possession verbs (e.g. *own, have, belong to*, etc.). Static Possession verbs do not evoke any change and use a different constructional metaphor. In this paper, we only discuss Dynamic Possession verbs.

speech act theory (Levinson, 2017), as opposed to physical force, to bring about change in the endpoint. The non-causal force-dynamic relation that characterizes the relation between Agent and Possession is CONTROL. The CONTROL relation prototypically describes a socially sanctioned relation between an Agent and an entity.[4] The Agent is construed as antecedent to the Possession in the causal chain, similar to the ordering of Figure and Ground in physical event structure representations. In the Possession and Transfer event structures, the CONTROL relation indicates that the Agent (or Possessor) either loses or gains control of the Possession.

The Possession participant is construed as an incremental theme in both verbal event structures. It is labeled MER to indicate change in possession. The type of incremental change undergone in possession events is the same as in physical Application events. Similarly to the Application network in the physical domain, we do not distinguish whether the verb describes a giving (placing) or taking (removal) event in the networks with possession verbs. Whether the incremental theme is +/-MER is not relevant to the verbal event structure representation, it is only relevant to the syntactic realization of participants.

The Possessor in the Transfer of Possession network is also identified as MER. The Possessor undergoes a mereological change by receiving or losing the Possession. Similarly to physical Application constructions, the Possessor in Transfer events may instead be construed as the incremental theme (and syntactically realized as a direct object), as shown in examples (3b) and (4b).

3.2 Metaphorical mappings

Our representation for constructional metaphors consists of a systematic mapping between constructional and verbal event structures in two domains. We show that there exists a set of correspondences between the physical (source domain) network and the social (target domain) network that motivates the metaphorical extension of the argument structure construction associated with events in the physical domain. Defining the type of change that each participant undergoes in the event as a domain-independent semantic feature allows us to identify commonalities in verbal event structures across domains. A structural overlap between the physical and social domain verbal networks does not immediately yield a metaphorical analysis but it shows that verbs in distinct domains share abstract semantic features in their representations. Common semantic features frequently motivate the use of constructional metaphors.

Figure 4 shows the semantic motivations for metaphorical mappings observed with Possession and Transfer verbs. The mappings show the source and target domain verbal networks, the correspondences between them, and the constructional causal chains that are metaphorically extended to the target domain.

A metaphorical mapping of the Constrain causal chain onto the Possession network is presented in Figure 4a. The Constrain metaphor is frequently used to describe events with Possession verbs which prototypically occur in the transitive argument structure construction. As shown in Figure 4a, the partici-

---

[4]*Obtaining* or *finding* events also correlate with a physical movement of the Possession in a prototypical transfer event (Goldberg, 1995). It has been argued that the correlation of spatial motion with control over the possessed entity motivates the metaphorical extension from the physical source domain (Grady, 1997). However, we do not represent a spatial Path relation between the participant with Possession verbs as literal motion between the Possessor and the Possession is not evoked by the verbal semantics.

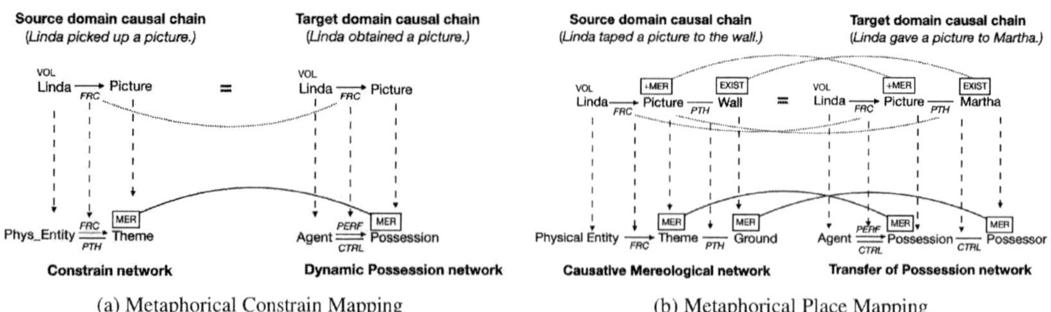

(a) Metaphorical Constrain Mapping   (b) Metaphorical Place Mapping

Figure 4: Metaphorical Mapping Representations

pants in the Constrain network and the Possession network undergo the same type of internal change. The correspondences between the two semantic domains are sufficient to motivate a metaphorical mapping in which the transitive Constrain argument structure construction is extended to Possession verbs.

Figure 4b demonstrates that the Application and Transfer verbal networks also share semantic features in their representations. The participants undergo the same type of internal change over the course of these semantically distinct events. Both networks consist of an initiator which is external to the non-causal relation between participants.

As shown in Figure 4, social domain force-dynamic relations are metaphorically construed as physical relations. In particular, the social PERFORM relation maps to the source domain physical FORCE relation and the social CONTROL relation maps onto the physical PATH relation. The mapping between force-dynamic relations across domains in metaphorical construals is not random: the causal and non-causal relations in the target domain map to the causal and non-causal relations in the source domain, respectively. Additional motivations for linking relations across domains may exist. For example, the CONTROL relation is frequently associated with a physical co-location relation between the Possession and the Possessor, which further motivates the metaphorical mapping to physical PATH.

Possession verbs can also be metaphorically construed as Transfer events in metaphorical Application argument structure constructions. For example, an *obtain* verb can be used to describe a metaphorical remove event, e.g. *She obtained the book from her friend*. The verbal event structure evokes that the Agent ends up in control of the Possession; however, the constructional semantics describes a removal event in which the Possession is taken away from the original Possessor. This metaphorical construal is not unexpected given that Constrain verbs are used analogously in the physical domain in removal or placing construals (e.g. *She picked it up from the floor*). The non-causal relation between the initiator and the theme in both the Possession and Constrain networks is semantically implied but it is not syntactically expressible in English. If a CONTROL relation is overtly expressed in the constructional causal chain with Possession verbs, the participant will always be distinct from the initiator of the network and will evoke a Transfer event.

Evidence for a close correspondence between the event structures of Constrain, Application, Possession, and Transfer verbs is the use of a single verb to describe these different types of events. For example, the English verb *take* can be used as a physical Constrain verb in *He took her hand*, a verb of Removal in *He took the cup from the cupboard*, a metaphorical Dynamic Possession verb in *He took the flower*, or a Transfer verb in *They took the book from him*.

3.3 Non-physical "Possession" in Transfer events

In their prototypical sense, Possession and Transfer verbs tend to be used with participants that denote physical entities that can be physically controlled. However, corpus data indicates that these verbs also frequently occur with non-physical entities that are metaphorically conceptualized as Possessions. MetaNet (Petruck, 2018) includes metaphors such as ATTRIBUTES ARE POSSESSIONS, BELIEFS ARE POSSESSIONS, or IDEAS ARE POSSESSIONS. Non-physical entities with Possession and Transfer verbs primarily include attributes that define a person's social status or role (e.g. *They gave him an important role*). They can also denote socially agreed upon artifacts that define a person's status (e.g. *They presented him with a diploma*). Another common type of non-physical Possession is knowledge or experience, which can be metaphorically conceptualized as being 'transferred' to a person (Fillmore et al., 2003). An example such as *We now present the kaoshikii dance* describes an event in which the experience of a dance or performance is transferred to the audience.

Transfer verbs can also be used to describe communication events, e.g. *They presented him with a plan*. In this example, the speaker's ideas are metaphorically conceptualized as a Possession that is being transferred to an addressee. This conceptualization of the event motivates the use of the Transfer verb and the metaphorical Provide argument structure construction. Although a communication event may be entailed contextually, it is not specified by verbal or constructional semantics in this example. The means of presentation is not explicitly stated with a Transfer verb. The constructional and verbal semantics only convey that the Recipient now has a knowledge of the *plan*. Our semantic representation and annotation does not aim to disambiguate whether the event describes communication, social role assignment, or some other event in the social domain when Possession or Transfer verb is used. The representation only depicts the mapping of the constructional semantics to verbal semantics.

4 Annotation exercise

To see how well our representation could be developed into an annotation scheme, we asked three linguistics graduate students who are familiar with our research to annotate a random sample of 123 examples from the RED and BOLT corpora[5]. The annotators did not participate in the development of the annotation scheme. Only one of the annotators had previous experience annotating linguistic corpora.

The annotation sample was restricted to verbs that describe Possession and Transfer events and physical Application and *send* verbs which can be used to describe physical events as well as social possession events. We used the VerbNet verb classification (Kipper et al., 2007) to extract examples with verbs from VerbNet's possession classes. We later added *send* examples and additional physical examples with Application verbs to have a more balanced number of physical and metaphorical examples in the dataset. The sample excluded idiomatic examples with possession verbs (e.g. *I'm pretty calm about things and like to **take** things as they come*), examples in which the verb was followed by the preposition *without* (e.g. *I had to **leave** without a refund*) and other examples with *leave* that describe metaphorical Motion, not Possession (e.g. *[...]only 15 months until we can **leave** nationwide and move over to a proper btl mortgage*). A carefully pre-sorted annotation sample was needed to ensure that annotators encountered only examples that were addressed in the guidelines. The primary goal of the exercise was to test how well annotators can correctly identify metaphorical events given that the constructions used with metaphorical and non-metaphorical events are the same and are annotated the same way. High inter-annotator agreement for the semantic domain (annotated as EVENT DOMAIN in the exercise) would support our proposed simplified representation for constructional semantics which relies on accurate semantic domain identification.

EVENT DOMAIN	FD1 labels	FD2 labels
Social:Possession	Autonomous	Control
Physical:Force	Instrument	Deprive
Physical:Mereology	Physical	Force
Physical:Motion	Self-volitional	Motion
	Volitional	Place
		Provide
		Remove

Table 1: Annotation labels

The annotation scheme used in the exercise is an extension of our existing annotation scheme devised for examples in VerbNet classes with verbs in the physical domain (Croft et al., 2016). Each example was annotated for EVENT DOMAIN and the constructional semantics by using FD1 and FD2 labels. EVENT DOMAIN was not previously used in our annotation scheme. It was introduced in the current scheme to distinguish metaphorical uses of argument structure constructions from non-metaphorical ones. The full inventory of annotation labels is listed in Table 1.

EVENT DOMAIN specifies the domain and the subdomain of the example. The target domain is frequently implicit in the verb, as is the case with *find* in (5). *Find* is a Possession verb and the EVENT DOMAIN of the example is annotated Social:Possession. However, verbal semantics alone cannot always accurately determine the target domain. For instance, the verb *take* can be used to describe a physical mereological event (6), annotated as Physical:Mereological, or a Possession event (7), annotated as Social:Possession.

(5) They seemed more interested in helping me **find** the right car.

(6) One can **take** white eggs out with a pipette or eyedropper.

---

[5]The BOLT English Discussion Forums corpus can be accessed here: https://catalog.ldc.upenn.edu/LDC2017T11. The Richer Event Description corpus can be accessed here: https://catalog.ldc.upenn.edu/LDC2016T23

(7)   He at least **took** the neighbor's bicycle.

The FD1 label identifies whether the initiator of the event is internal or external to the core event. It also specifies whether the initiator acts volitionally or not.[6] The FD2 label describes the 'core' event, i.e. the event that the incremental theme is engaged in. For instance, example (6) was annotated Volitional Remove. The constructional semantics describes a causal chain in which the subject *one* is an external (Volitional) initiator that causes the Remove event in which the direct object *white eggs* is removed from a container, a null-instantiated participant.

The annotators were presented with written annotation guidelines[7]. Due to time constraints, we did not verbally go over the guidelines nor did we do a trial annotation prior to this annotation exercise. The types of disagreements detected in the test annotation indicate that improved annotation guidelines could lead to higher inter-annotator agreement scores in the future. To assess inter-annotator agreement, we used Cohen's Kappa on each of the annotated units. The reported values are averages of the Cohen's Kappa scores for each annotator. The EVENT DOMAIN annotation was the most accurate (0.73). Lower FD1 (0.47) and FD2 (0.57) agreement scores resulted from recurring errors that could be prevented with improved annotation guidelines, as discussed below.

5   Error analysis

About 40% of errors in the EVENT DOMAIN annotation resulted from incorrectly identifying whether an event was Physical or Social with *take* and *grab* verbs. This was particularly problematic when these verbs occurred with a theme that referred to a physical object. In such contexts, both verbs evoke temporary control over the object as well as a physical force event. There were two main types of these errors. In one case, the error with *take* and *grab* verbs resulted from incorrectly recognizing whether the physical event or the social control relation was more salient to the interpretation of the event. For instance, in *I quickly **grabbed** sentence strips out of the closet*, the verb describes a physical removal event; however, the event also evokes that the Agent has control over the object by being spatially co-located with it. The annotation of this example as Physical:Mereology reflects that the physical event is more salient in the interpretation when compared to the control relation between the Agent and the moved entity, which is only a precondition for the physical event to take place. In other cases, *take* occurred in a context in which the verb described a use-type relation, e.g. *If you **take** a flash light and shine it through the eggs [...]*. Alerting the annotators to the fact that *take* could be used to describe a FORCE relation in physical manipulation events in the annotation guidelines should result in fewer errors of this type. Additionally, including a more detailed description of how to annotate physical verbs that evoke both domains at the same time should lead to higher inter-annotator agreement.

Another common type of error (about 15%) in the EVENT DOMAIN resulted from choosing the wrong subdomain label when an event took place in the physical domain. Many *take* verbs were incorrectly annotated as Physical:Mereology when they occurred in Constrain events, e.g. *I was told to **take** my coffee to go*.

FD1 and FD2 labels were more challenging to annotate given the larger inventory of annotation labels associated with these categories. To correctly annotate the FD2 label, the annotators had to correctly determine the core event and, in many cases, take into account null instantiated participants. Additionally, the choice of FD2 impacted the annotation of FD1. Approximately 37% of all FD1 errors were due to an incorrect choice of an FD2 label. About 43% of FD1 errors resulted from annotators incorrectly distinguishing internal initiators from external initiators.

Many of the FD1 errors had to do with distinguishing external and internal initiators. For example, various examples with Force FD2, e.g. *I just **grab** the blender and pop in some other stuff*, were

---

[6]FD1 labels distinguish different types of initiators. Autonomous is used when the initiator is internal to the event, similarly to Self-volitional. However, unlike Self-volitional, the Autonomous initiator does not act volitionally. Physical is used analogously to Volitional and describes an external initiator that doesn't act volitionally. Instrument is used when an Agent uses an intermediary object, i.e. an instrument, to carry out an action. Instruments are common with physical Application and *send* verbs but infrequent in metaphorical construals with Application verbs.

[7]A revised version of the annotation guidelines can be accessed online at https://github.com/fd-semantics-unm/coling-metaphors. Revisions to the guidelines were made after the annotation exercise to address common errors, see Section 5.

annotated `Volitional FD1` despite the semantic incompatibility of `Force` and the presence of an external initiator in transitive argument structure constructions.[8]

As noted above, annotators sometimes chose a wrong `FD2` label which then led to an incorrect `FD1` annotation. About 14% of `FD2` errors resulted from annotators incorrectly including a null instantiated participant in the annotation. For example, some annotators annotated the example *What year did Mussolini seize power in Italy?* as `Volitional Remove`, assuming that an original possessor was part of the constructional semantics. However, in this context, *take* does not describe a removal event, it describes an obtaining event, i.e. Mussolini gaining power. The correct annotation label for `FD1` and `FD2` was therefore `Self-volitional Force`. Approximately 25% of `FD2` errors resulted from a null instantiated participant not being included in the annotation when it should have been. For example, in *we are **collecting** a premium up front and their total cost is known up front*, the original possessor from whom the premium is collected should be part of the constructional semantics leading to the annotation `Volitional Remove`. If an annotator did not recognize that a null instantiated participant was semantically evoked, the `FD2` label would have been incorrectly annotated as `Force`. The guidelines should clarify when a null instantiated participant ought to be included in the annotation and provide more examples to supplement the explanations.

About 16% of `FD2` errors included a wrong incremental theme construal. Annotators frequently annotated a `Remove FD2` example (e.g. *[they] actually care about the customers safety rather than **taking** their money*) as `Deprive FD2`. This error resulted from incorrectly identifying the original Possessor as the incremental theme, rather than the Possession. This type of error was also common with `Place` and `Provide` construals. The decision which of the participants is the incremental theme should be guided by which participant is expressed as the direct object in the construction.

Another 17% of `FD2` errors resulted from interpreting a motion event as mereological. Some annotators incorrectly identified examples with *send* verbs as mereological, rather than motion events. Although it was clearly stated in the annotation guidelines that the `FD2` label in examples such as *He might have **sent** it to me today* is `Motion`, having more time to go over the guidelines with the annotators would have probably resulted in fewer errors. The guidelines should also include a more detailed description of various application examples and the syntactic realization of the incremental theme.

6   Conclusion

The use of constructional metaphors in the social domain is pervasive. Communication verbs use the same inventory of Application argument structure constructions as Transfer of Possession verbs. Other common constructional metaphors in the social domain include Motion metaphors with verbs that describe entering or leaving a social role, status, or an institution. For example, *firing* and *resigning* verbs occur in Motion argument structure constructions (e.g. *He resigned from the military*). Locative metaphors are common with verbs of social membership and employment (e.g. *He is employed at IBM*). Recognition of the many metaphorical argument structure constructions in social events will allow us to simplify the annotation of the semantic contribution of argument structure constructions to event structures for social events. It will also allow us to capture an important dimension of meaning that will be useful for building computational models that reason over social events, a goal of future work.

The annotation exercise indicates that annotators can reliably identify a literal use of argument structure constructions from their metaphorical use. This finding supports our hypothesis that a simplified representation of constructional metaphors that relies on a correct identification of the semantic domain of the example can be used to determine the event structure of a particular example.

Acknowledgements

This research was partly funded by grant number HDTRA1-15-0063 from the Defense Threat Reduction Agency to the last author.

---

[8]The dataset included only examples in which `Force` had an internal initiator since we focused on Constrain events. `Place` and `Remove` events, on the other hand, always evoked an external initiator when metaphorically used with Transfer of Possession verbs. In the physical domain, `Place` and `Remove` may occur with an external or internal initiator. The annotators were not informed about the correlation of internal and external initiators with `FD2` labels in this dataset.

References

Omri Abend and Ari Rappoport. 2013. Universal conceptual cognitive annotation (UCCA). In *Proceedings of the 51st Annual Meeting of the Association for Computational Linguistics*, volume 1, pages 228–238.

Laura Banarescu, Claire Bonial, Shu Cau, Madalina Georgescu, Kira Griffitt, Ulf Hermjakob, Kevin Knight, Phillipp Koehn, Martha Palmer, and Nathan Schneider. 2013. Abstract meaning representation for sembanking. In *Proceedings of the 7th Linguistic Annotation Workshop*.

Marianna Bolognesi, Mario Brdar, and Kristina Despot, editors. 2019. *Metaphor and Metonymy in the Digital Age: Theory and methods for building repositories of figurative language*. John Benjamins Publishing Company.

William Croft, Pavlína Pešková, and Michael Regan. 2016. Annotation of causal and aspectual structure of events in RED: a preliminary report. In *4th Events Workshop, 15th Annual Conference of the North American Chapter of the Association of Computational Linguistics: Human Language Technologies*, NAAACL-HLT 2016, pages 8–17. Stroudsburg, Penn: Association for Computational Linguistics.

William Croft. 1991. *Syntactic categories and grammatical relations: the cognitive organization of information*. Chicago: University of Chicago Press.

William Croft. 2012. *Verbs: aspect and causal structure*. Oxford University Press.

Francisco José Ruiz de Mendoza Ibáñez and Ricardo Mairal Usén. 2007. High-level metaphor and metonymy in meaning construction. *Aspects of meaning construction*, pages 33–49.

David Dowty. 1991. Thematic proto-roles and argument selection. *Language*, 67:547–619.

Vyvyan Evans. 2009. *How words mean: lexical concepts, cognitive models, and meaning construction*. Oxford University Press on Demand.

Gilles Fauconnier and Mark Turner. 2008. Rethinking metaphor. In *Cambridge Handbook of Metaphor and Thought*, pages 53–66. Cambridge University Press.

Charles J. Fillmore, Christopher R. Johnson, and Miriam R. Petruck. 2003. Background to FrameNet. *International Journal of Lexicography*, 16:235–50.

Charles J. Fillmore. 1985. Frames and the semantics of understanding. *Quaderni di semantica*, 6:622–54.

Raymond W. Gibbs Jr. and Gerard J. Steen, editors. 1997. *Metaphor in cognitive linguistics: Selected papers from the 5th international cognitive linguistics conference*, volume 175. John Benjamins Publishing.

Adele E. Goldberg. 1995. *Constructions: A Construction Grammar Approach to Argument Structure*. Chicago: University of Chicago Pres.

Joseph E. Grady. 1997. *Foundations of Meaning: Primary Metaphors and Primary Scenes*. Ph.D. thesis, University of California, Berkeley.

Jan Hajič, Eva Hajičová, Jarmila Panevová, Petr Sgall, Ondřej Bojar, Silvie Cinková, Eva Fučíková, Marie Mikulová, Petr Pajas, Jan Popelka, Jiří Semecký, Jana Šindlerová, Jan Štěpánek, Josef Toman, Zdeňka Urešová, and Zdeněk Žabokrtský. 2012. Announcing prague czech-english dependency treebank 2.0. In *LREC*, pages 3153–3160.

Jena D. Hwang, Archna Bhatia, Na-Rae Han, Tim O'Gorman, Vivek Srikumar, and Nathan Schneider. 2017. Double trouble: the problem of construal in semantic annotation of adpositions. *Proceedings of the 6th Joint Conference on Lexical and Computational Semantics*, pages 178–188.

Ray S. Jackendoff. 1972. *Semantic interpretation in generative grammar*. The MIT Press.

Pavlina Kalm, Michael Regan, and William Croft. 2019. Event Structure Representation: Between Verbs and Argument Structure Constructions. *Proceedings of the First International Workshop on Designing Meaning Representations*, pages 100–109.

Karin Kipper, Anna Korhonen, Neville Ryant, and Martha Palmer. 2007. A large-scale classification of English verbs. *English Resources and Evaluations*, 42:21–40.

George Lakoff and Mark Johnson. 1980. *Metaphors We Live By*. Chicago: University of Chicago Pres.

George Lakoff. 1993. *Metaphor and thought*. Cambridge, UK: Cambridge University Press, 2nd edition.

Beth Levin. 1993. *English verb classes and alternations: a preliminary investigation*. Chicago: University of Chicago Press.

Stephen C. Levinson. 2017. Speech acts. In Y Huang, editor, *Oxford handbook of pragmatics*, pages 199–216. Oxford University Press.

Miriam R.L. Petruck, editor. 2018. *MetaNet*. John Benjamins Publishing.

Leonard Talmy. 1988. Force dynamics in language and cognition. *Cognitive Science*, 2:49–100.